Oh My Goddess!

あああっ女神さまっ

26

STORY AND ART BY
Kosuke Fujishima

TRANSLATION BY
Christopher Lewis, Dana Lewis AND Lea Hernandez

LETTERING AND TOUCH-UP BY
Susie Lee AND Betty Dong WITH Tom2K

DARK HORSE MANGA™

CHAPTER 163

Flight of the Fighting Wings

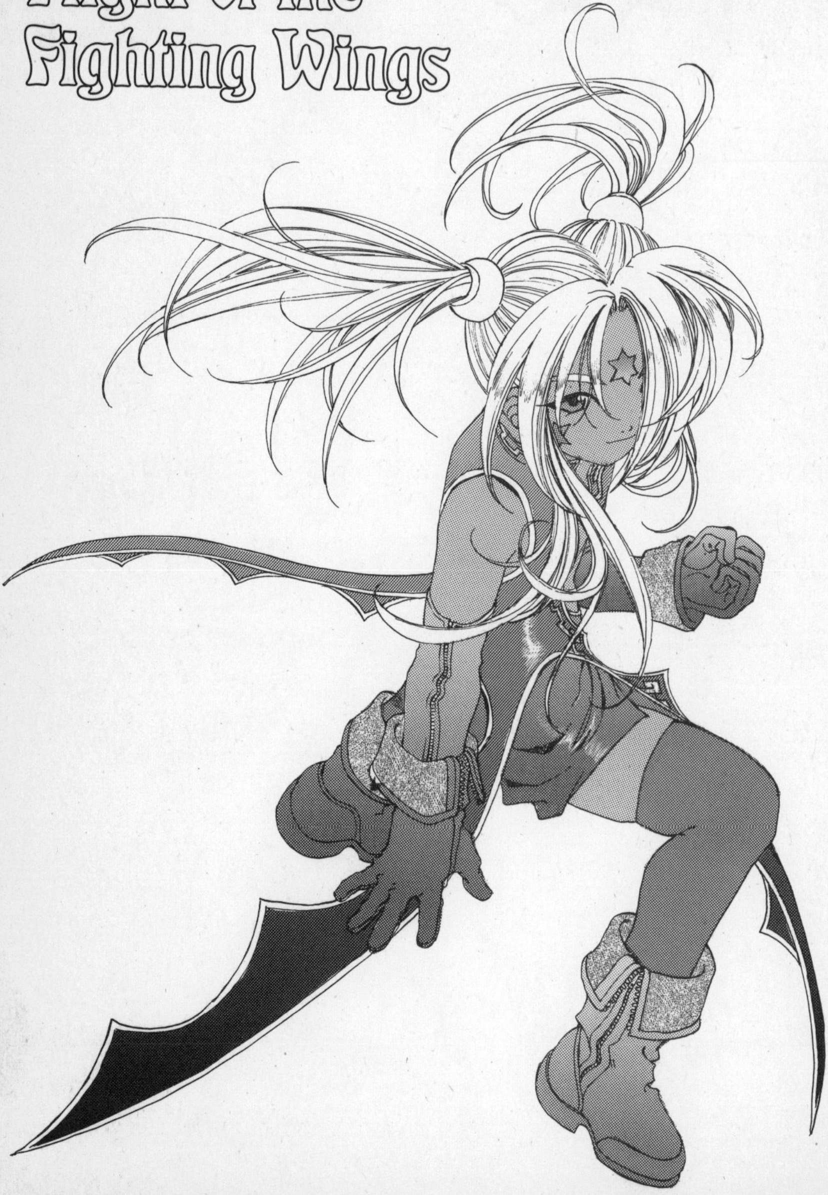

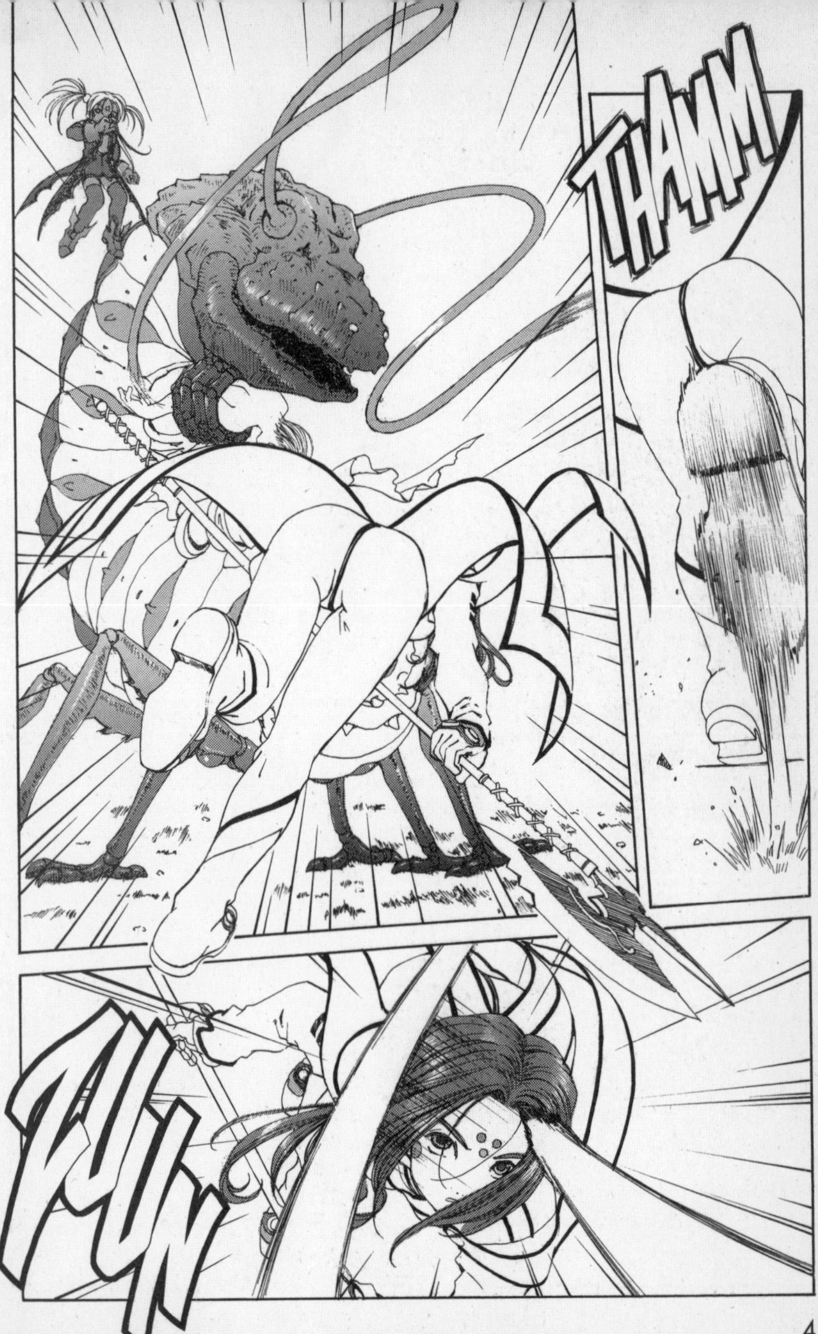
THAMM
ZUN

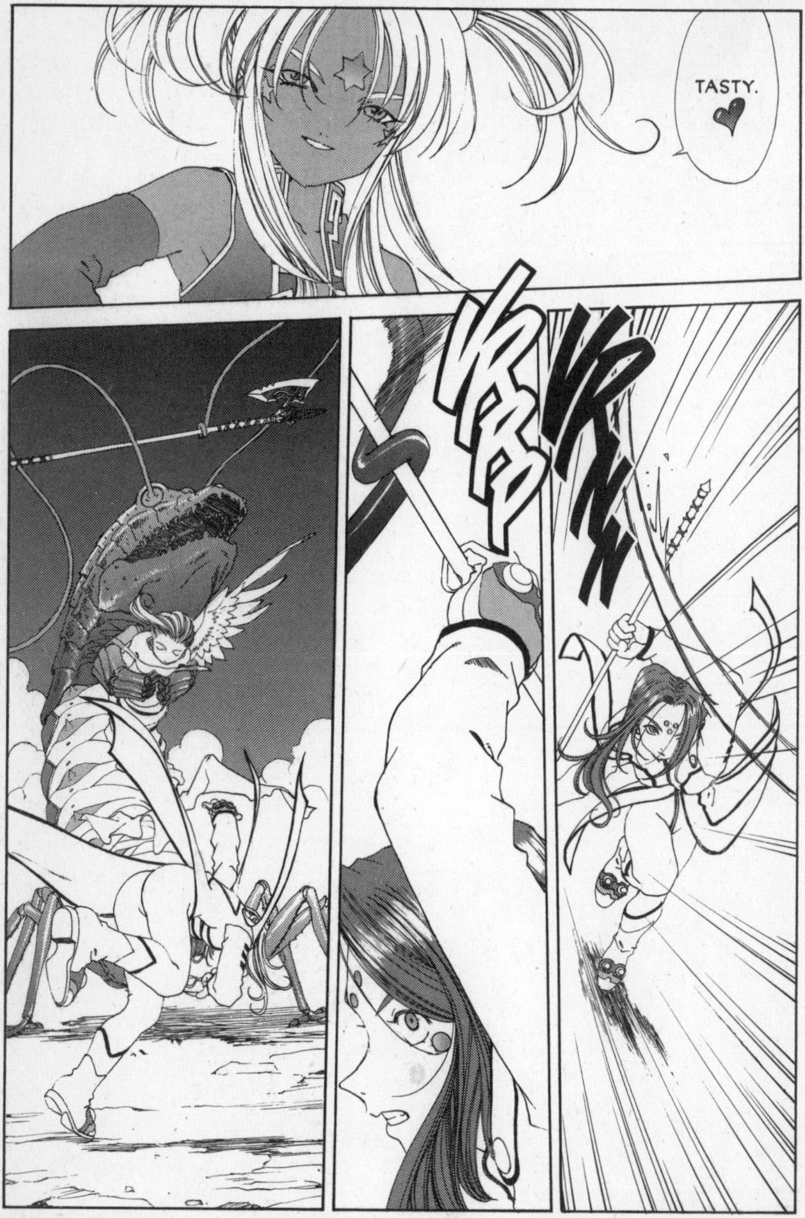
TASTY.

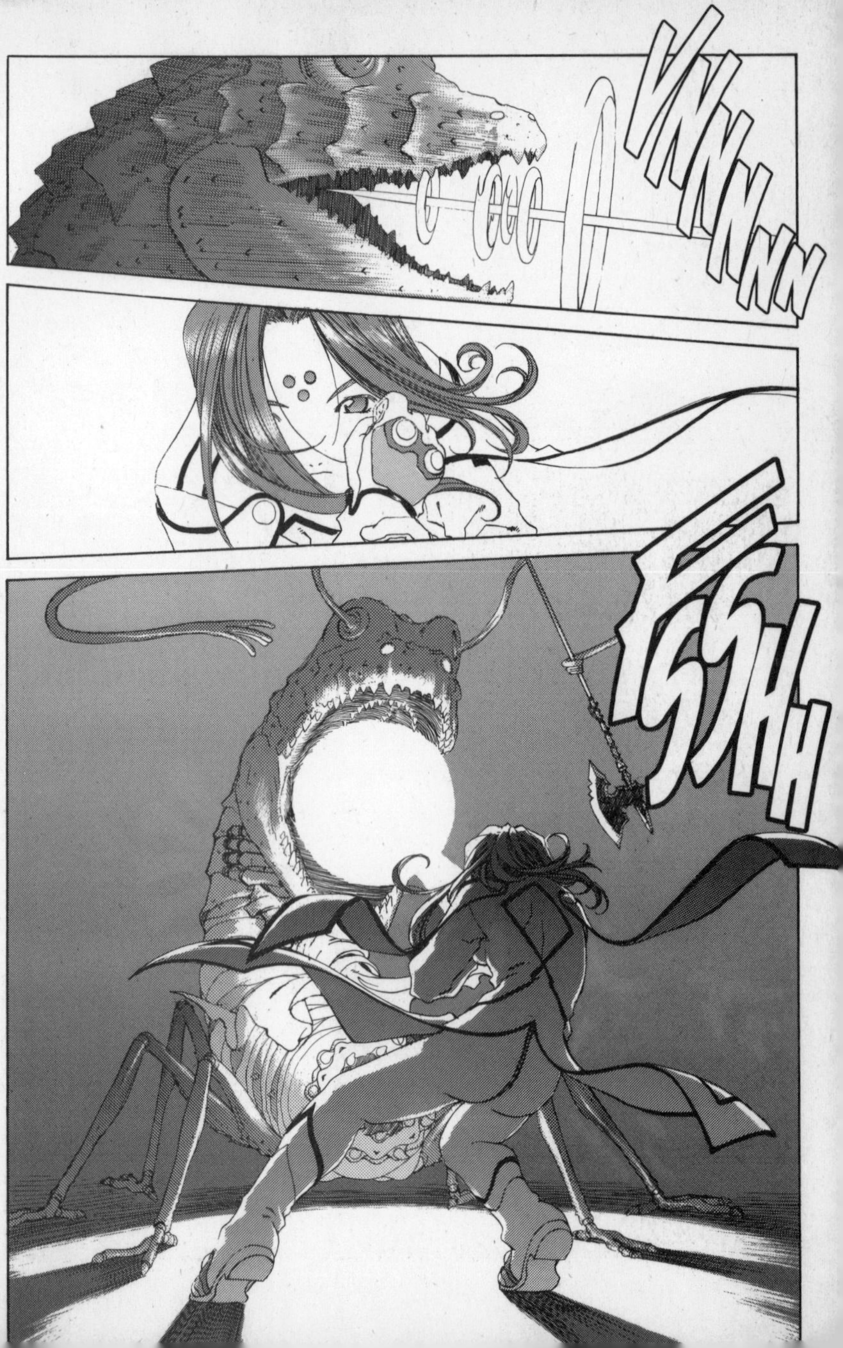
VNNNNN
FSSHH

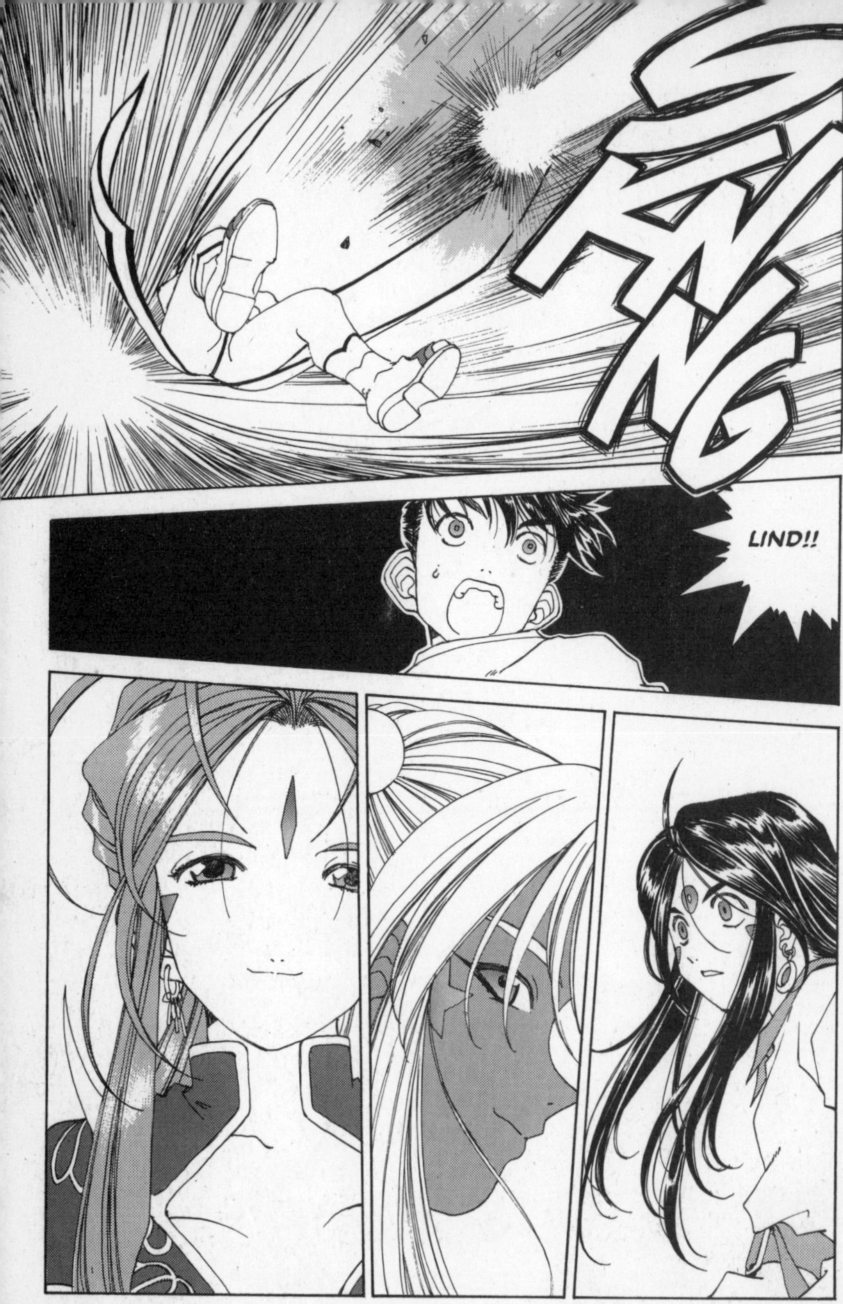
LIND!!

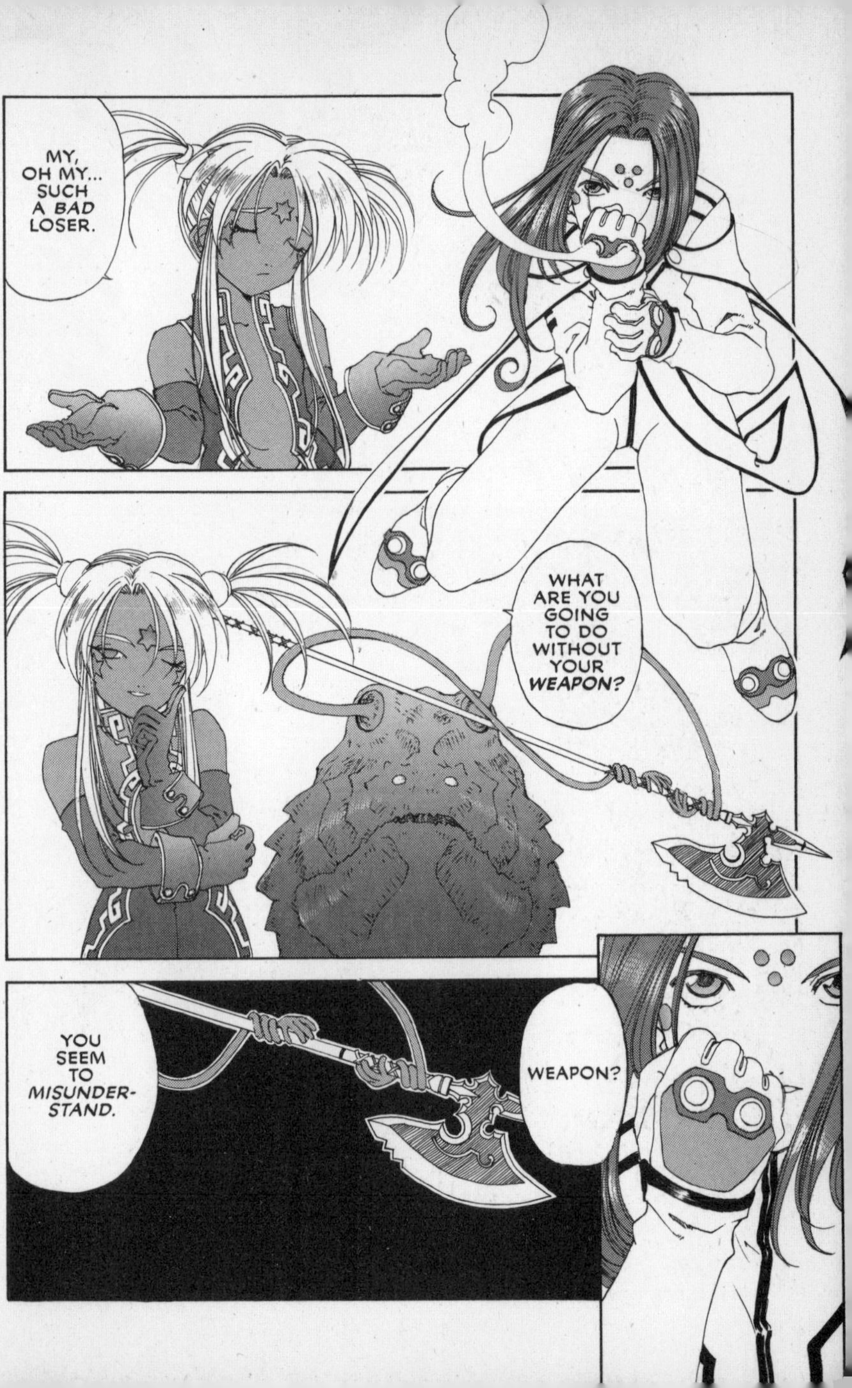
MY, OH MY... SUCH A *BAD* LOSER.
WHAT ARE YOU GOING TO DO WITHOUT YOUR *WEAPON?*
WEAPON?
YOU SEEM TO *MISUNDERSTAND.*

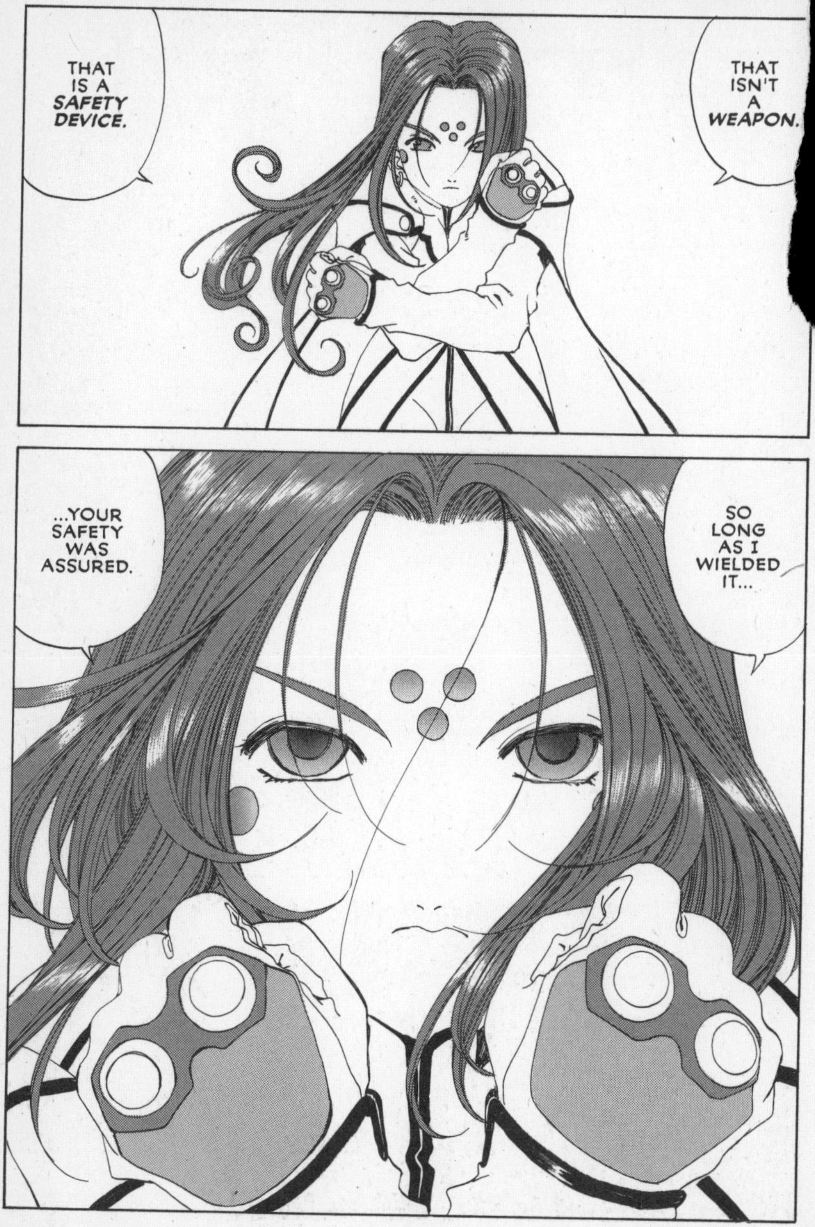
THAT ISN'T A WEAPON.
THAT IS A SAFETY DEVICE.
SO LONG AS I WIELDED IT...
...YOUR SAFETY WAS ASSURED.

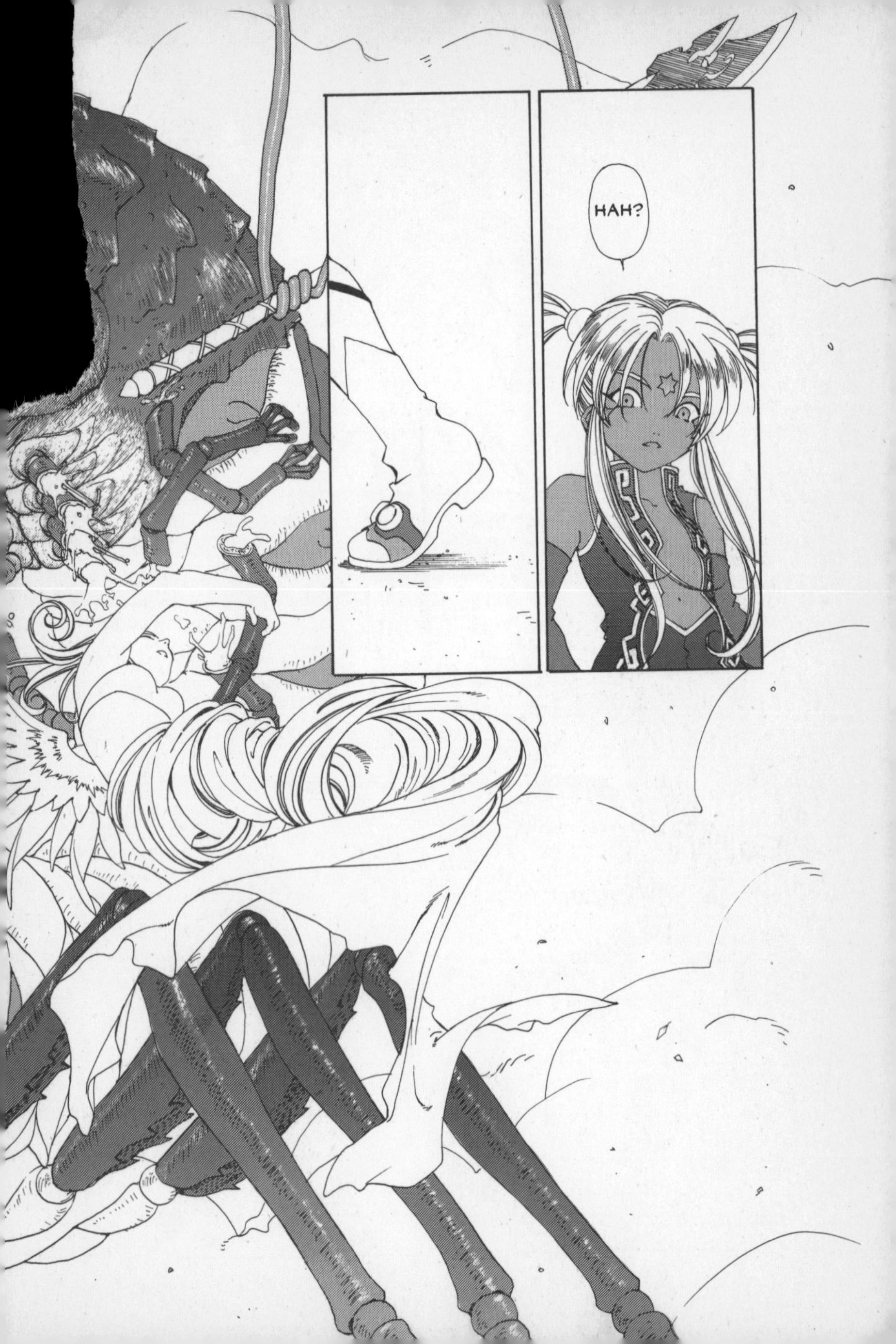
HAH?

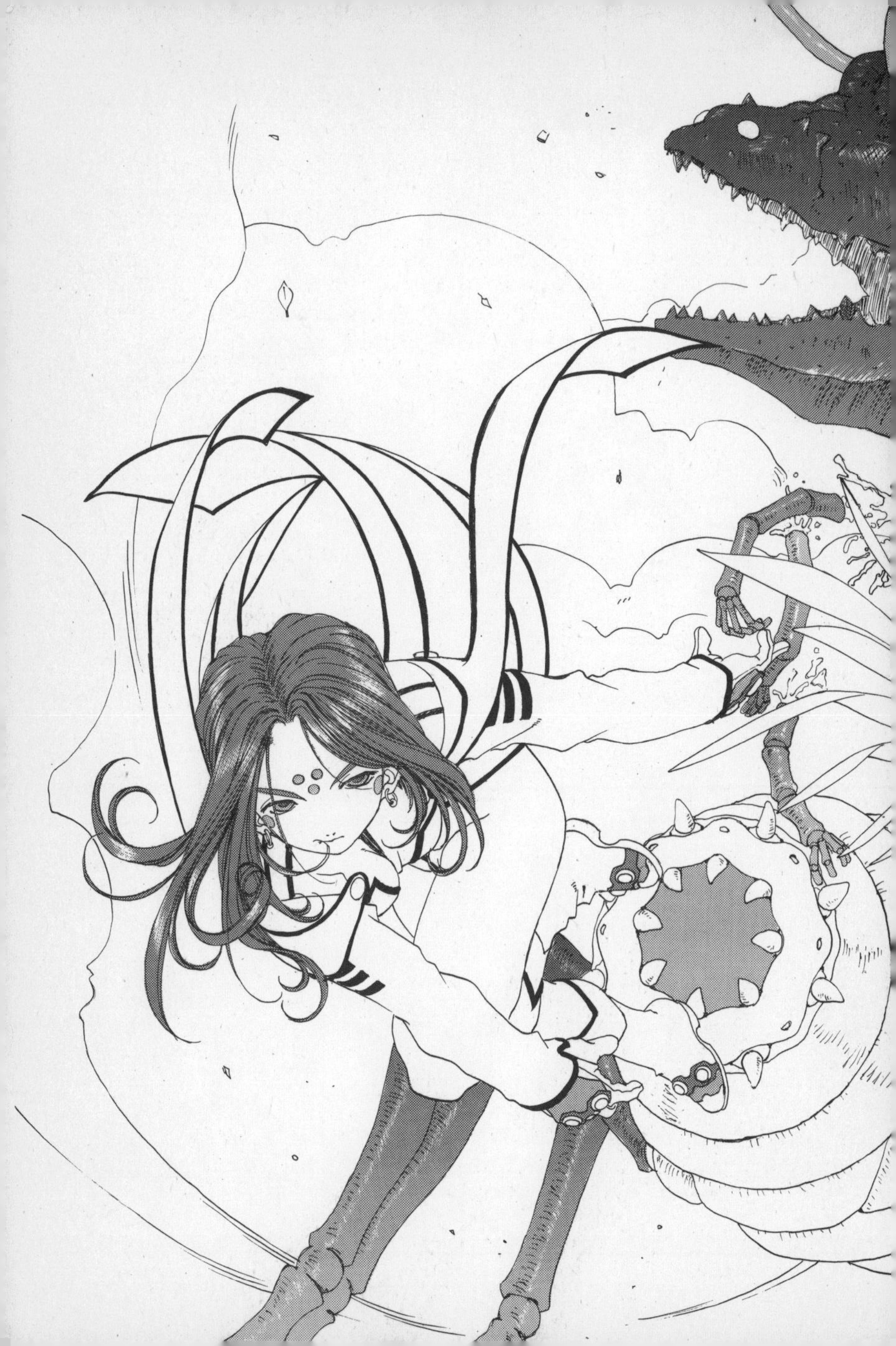

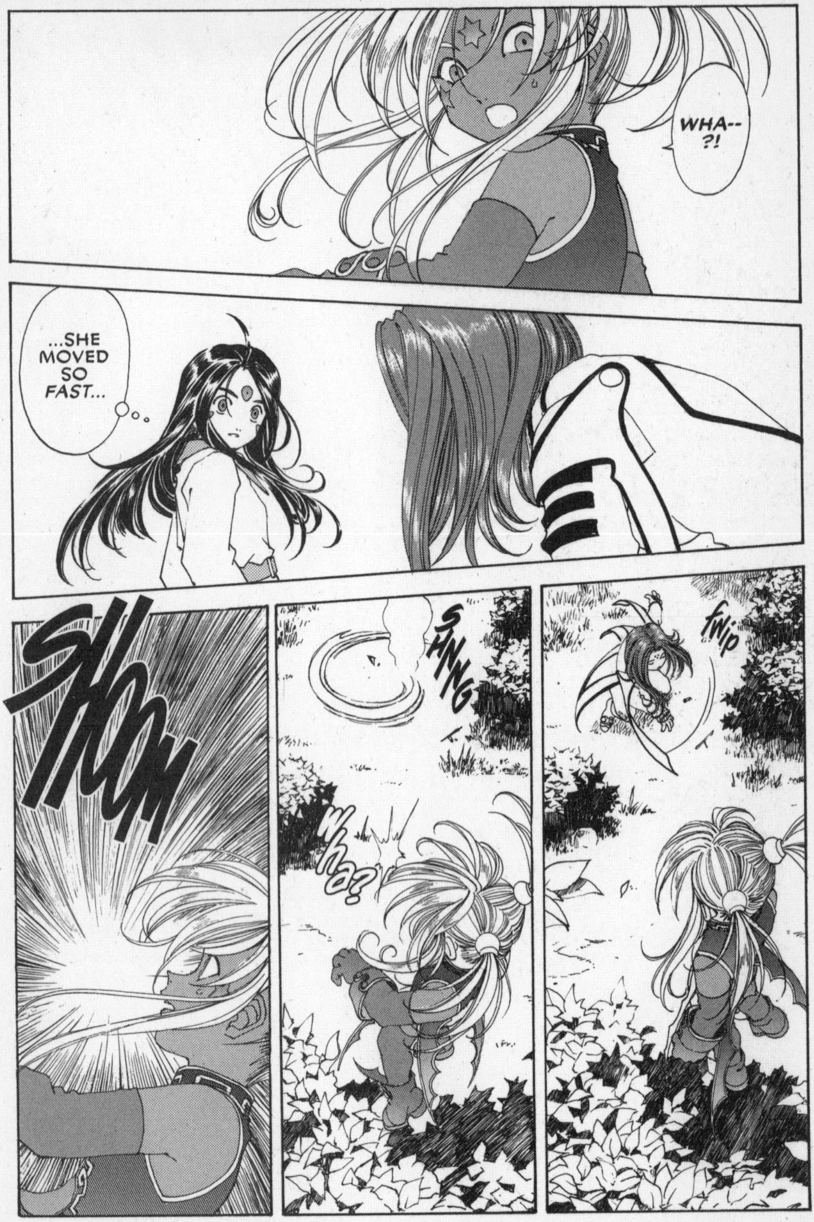
WHA-- ?!
...SHE MOVED SO FAST...
fwip
SHANNG
wha?
SHOOM

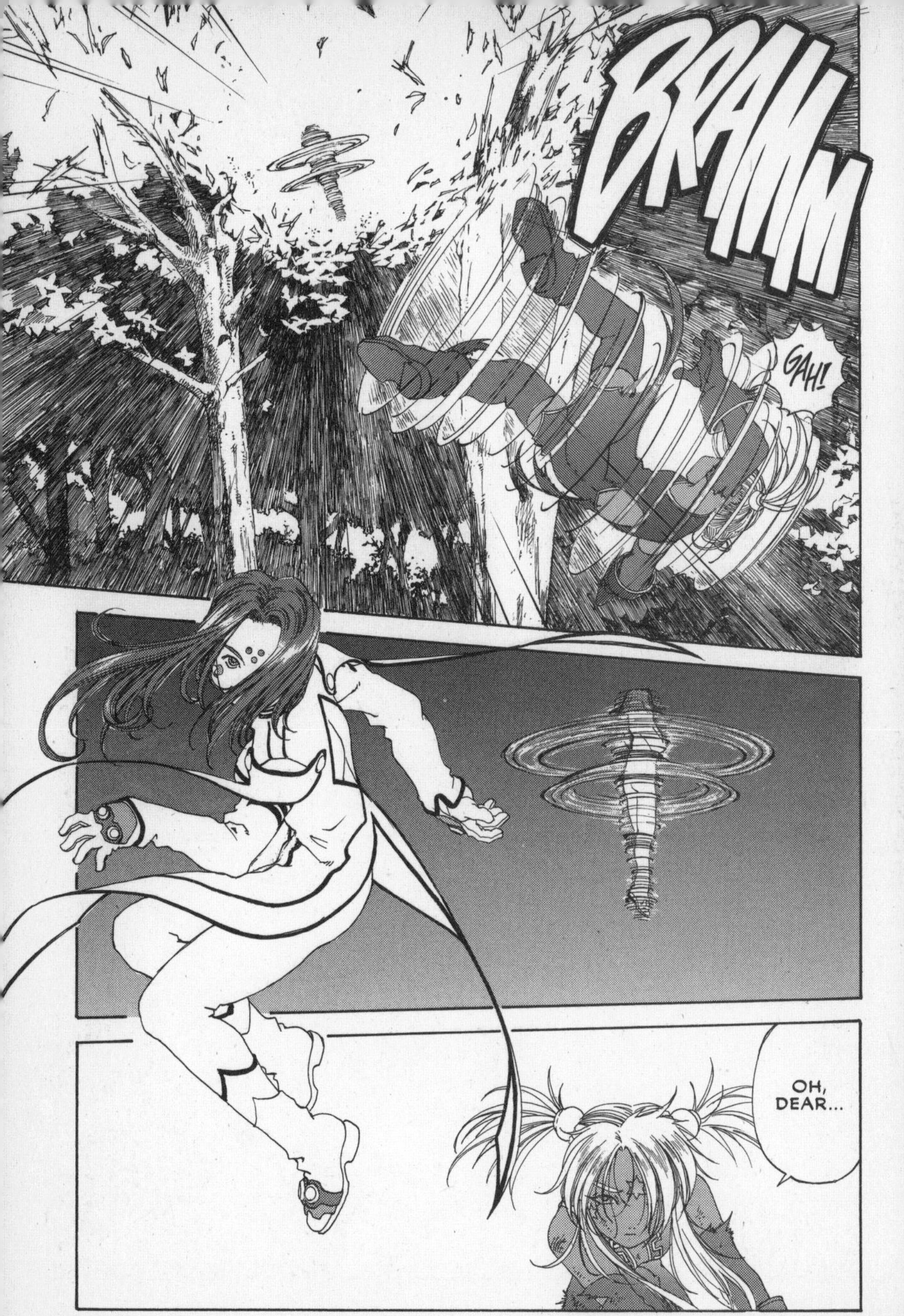
BRAMM
GAH!
OH, DEAR...

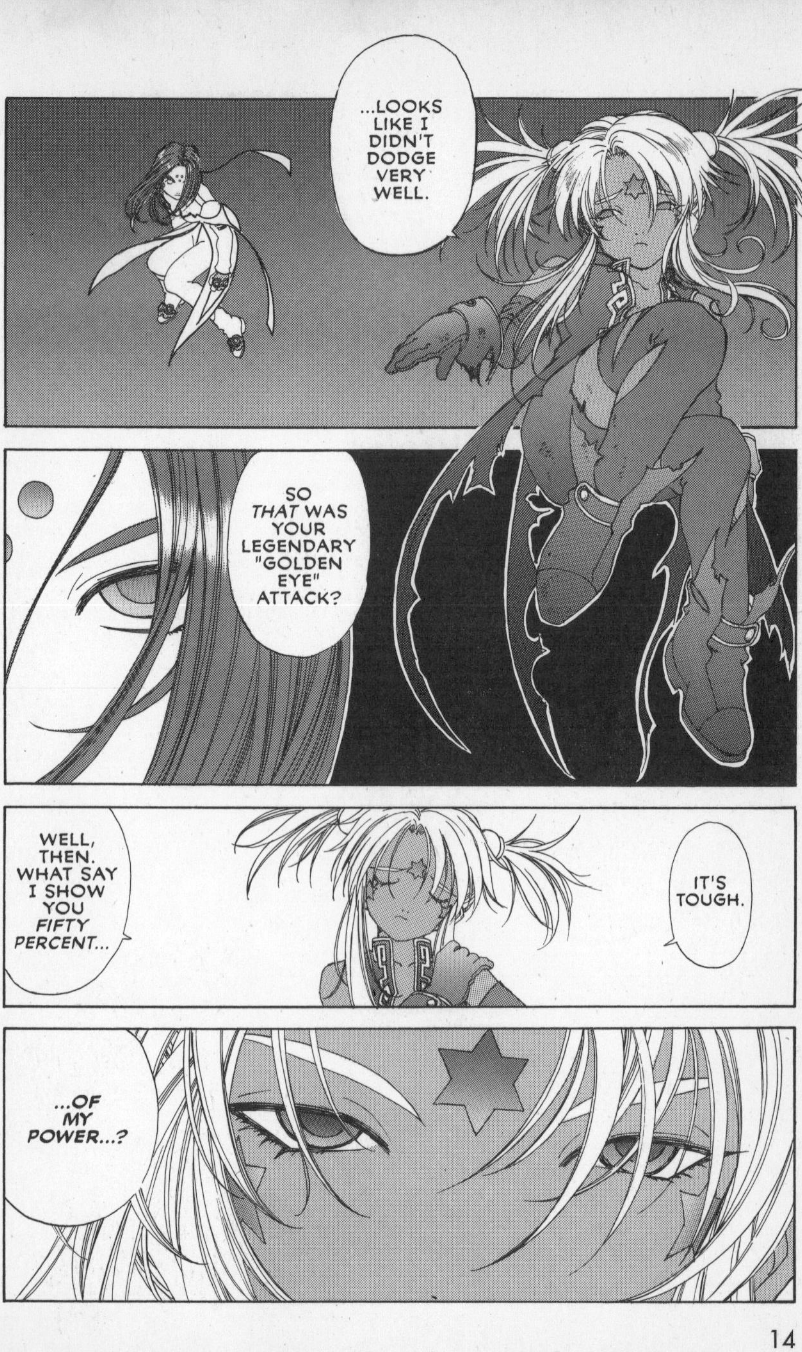
...LOOKS LIKE I DIDN'T DODGE VERY WELL.
SO *THAT* WAS YOUR LEGENDARY "GOLDEN EYE" ATTACK?
IT'S TOUGH.
WELL, THEN. WHAT SAY I SHOW YOU *FIFTY PERCENT...*
...OF MY POWER...?

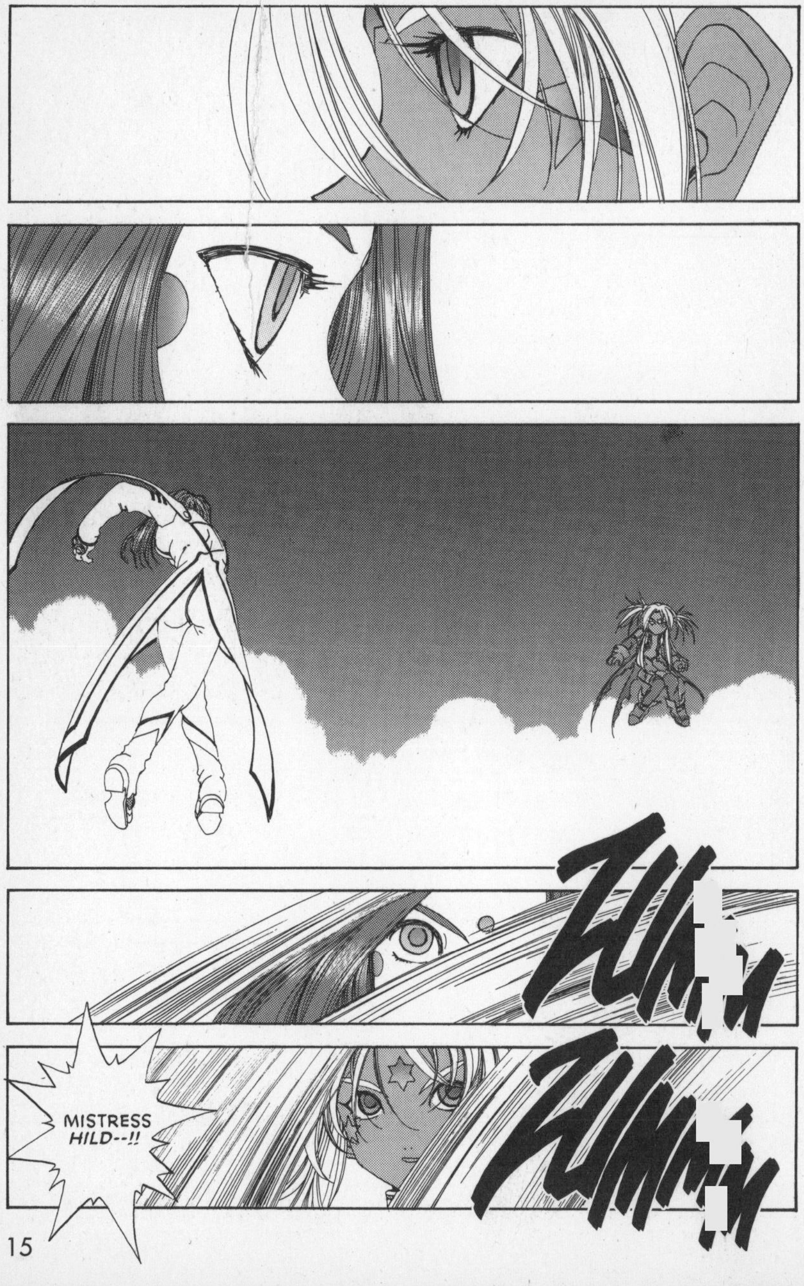
MISTRESS
HILD--!!

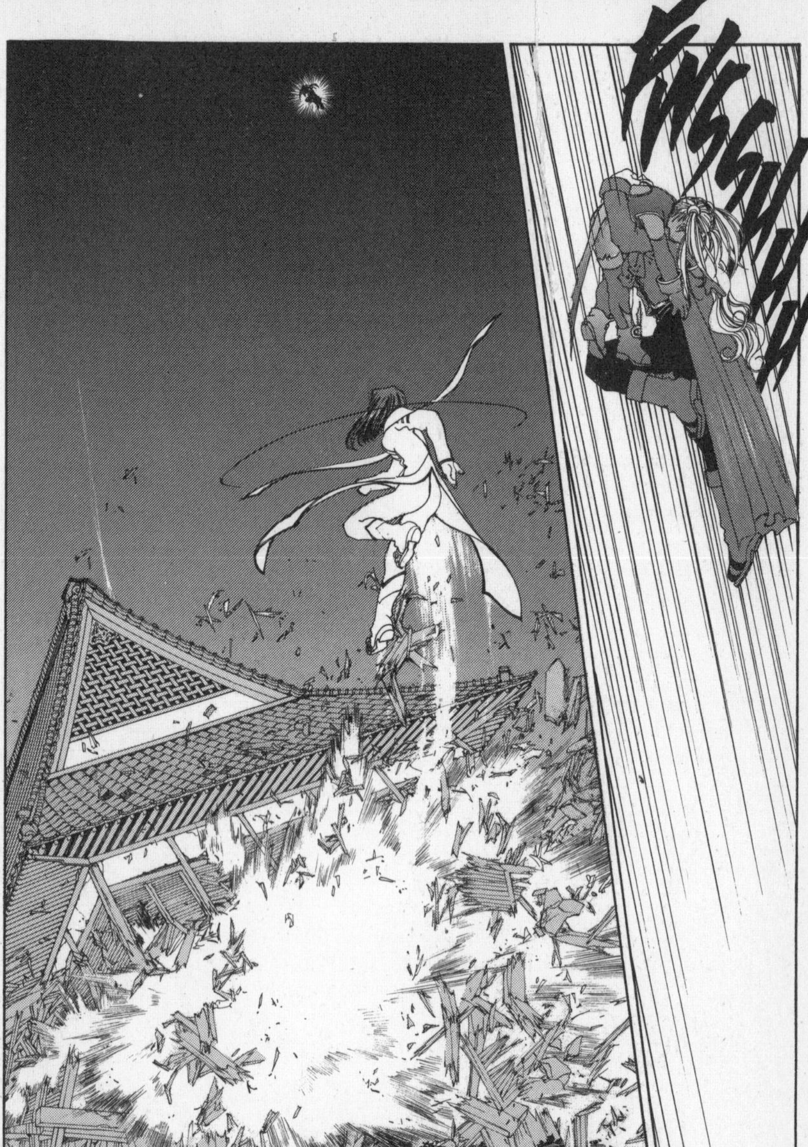
FWSSHHH

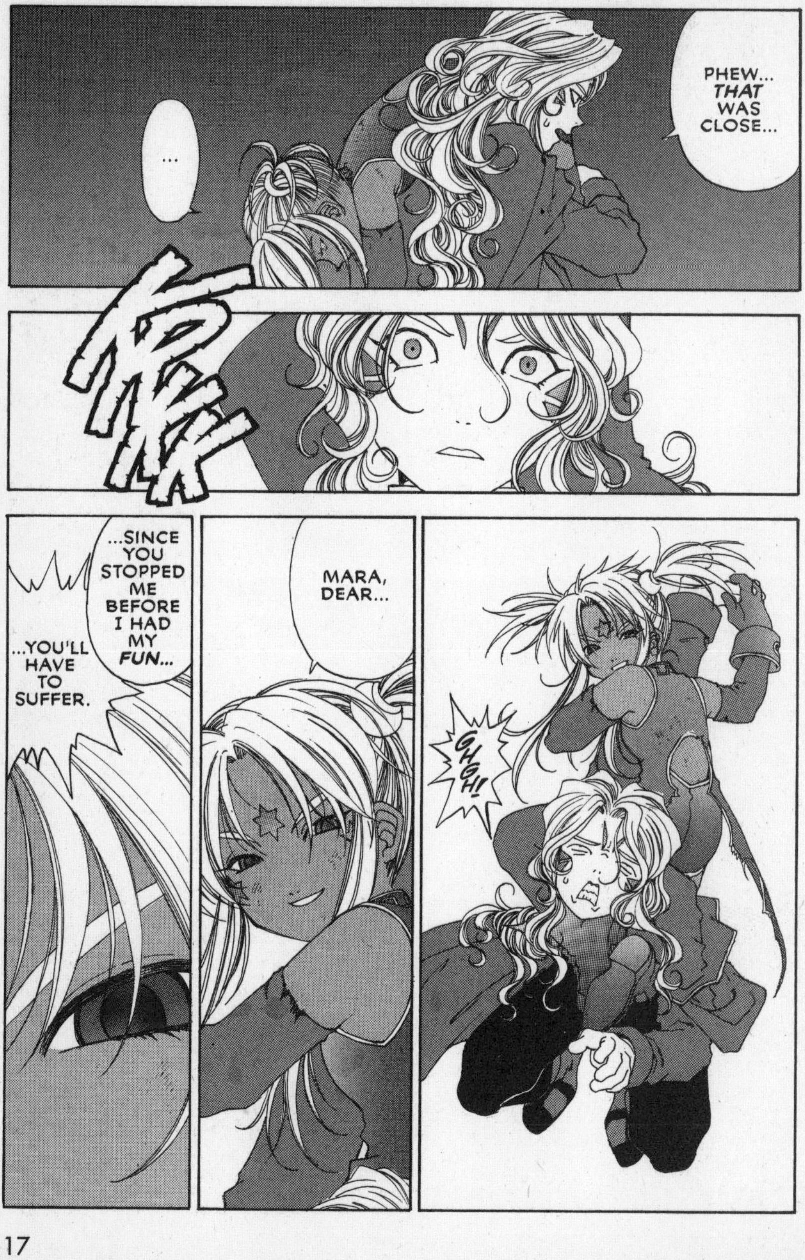
PHEW... *THAT* WAS CLOSE...
...
GHGH!
MARA, DEAR...
...SINCE YOU STOPPED ME BEFORE I HAD MY *FUN*...
...YOU'LL HAVE TO SUFFER.

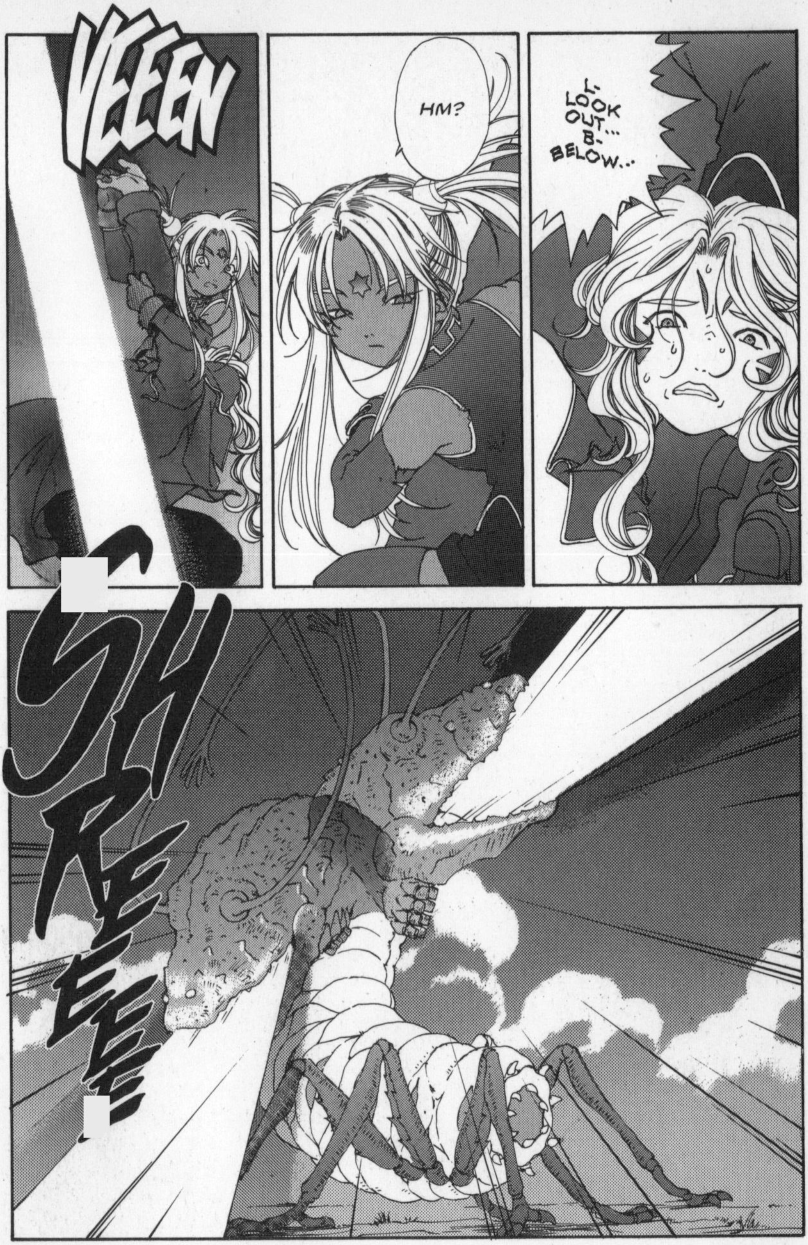
L-LOOK OUT... B-BELOW...
HM?
VEEEN
SHREEEEE

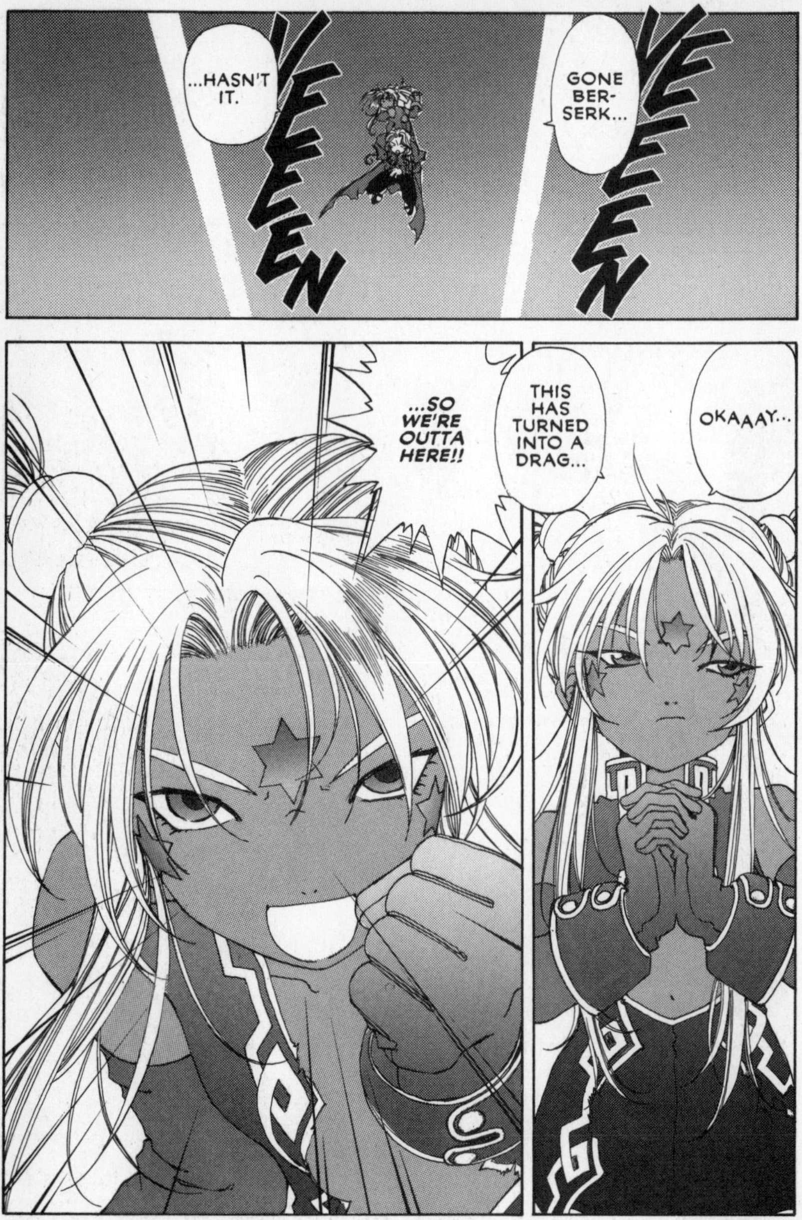
GONE BER-SERK...
...HASN'T IT.
OKAAAY...
THIS HAS TURNED INTO A DRAG...
...SO WE'RE OUTTA HERE!!

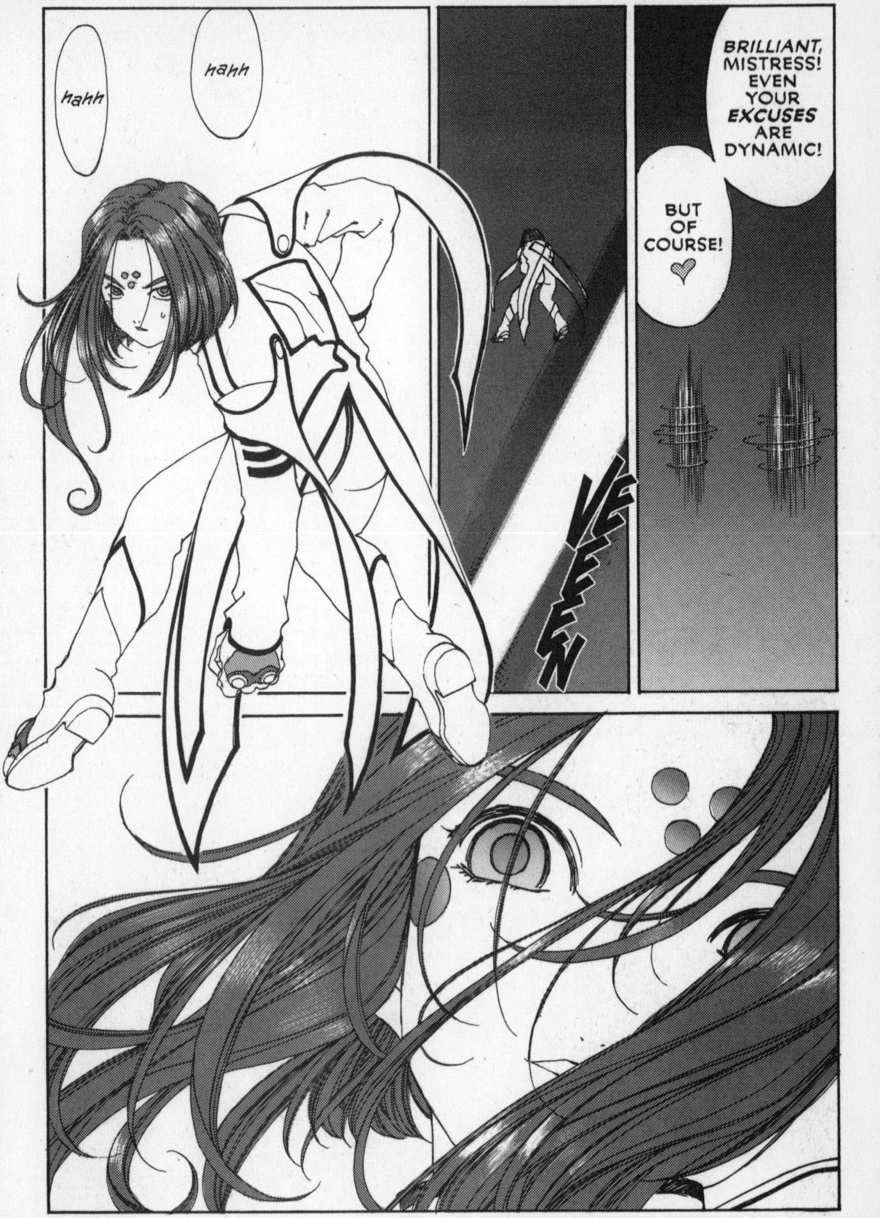

BRILLIANT, MISTRESS! EVEN YOUR ***EXCUSES*** ARE DYNAMIC!
BUT OF COURSE! ♡
VEEEEEN
hahh
hahh

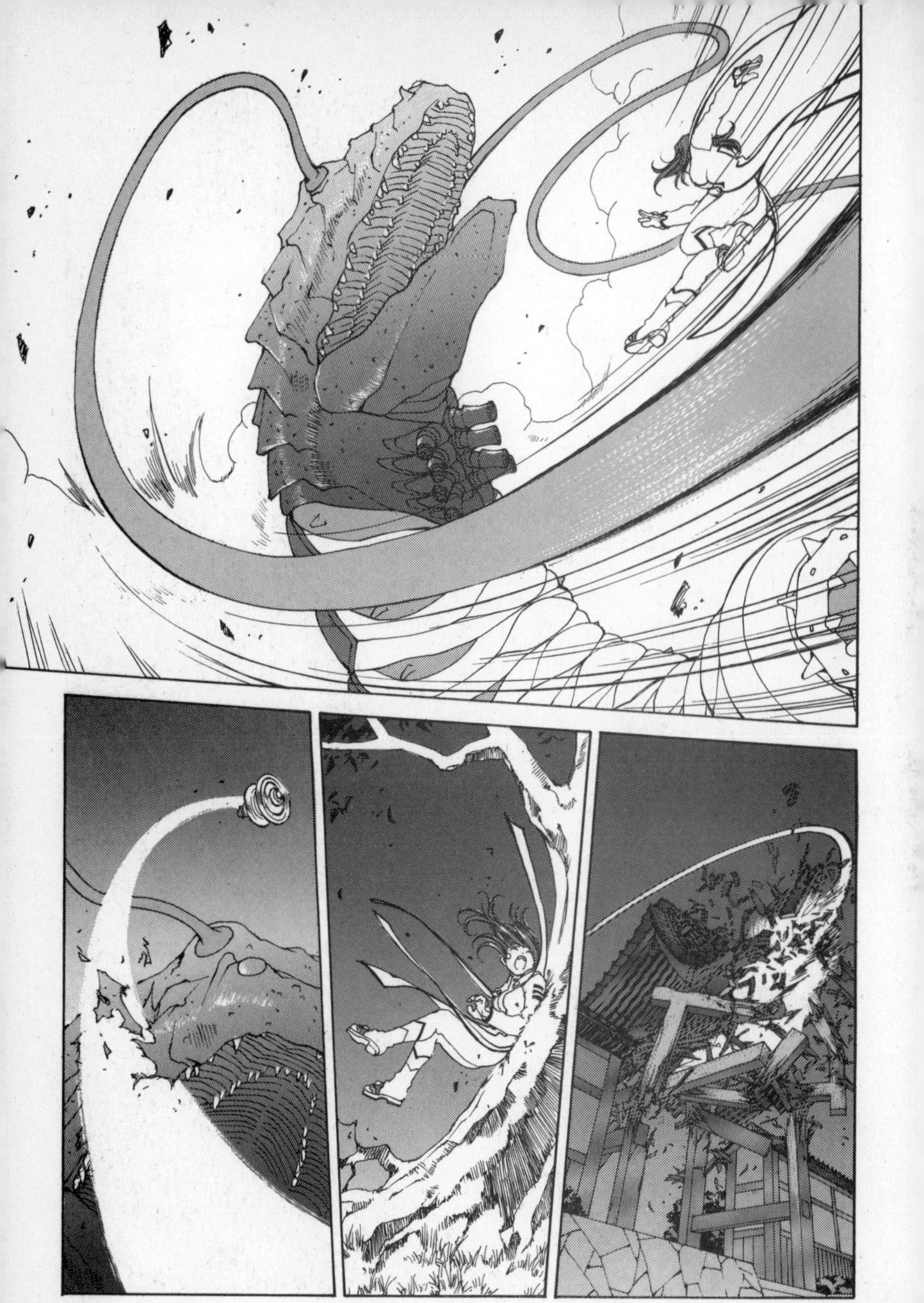

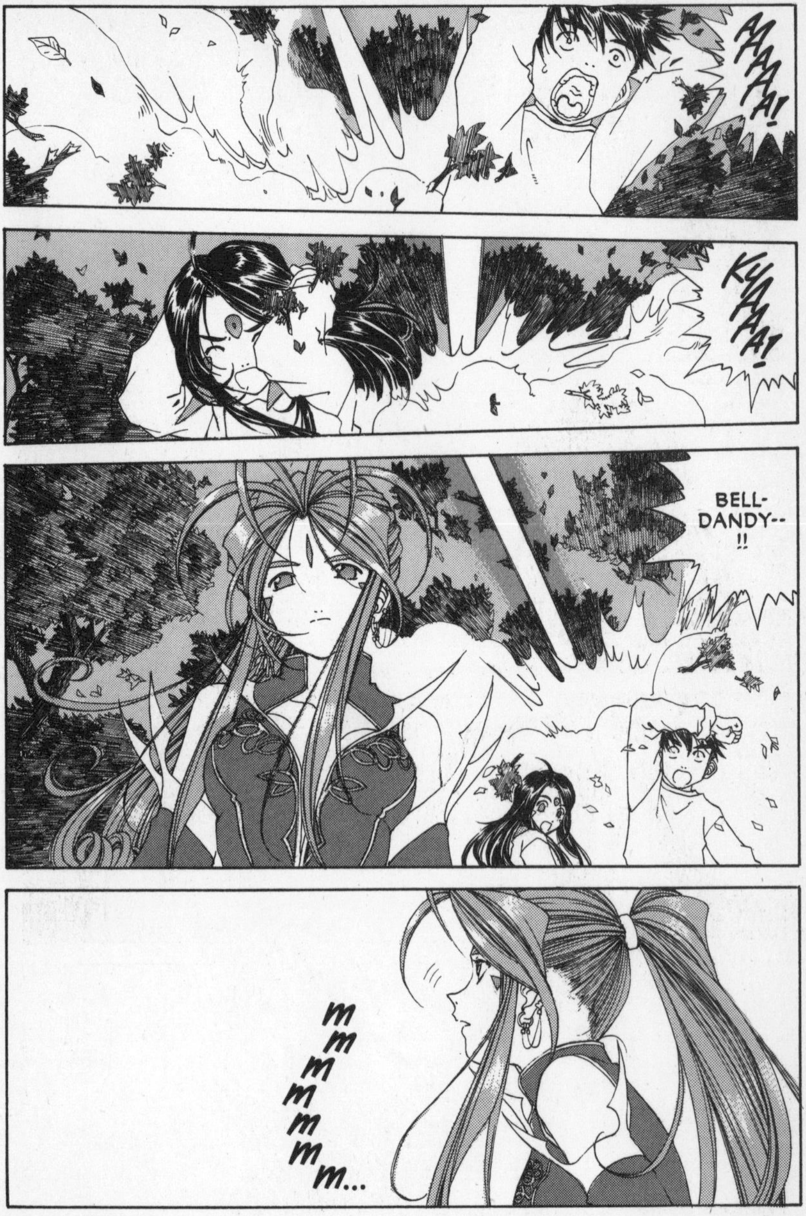
AAAAAA!
KYAAAA!
BELL-DANDY--!!
mmmmmmmm...

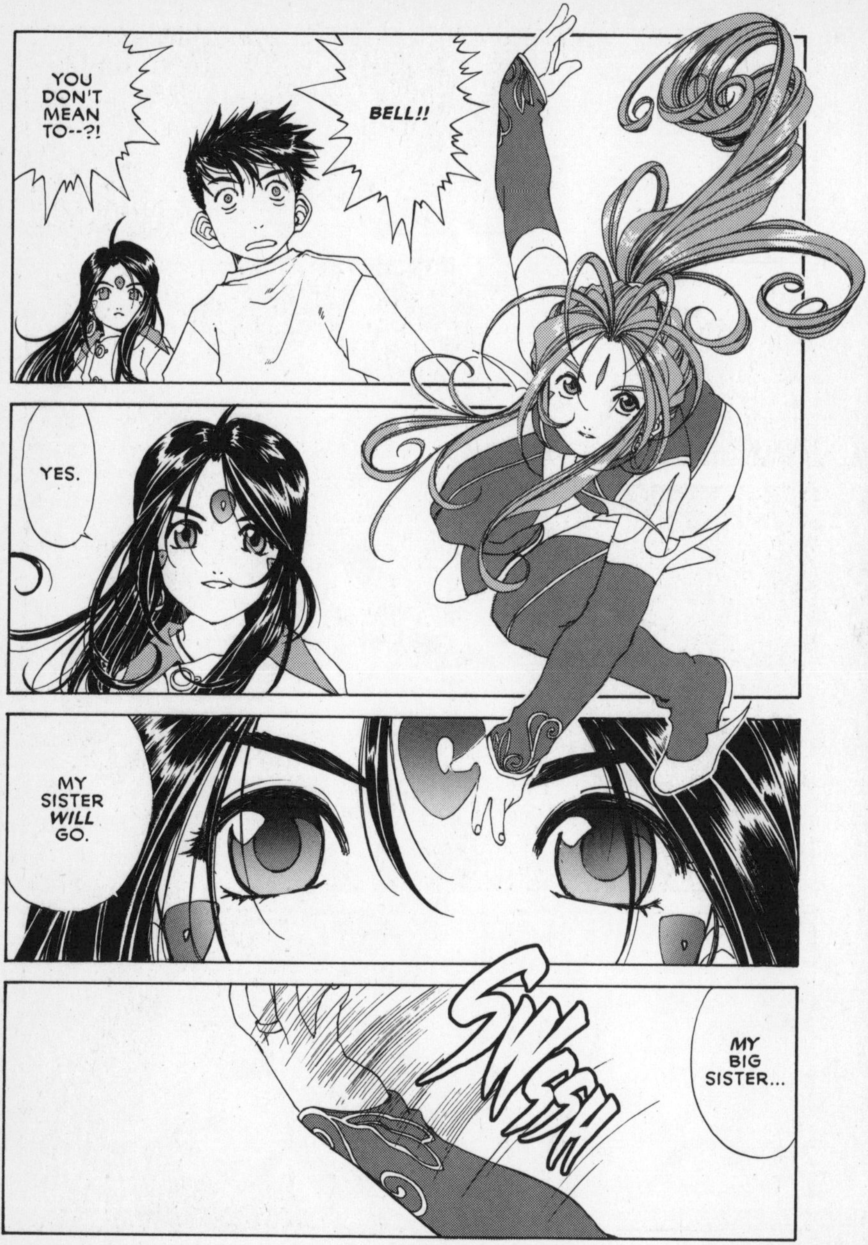
BELL!!
YOU DON'T MEAN TO--?!
YES.
MY SISTER *WILL* GO.
MY BIG SISTER...
SWISH

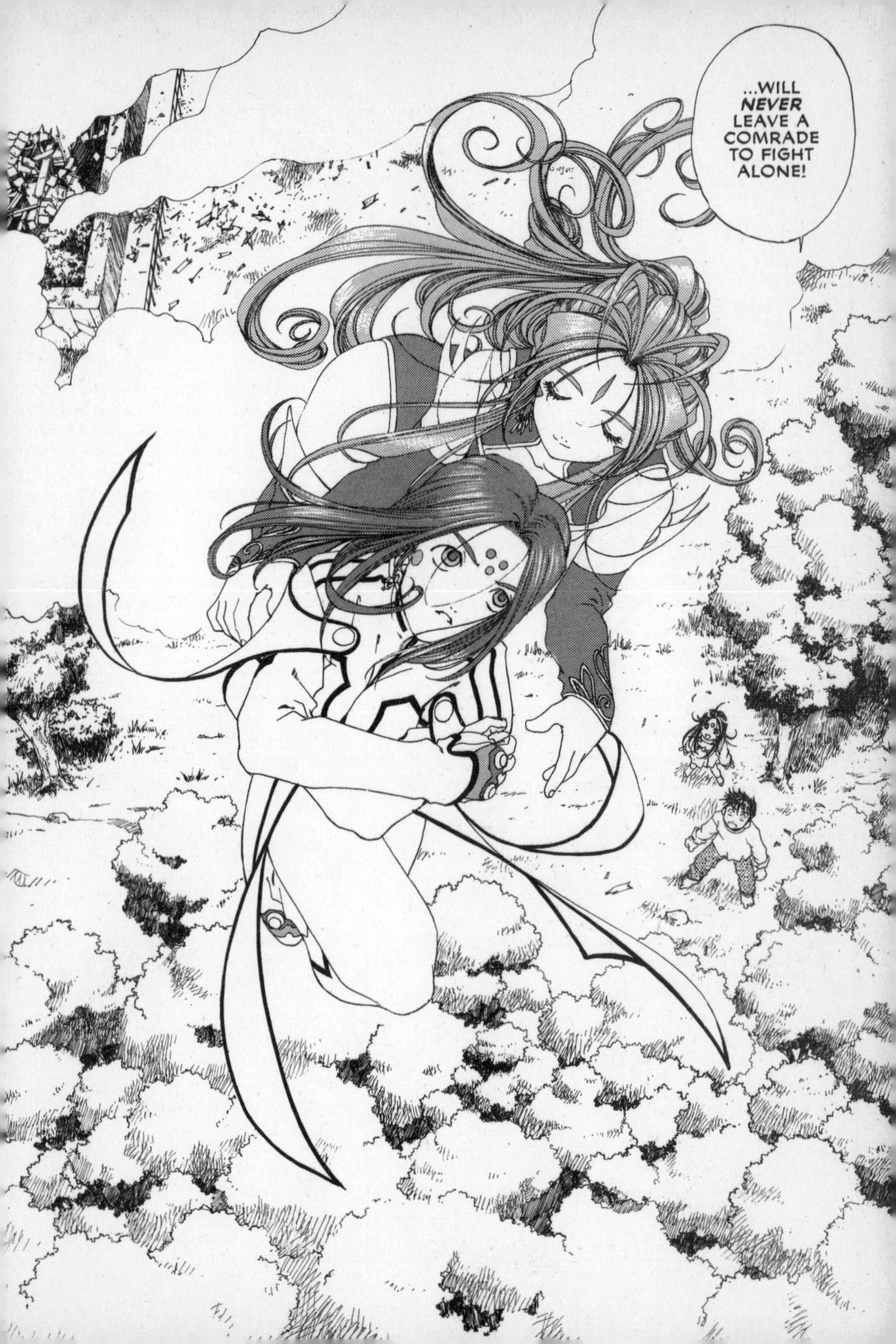
...WILL NEVER LEAVE A COMRADE TO FIGHT ALONE!

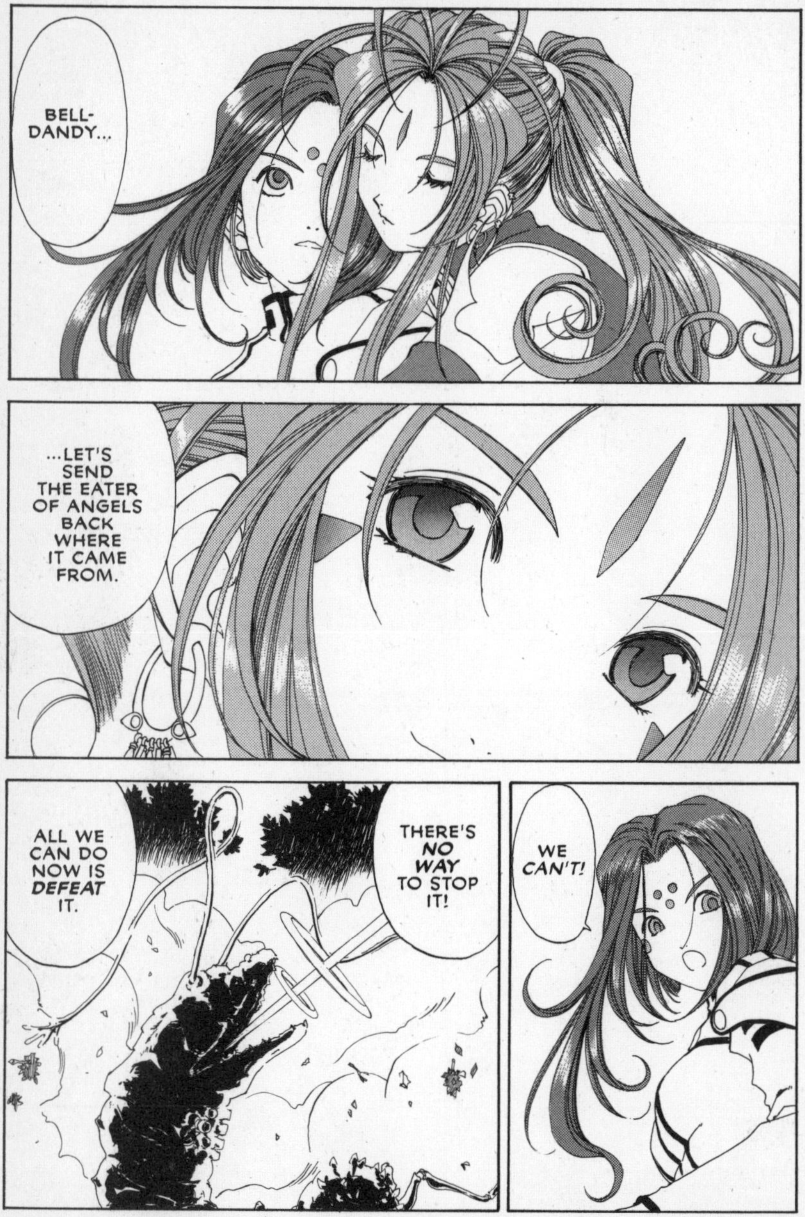
BELL-DANDY...
...LET'S SEND THE EATER OF ANGELS BACK WHERE IT CAME FROM.
WE *CAN'T!*
THERE'S ***NO WAY*** TO STOP IT!
ALL WE CAN DO NOW IS ***DEFEAT*** IT.

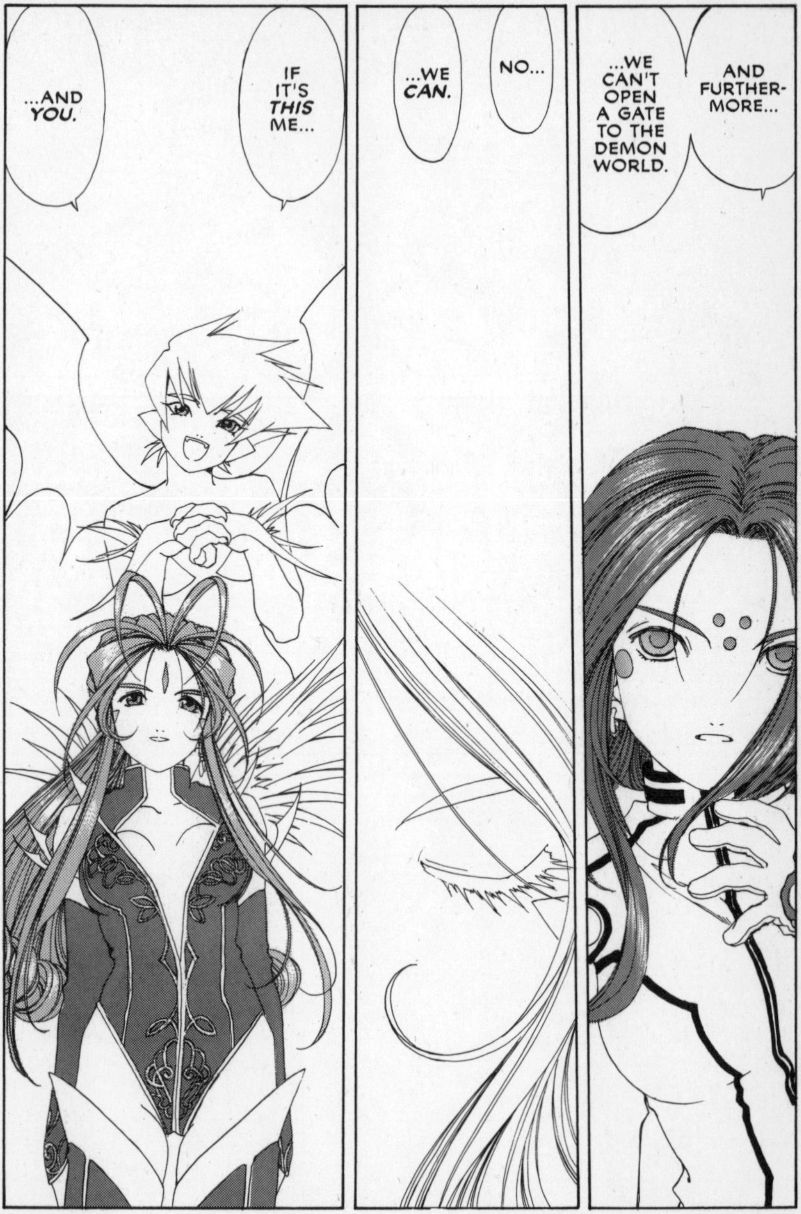
AND FURTHER-MORE...
...WE CAN'T OPEN A GATE TO THE DEMON WORLD.
NO...
...WE *CAN.*
IF IT'S *THIS* ME...
...AND *YOU.*

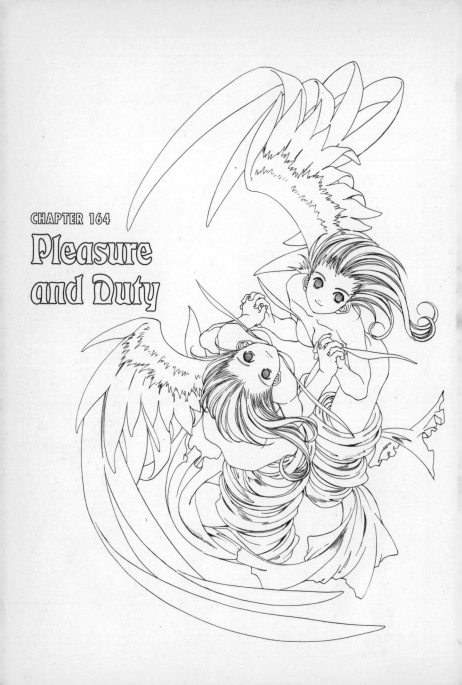

CHAPTER 164

Pleasure and Duty

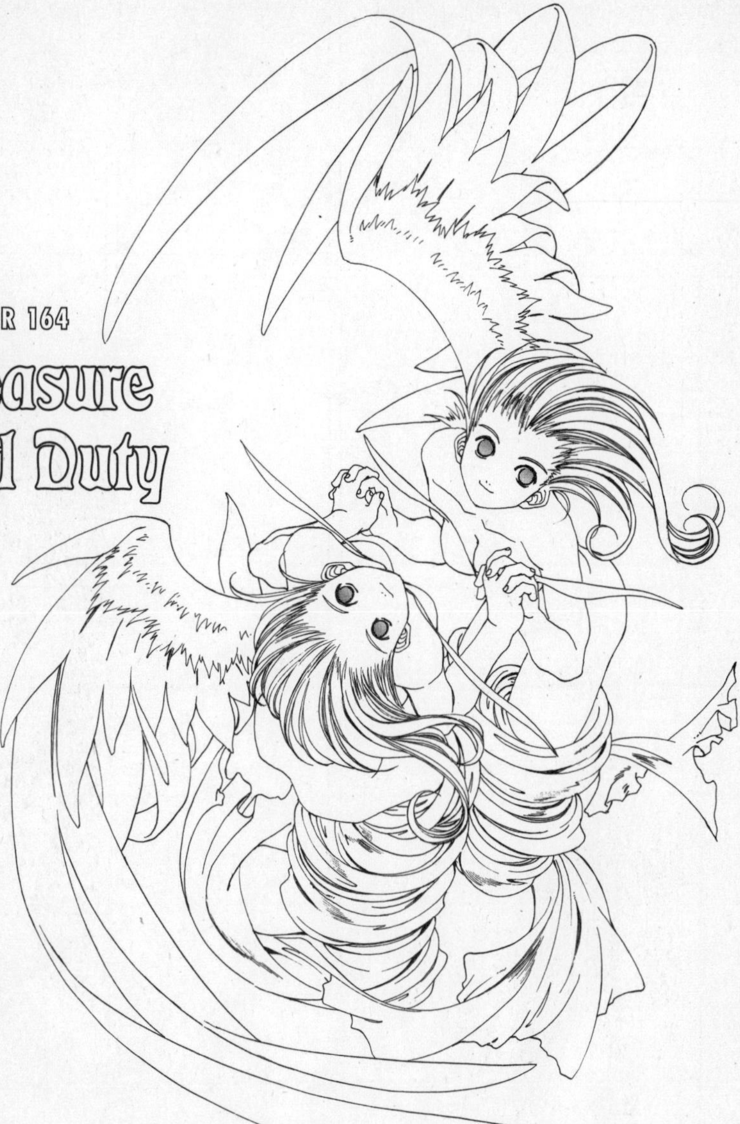

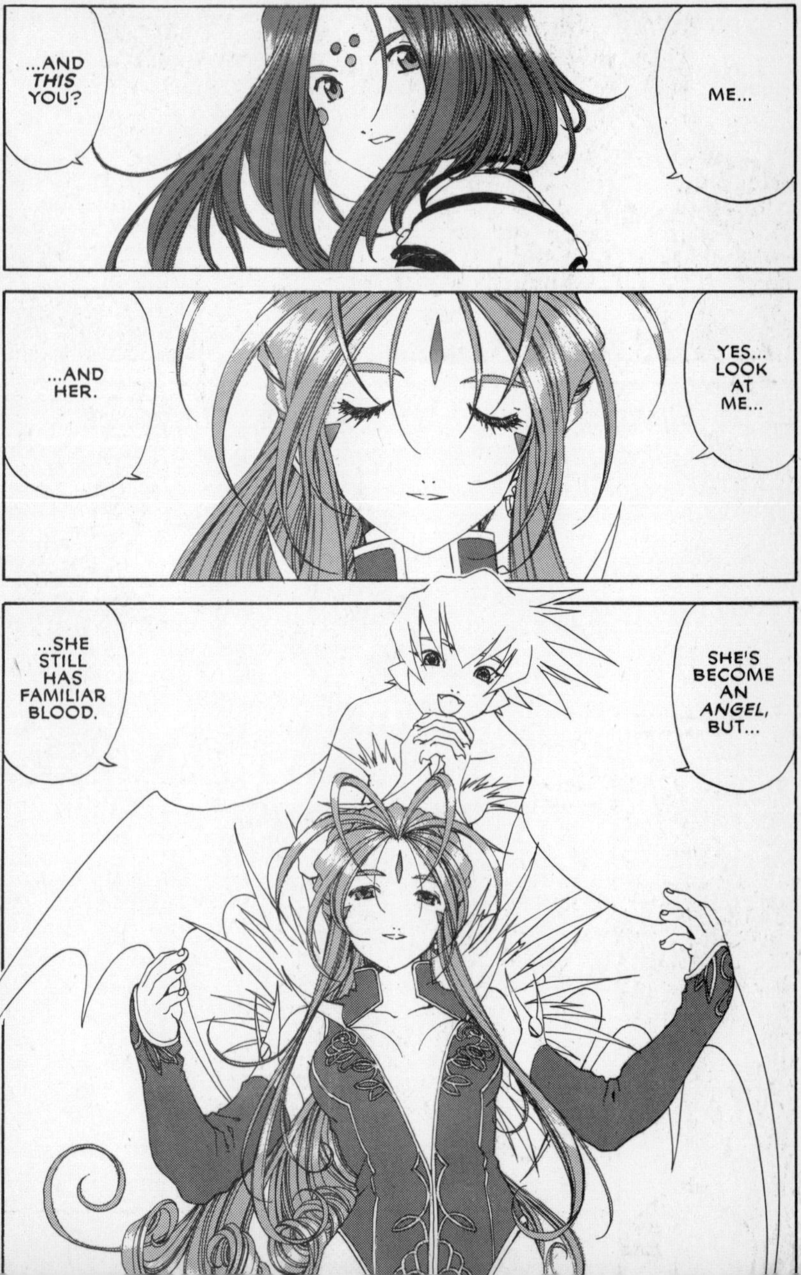
ME...
...AND *THIS* YOU?
YES... LOOK AT ME...
...AND HER.
SHE'S BECOME AN *ANGEL*, BUT...
...SHE STILL HAS FAMILIAR BLOOD.

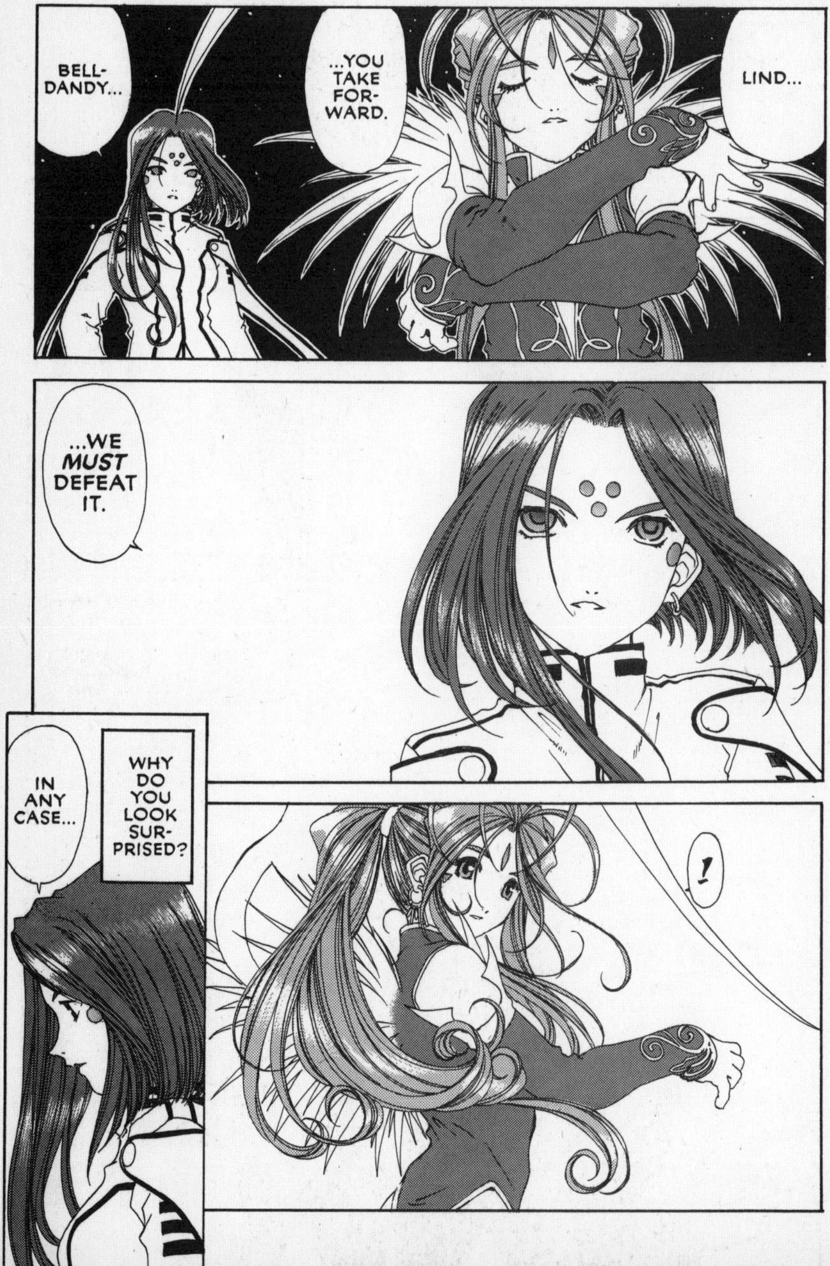
LIND...
...YOU TAKE FOR-WARD.
BELL-DANDY...
...WE *MUST* DEFEAT IT.
!
WHY DO YOU LOOK SUR-PRISED?
IN ANY CASE...

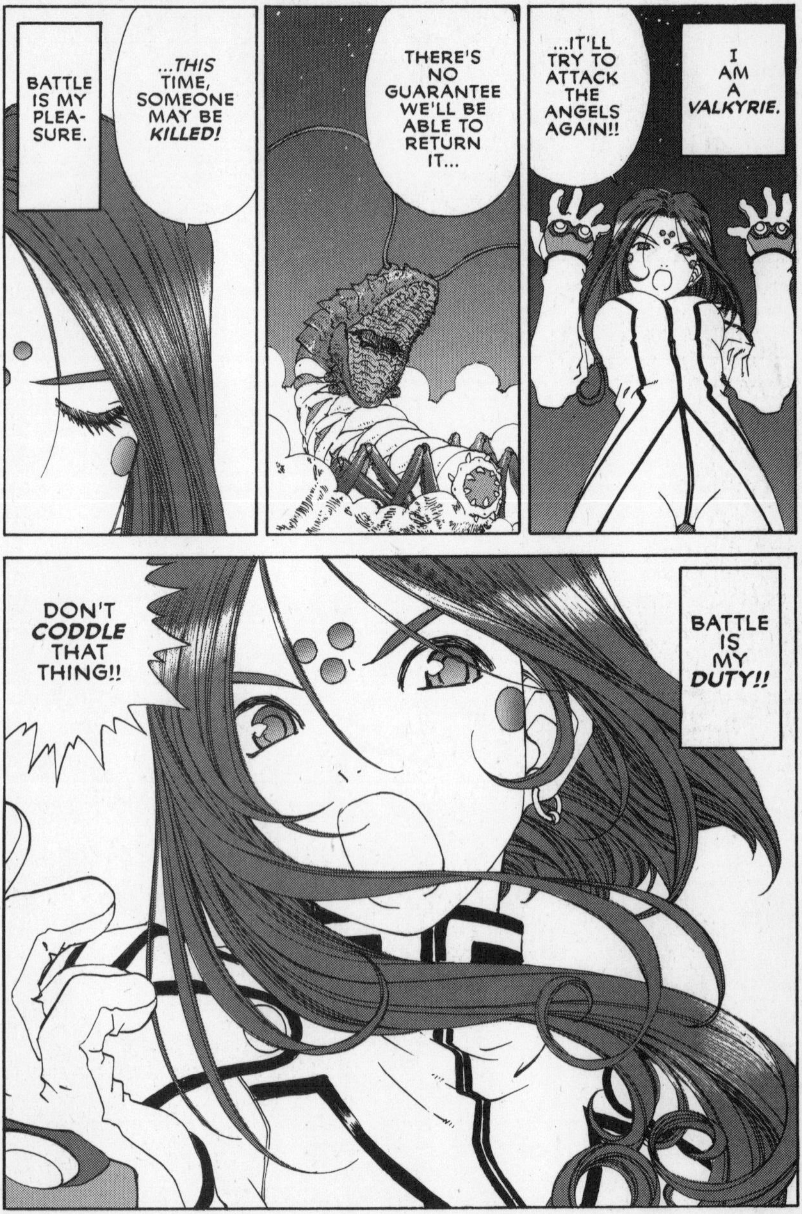
I AM A VALKYRIE.
...IT'LL TRY TO ATTACK THE ANGELS AGAIN!!
THERE'S NO GUARANTEE WE'LL BE ABLE TO RETURN IT...
...THIS TIME, SOMEONE MAY BE KILLED!
BATTLE IS MY PLEA-SURE.
BATTLE IS MY DUTY!!
DON'T CODDLE THAT THING!!

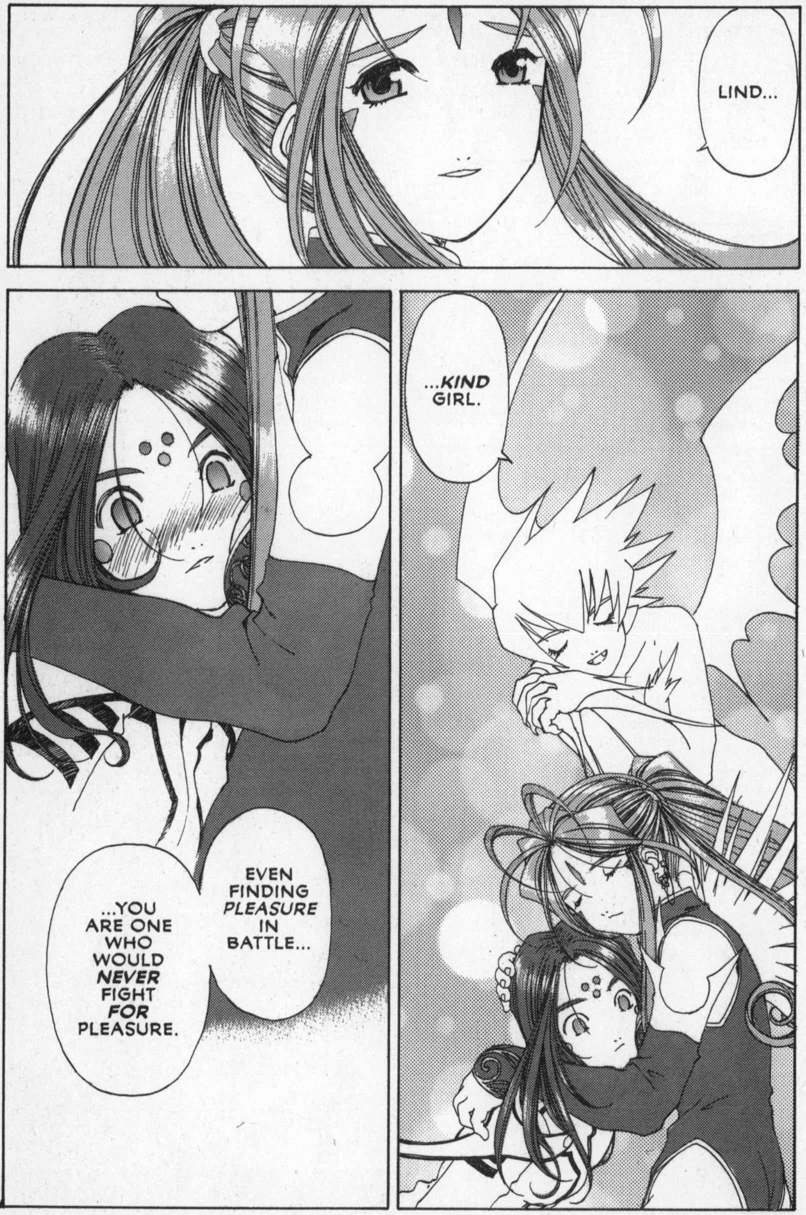
LIND...
...*KIND* GIRL.
EVEN FINDING *PLEASURE* IN BATTLE...
...YOU ARE ONE WHO WOULD *NEVER* FIGHT *FOR* PLEASURE.

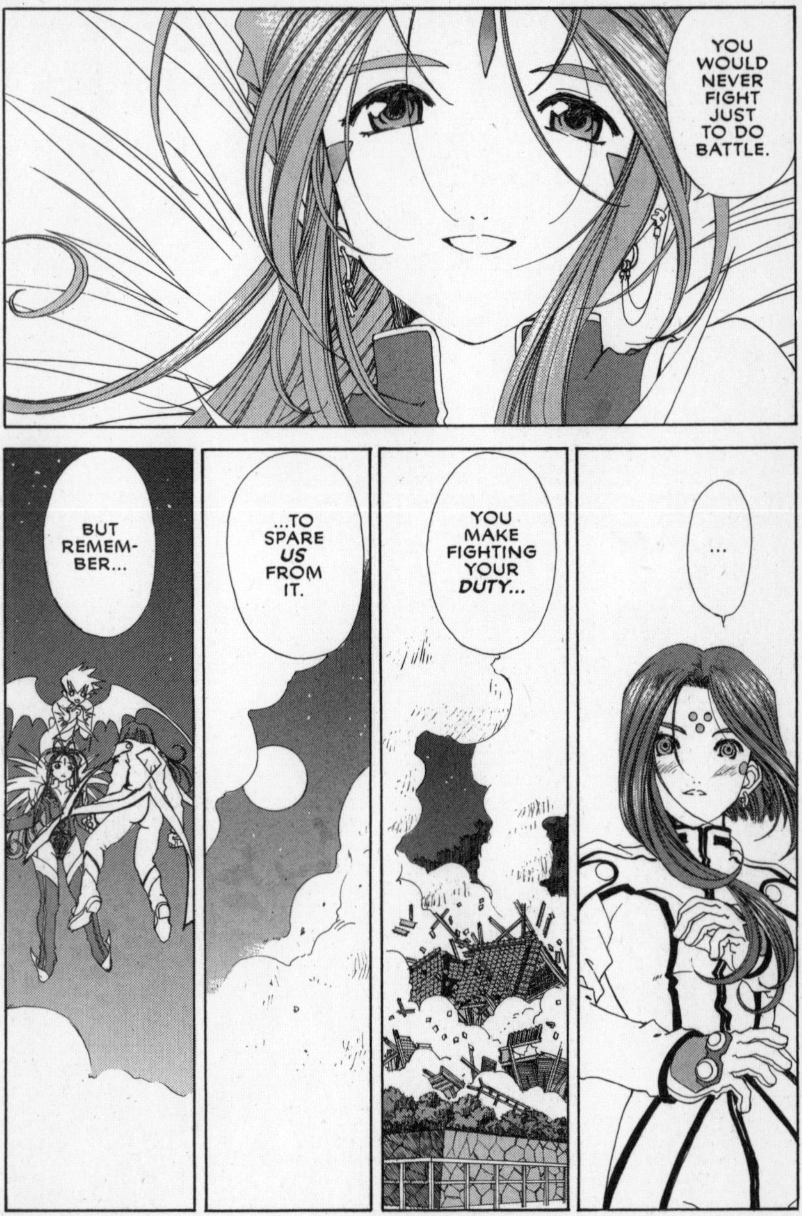
YOU WOULD NEVER FIGHT JUST TO DO BATTLE.
...
YOU MAKE FIGHTING YOUR *DUTY*...
...TO SPARE *US* FROM IT.
BUT REMEM-BER...

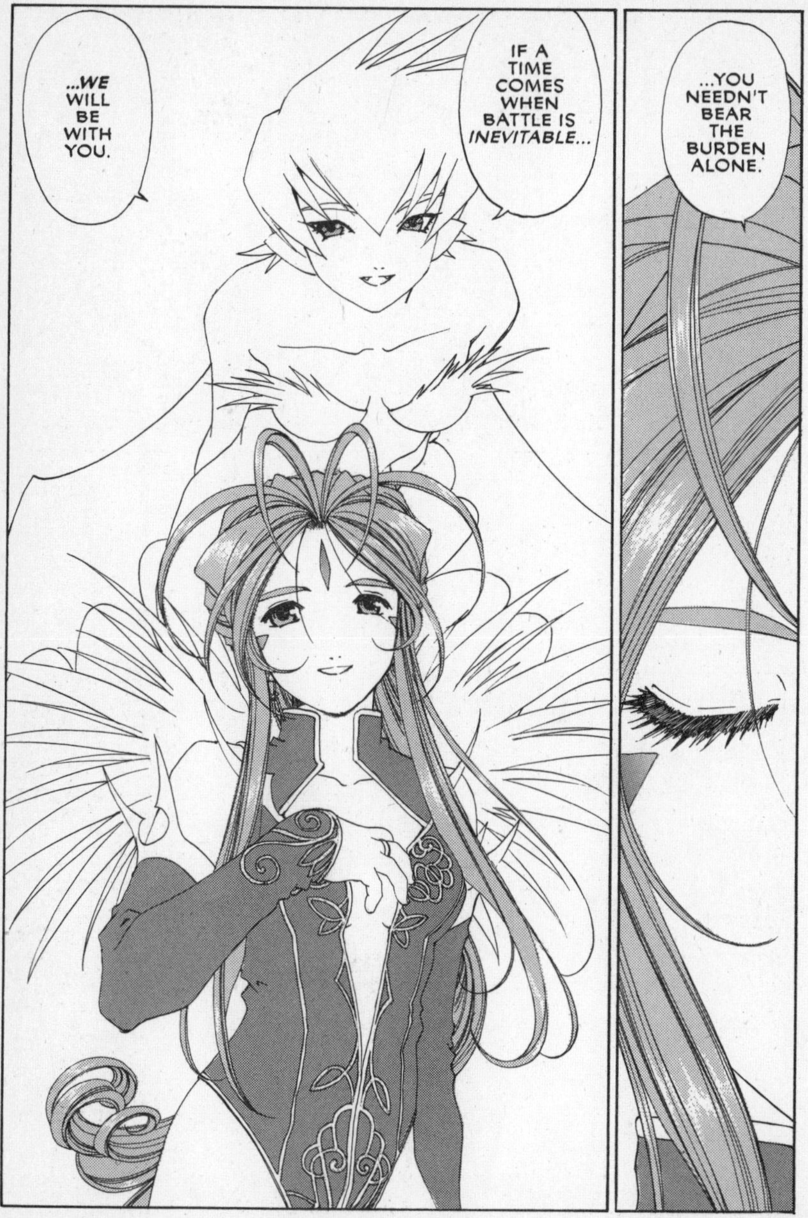
...YOU NEEDN'T BEAR THE BURDEN ALONE.
IF A TIME COMES WHEN BATTLE IS *INEVITABLE*...
...***WE*** WILL BE WITH YOU.

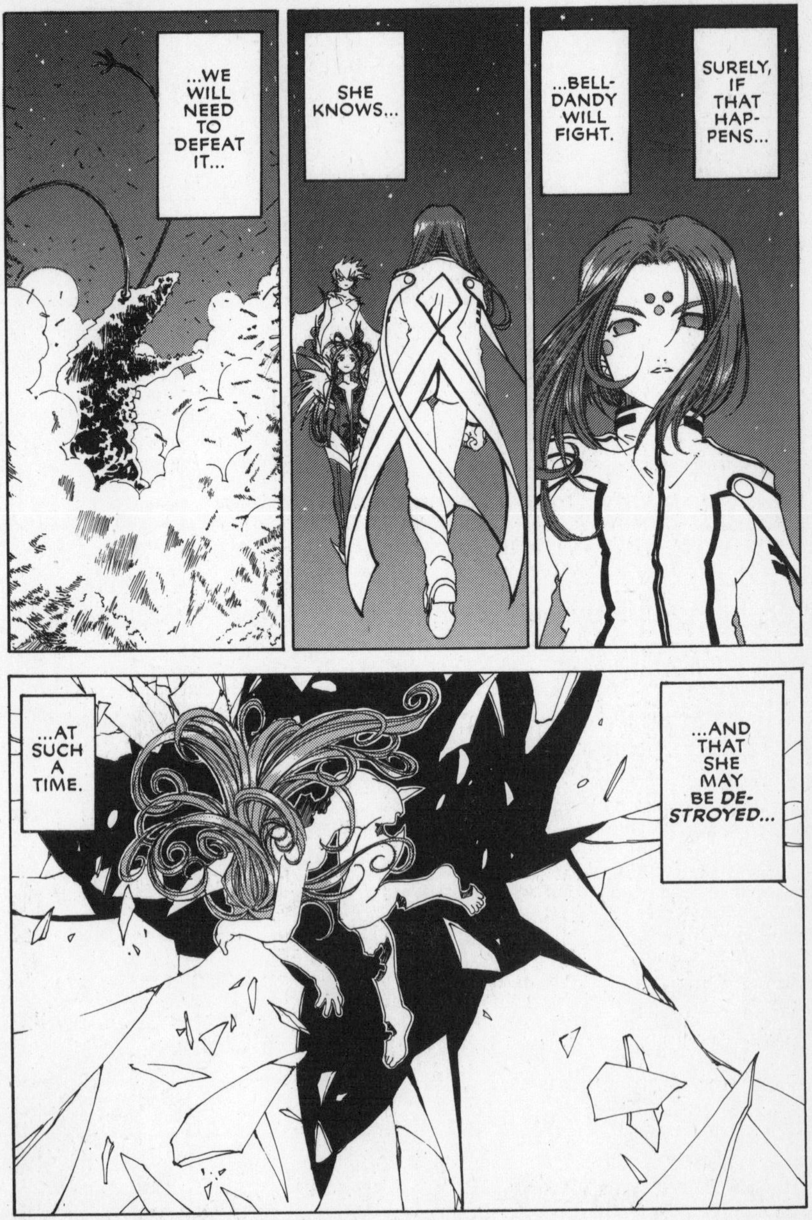
SURELY, IF THAT HAP-PENS...
...BELL-DANDY WILL FIGHT.
SHE KNOWS...
...WE WILL NEED TO DEFEAT IT...
...AND THAT SHE MAY BE *DE-STROYED*...
...AT SUCH A TIME.

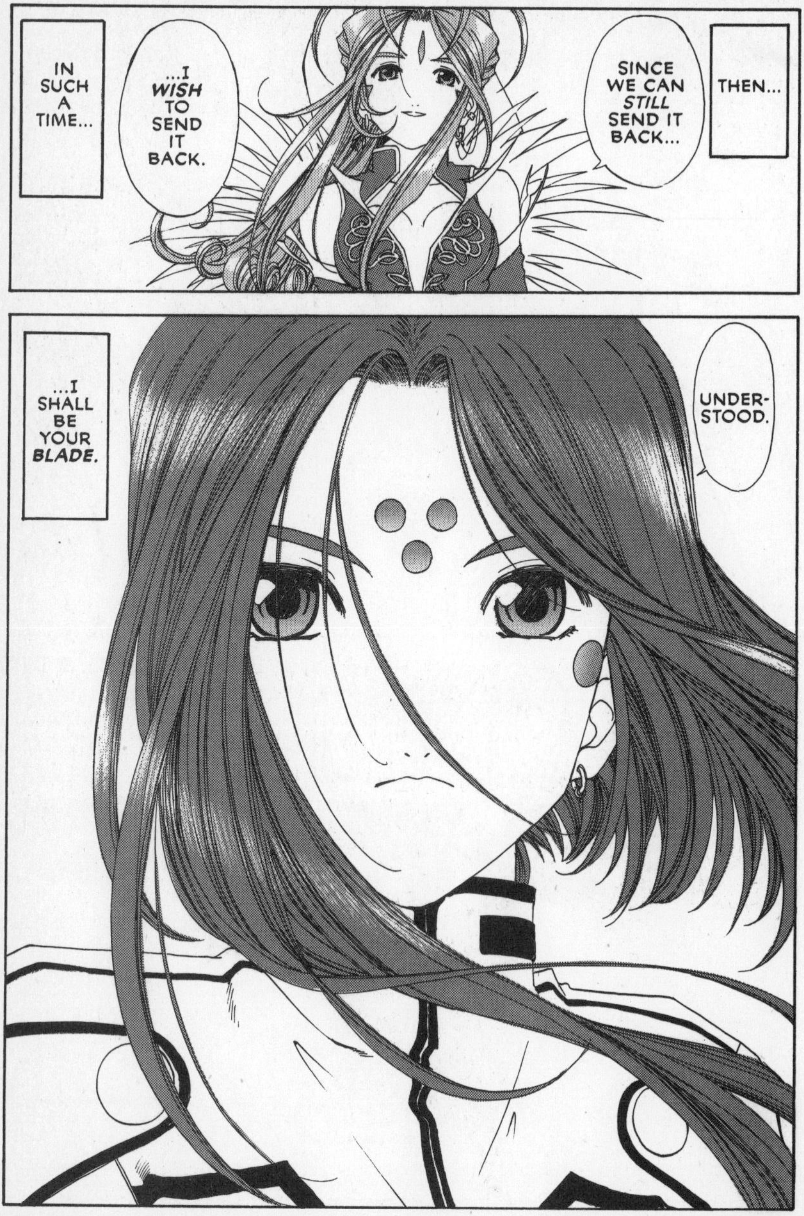
THEN...
SINCE WE CAN *STILL* SEND IT BACK...
...I *WISH* TO SEND IT BACK.
IN SUCH A TIME...
UNDER-STOOD.
...I SHALL BE YOUR *BLADE.*

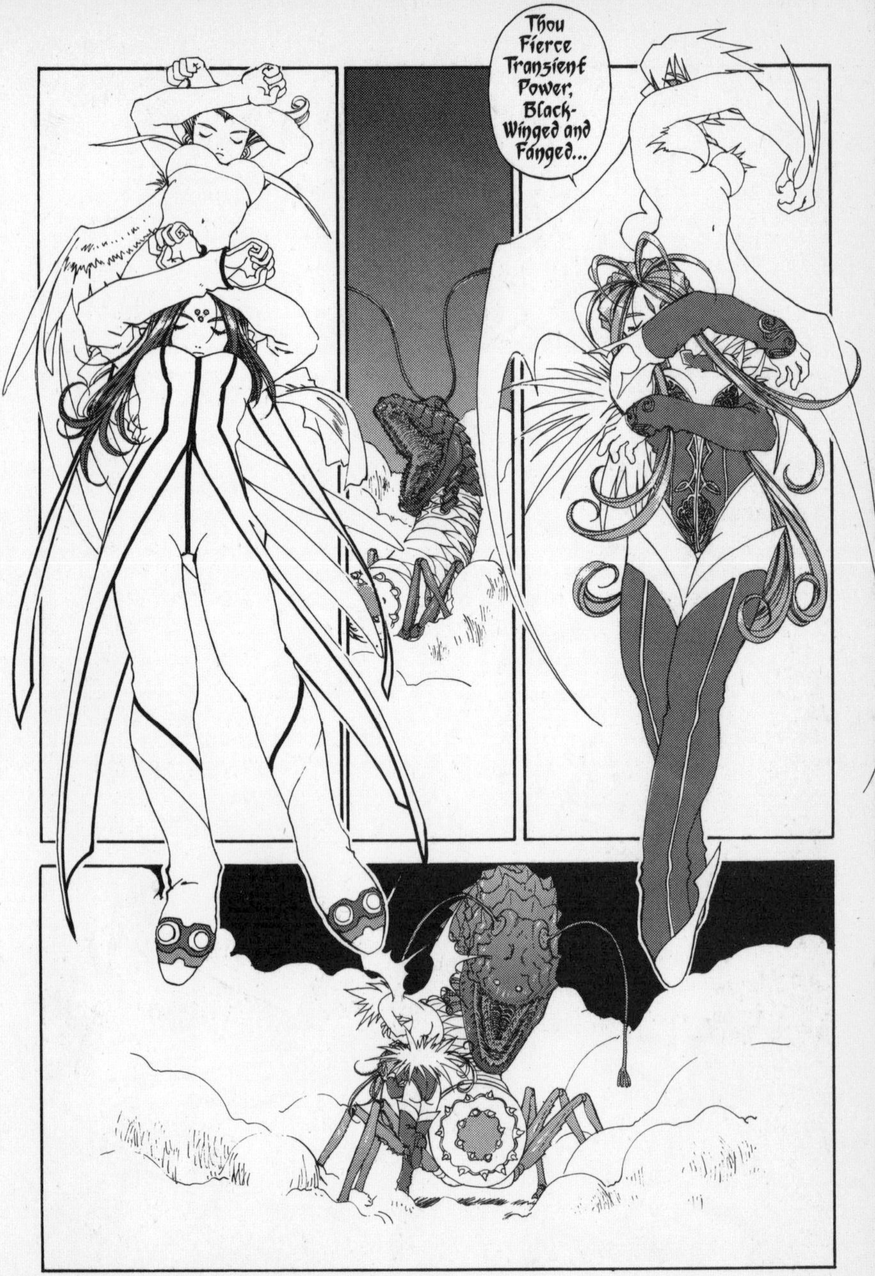
Thou Fierce Transient Power, Black-Winged and Fanged...

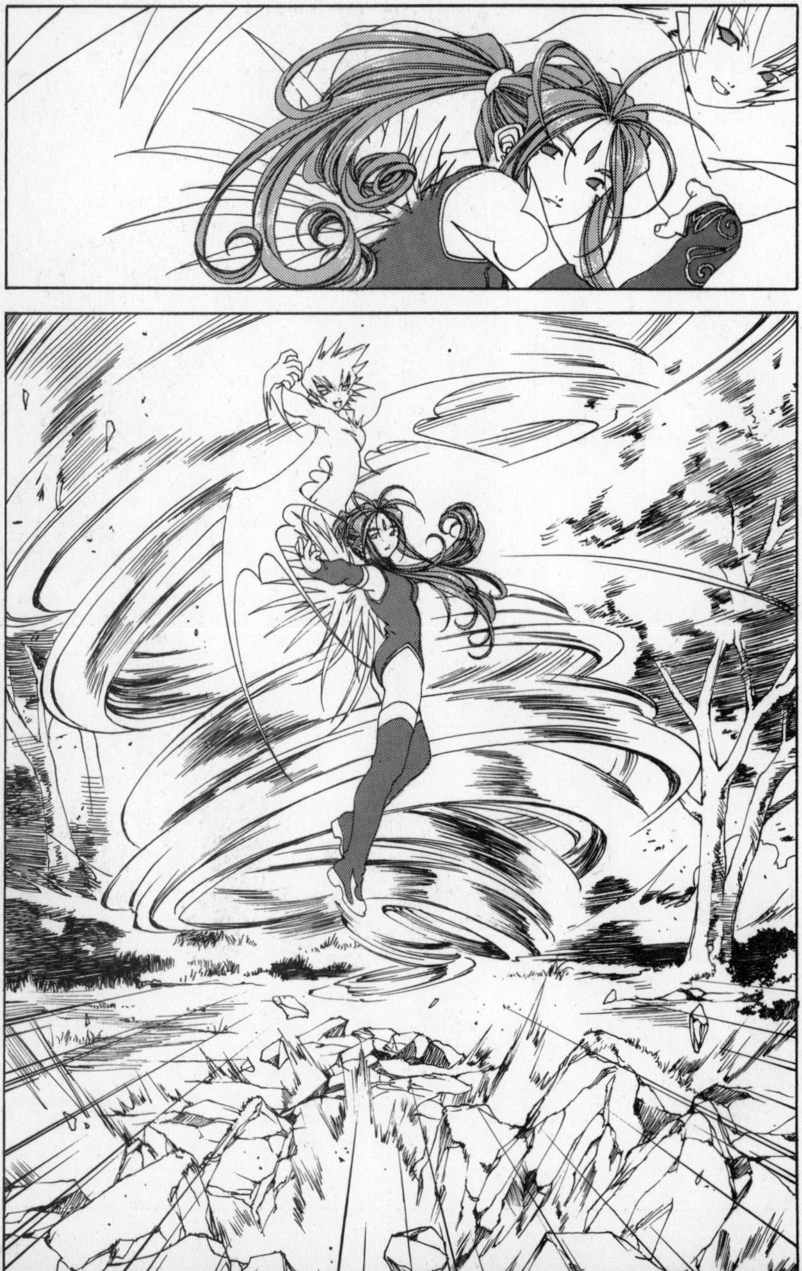

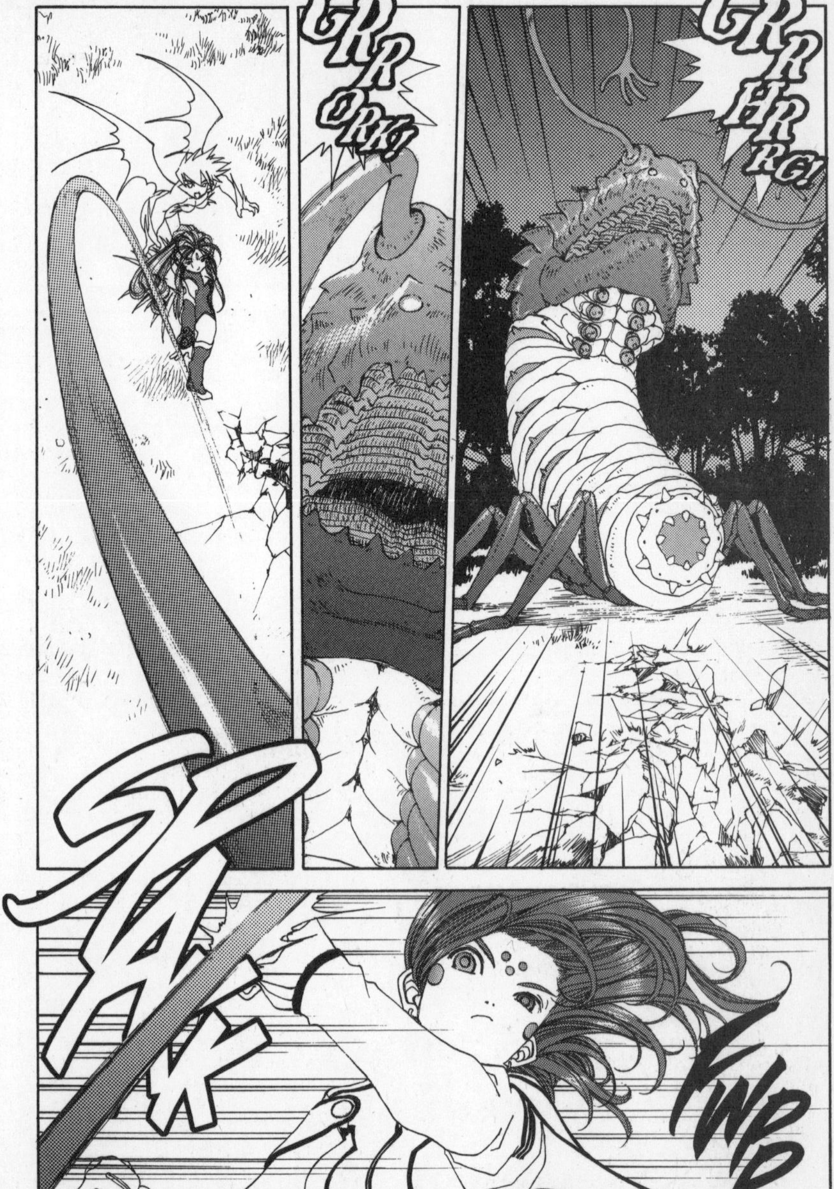
GRRFRRG!
GRRORK!
FWDD
SKAK

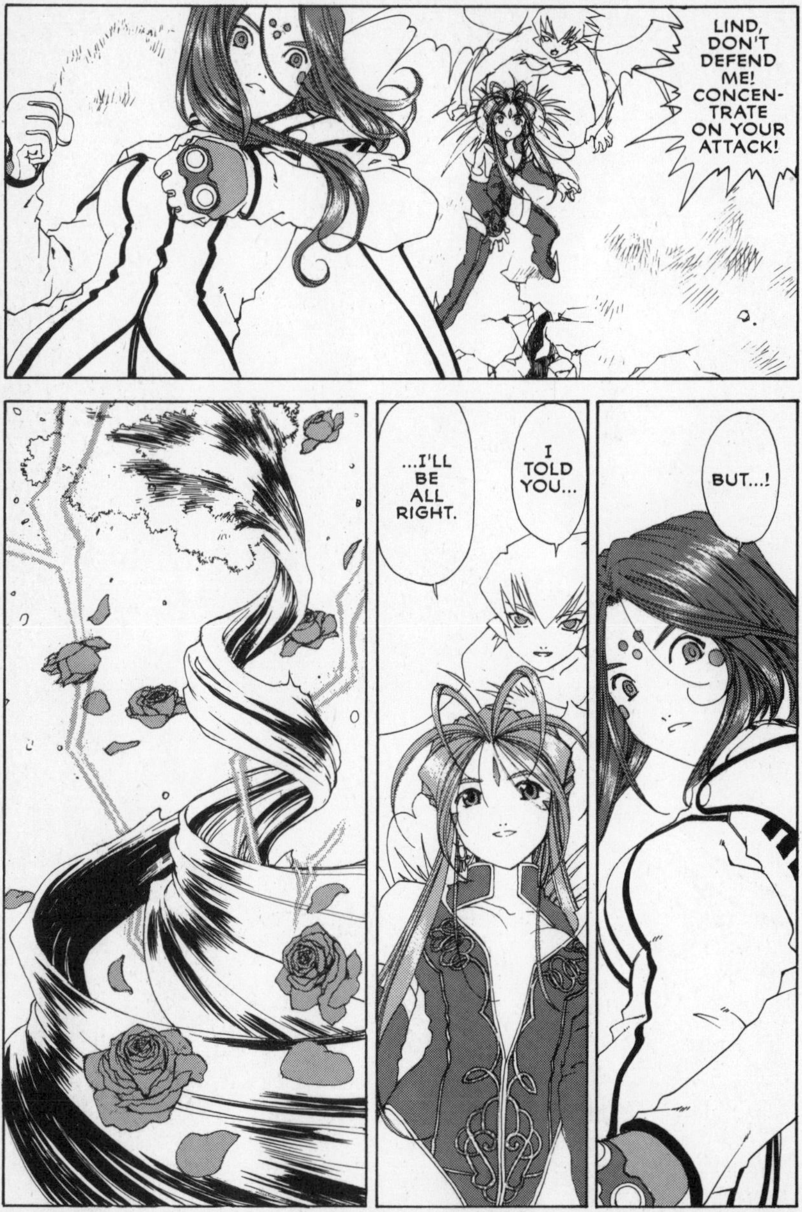
LIND, DON'T DEFEND ME! CONCENTRATE ON YOUR ATTACK!
BUT...!
I TOLD YOU...
...I'LL BE ALL RIGHT.

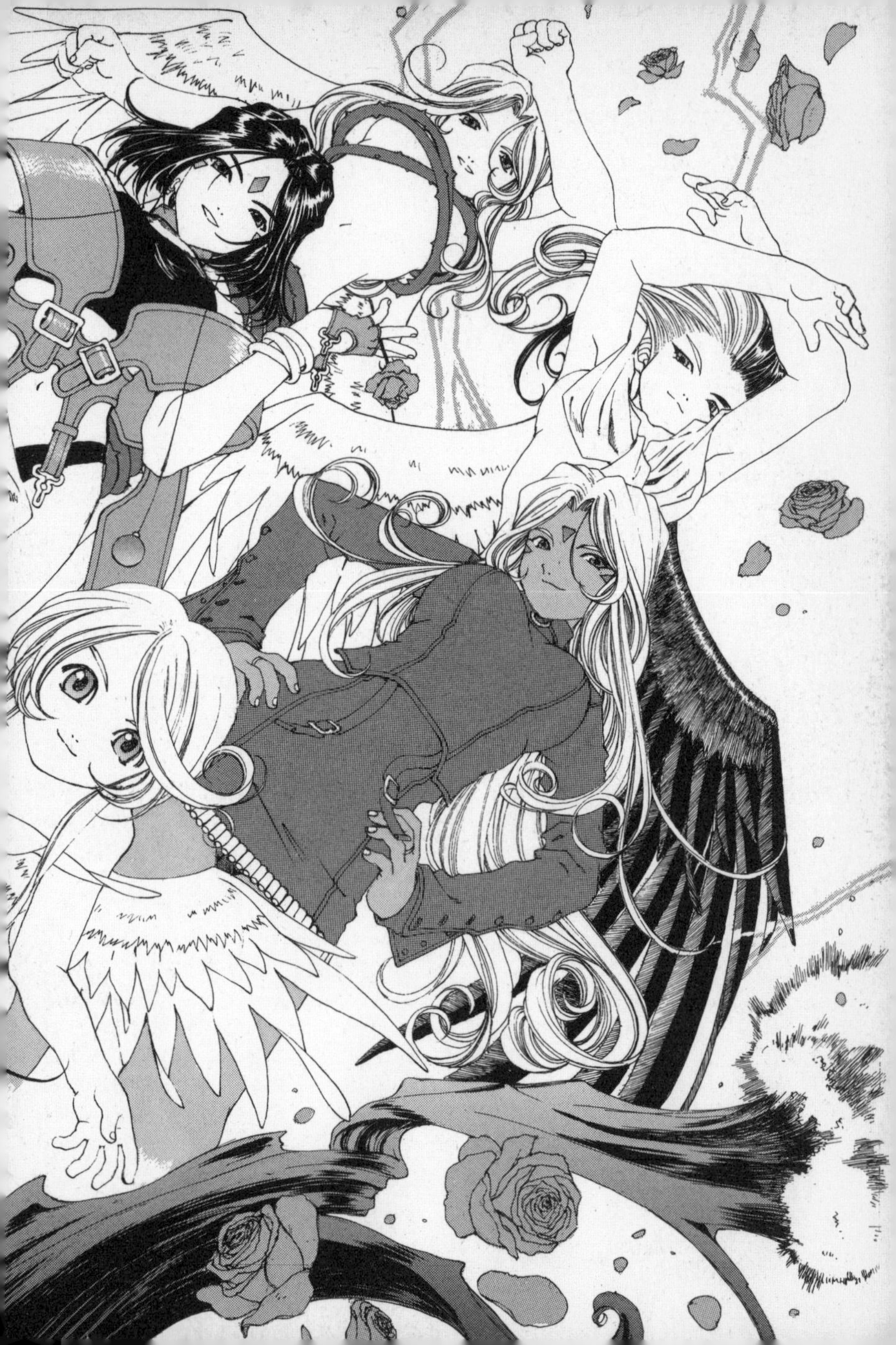

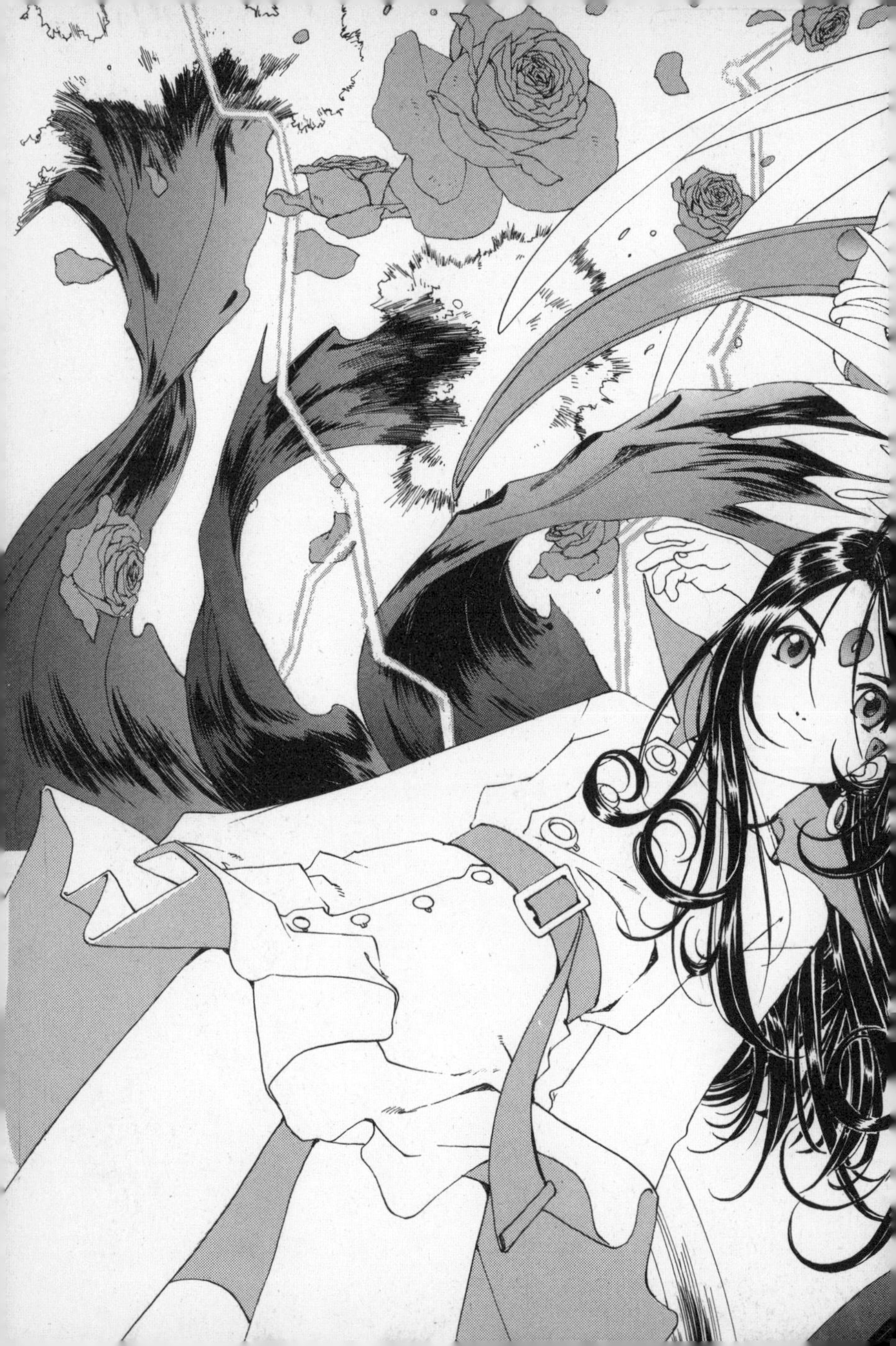

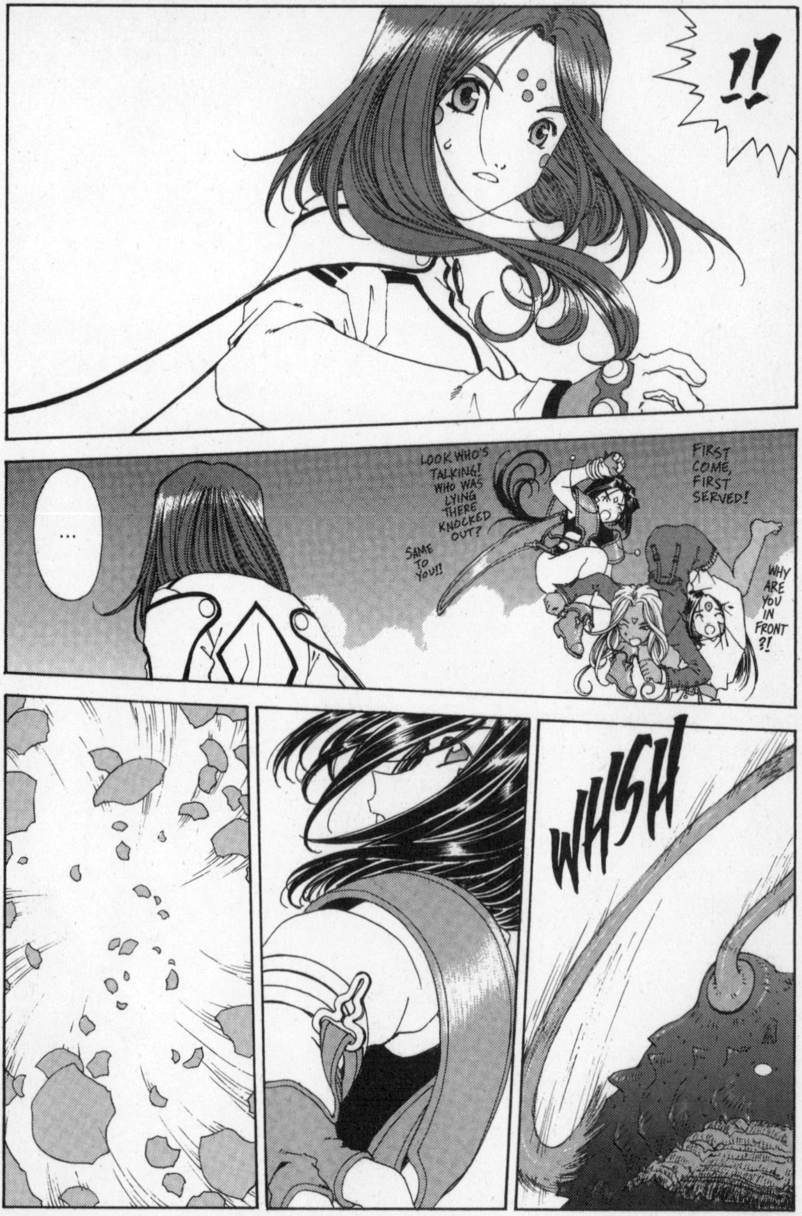
!!
WHY ARE YOU IN FRONT?!
FIRST COME, FIRST SERVED!
LOOK WHO'S TALKING! WHO WAS LYING THERE KNOCKED OUT?
SAME TO YOU!!
...
WHSH

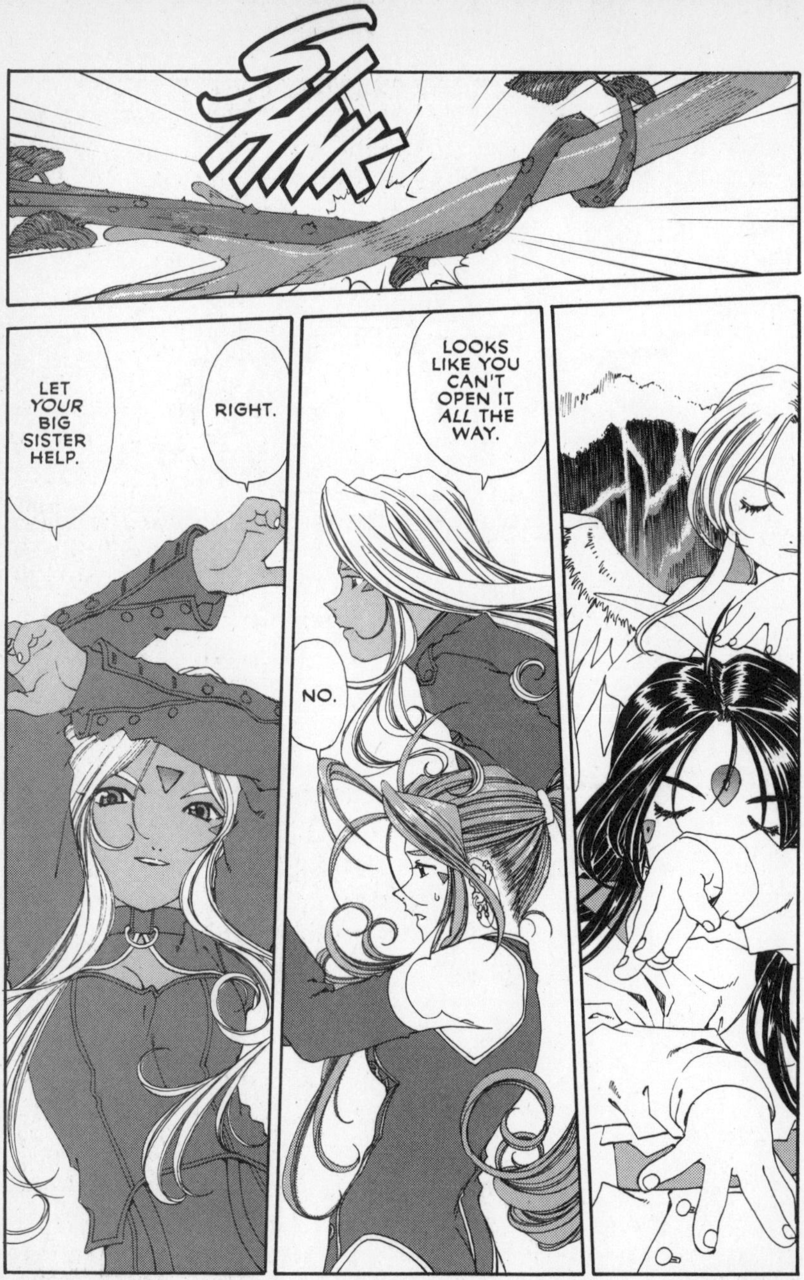
SHINK
LOOKS LIKE YOU CAN'T OPEN IT *ALL* THE WAY.
NO.
RIGHT.
LET *YOUR* BIG SISTER HELP.

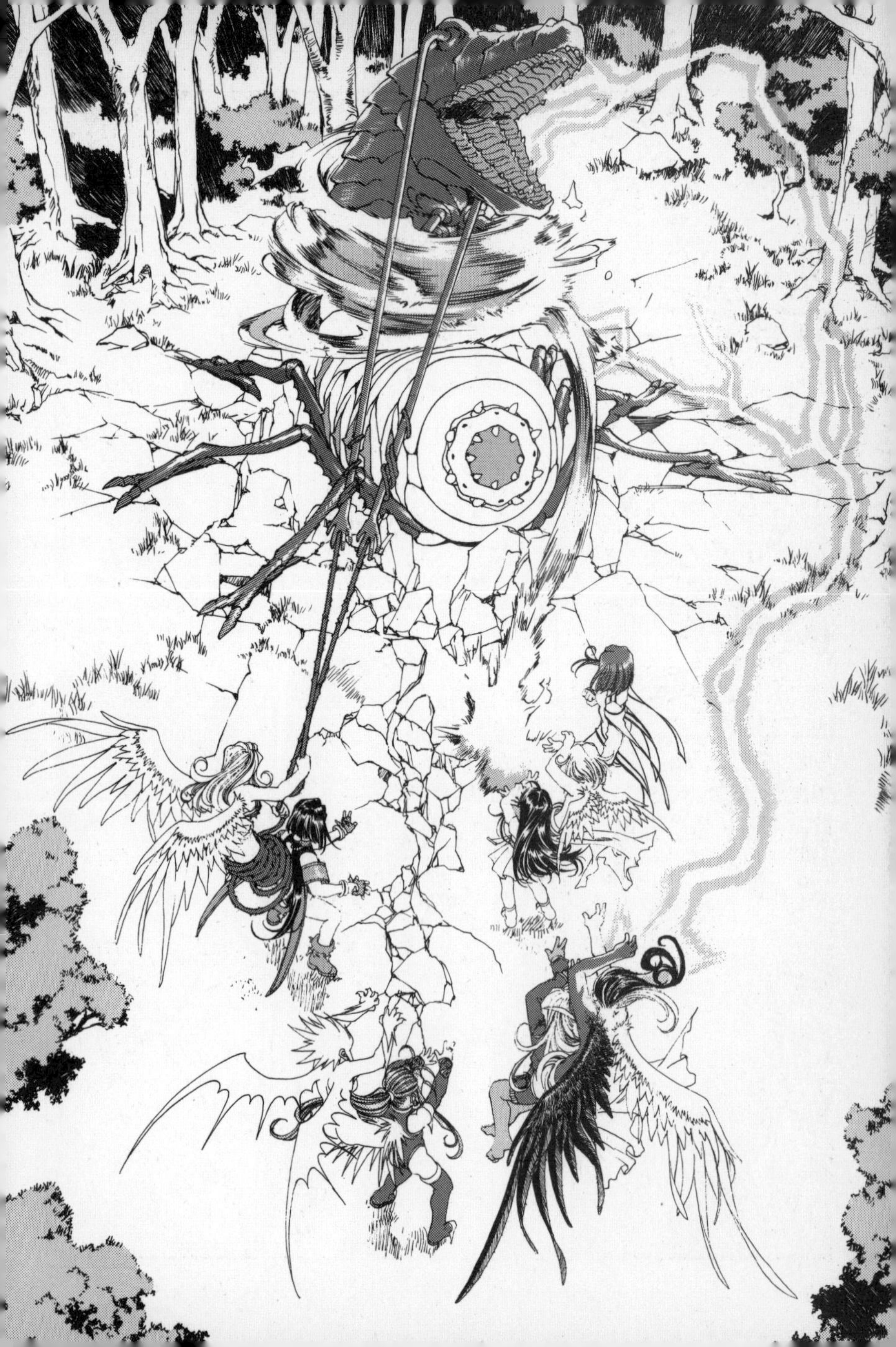

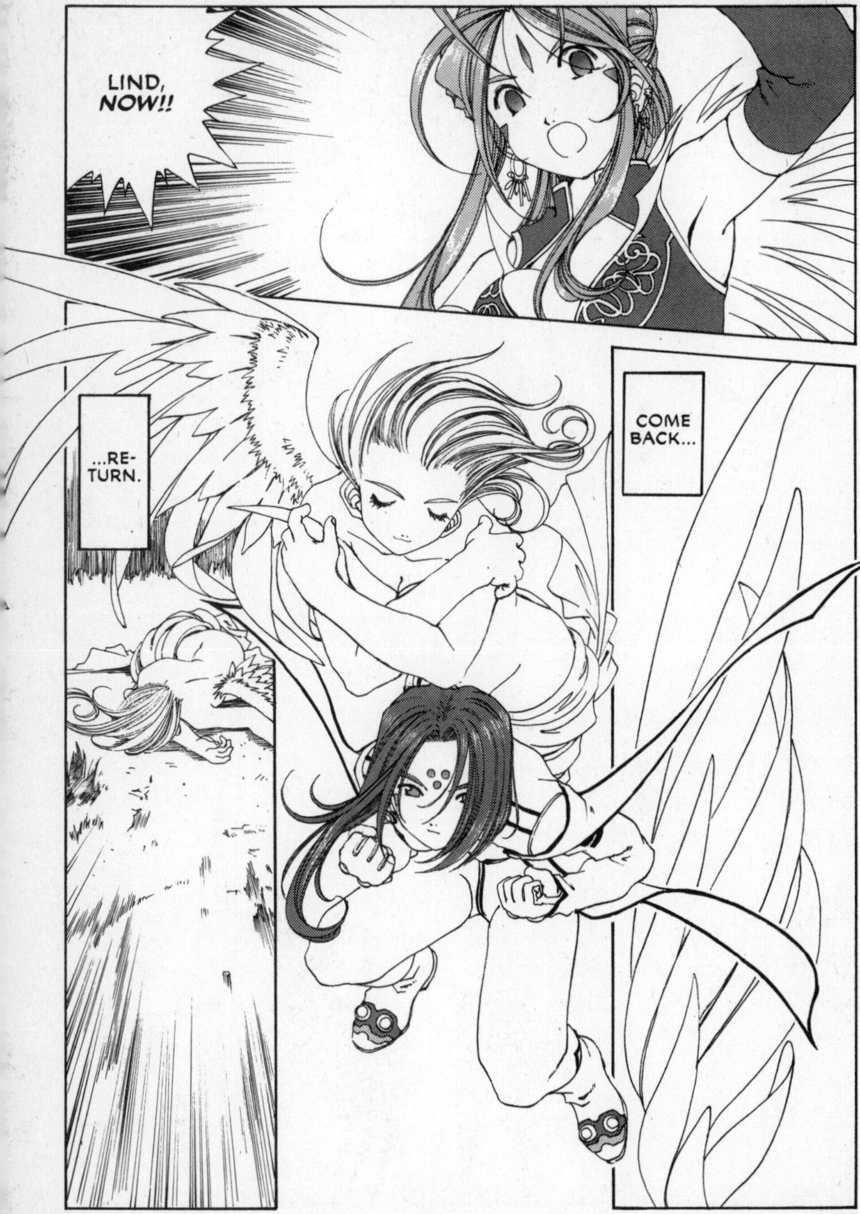
LIND, NOW!!
COME BACK...
...RE-TURN.

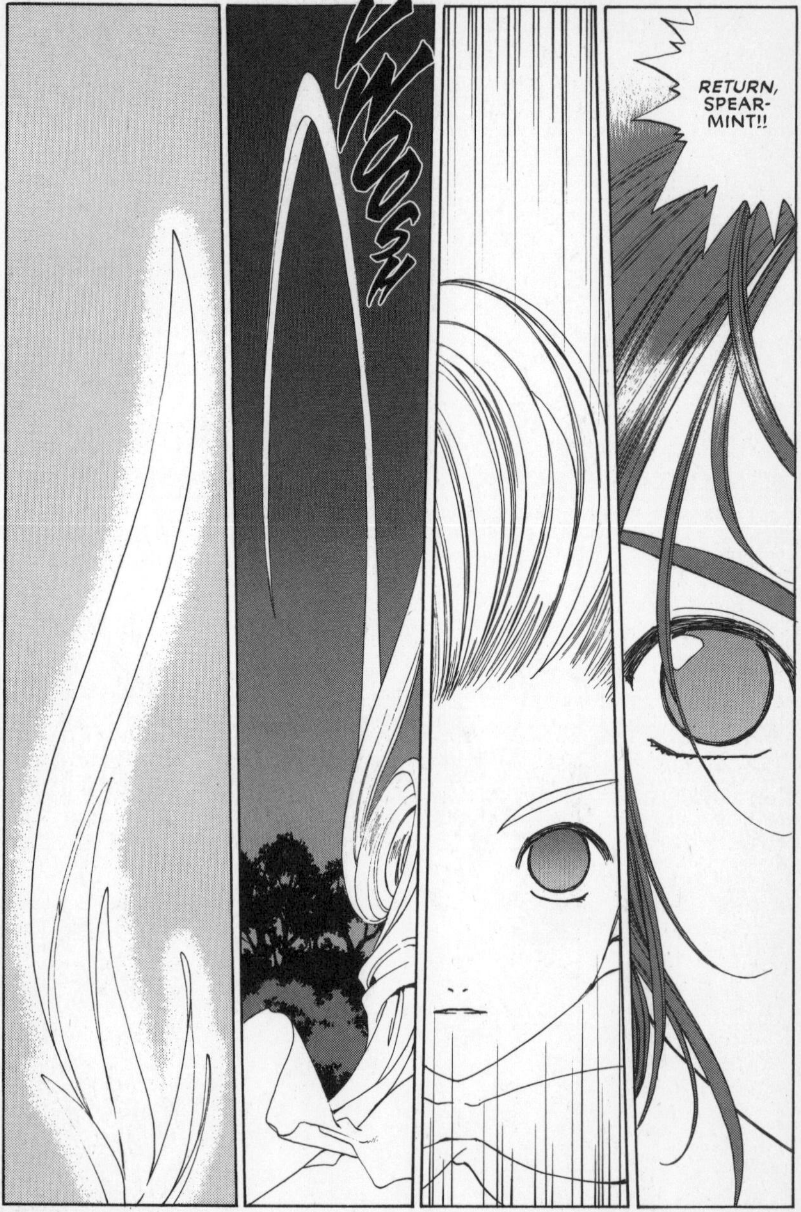
RETURN, SPEAR-MINT!!
VWOOSH

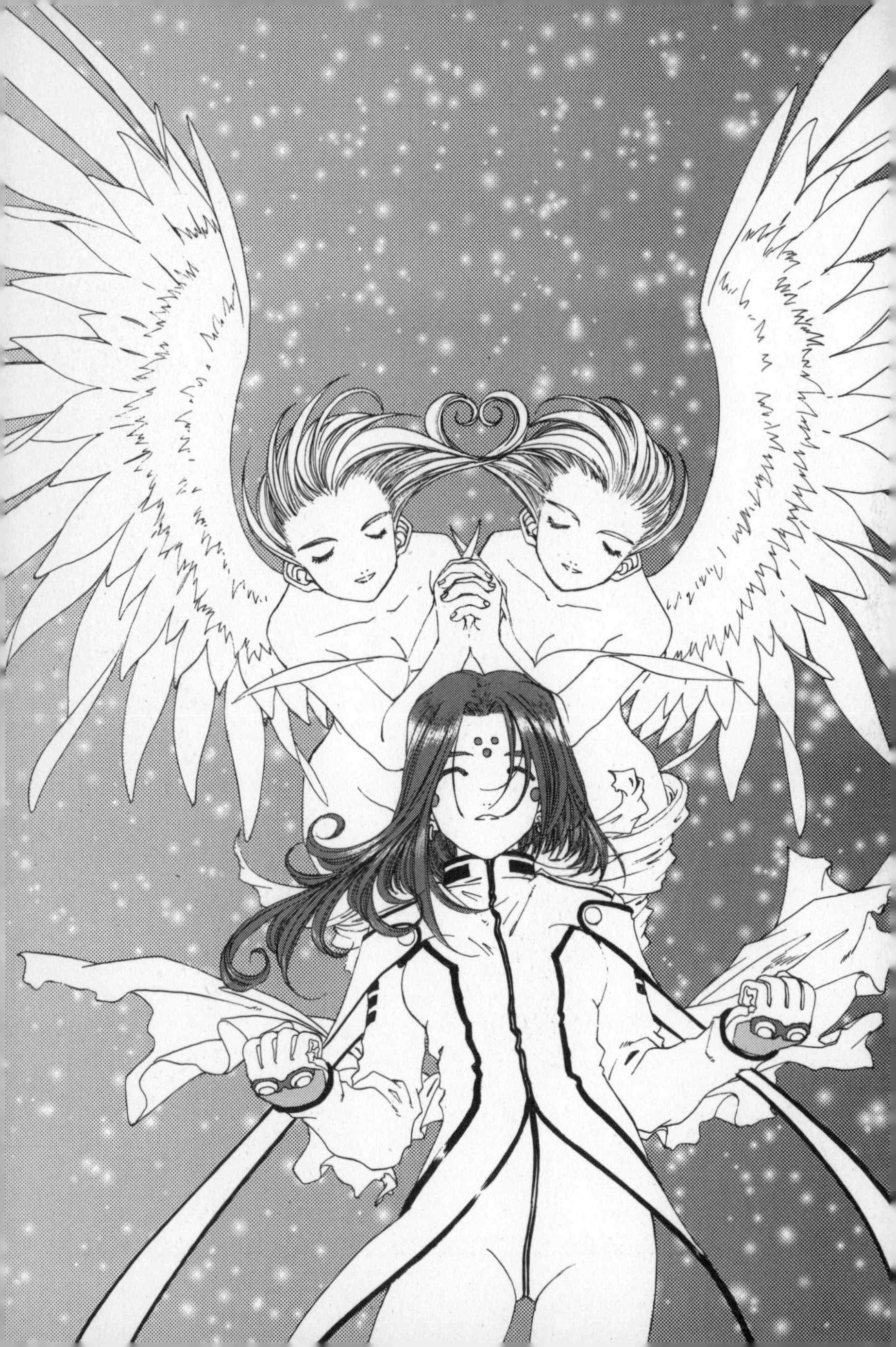

OH MY GODDESS!
BELLDANDY

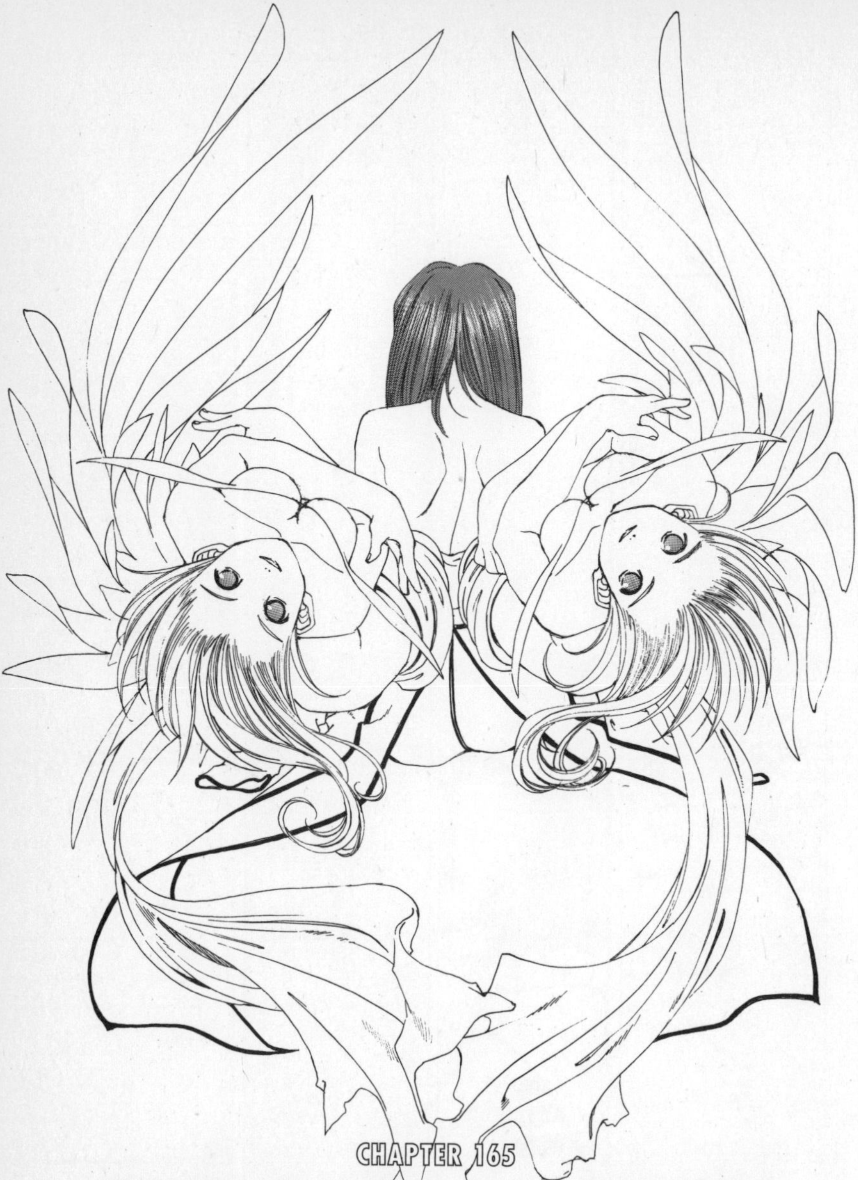

CHAPTER 165

With the Binary Angels

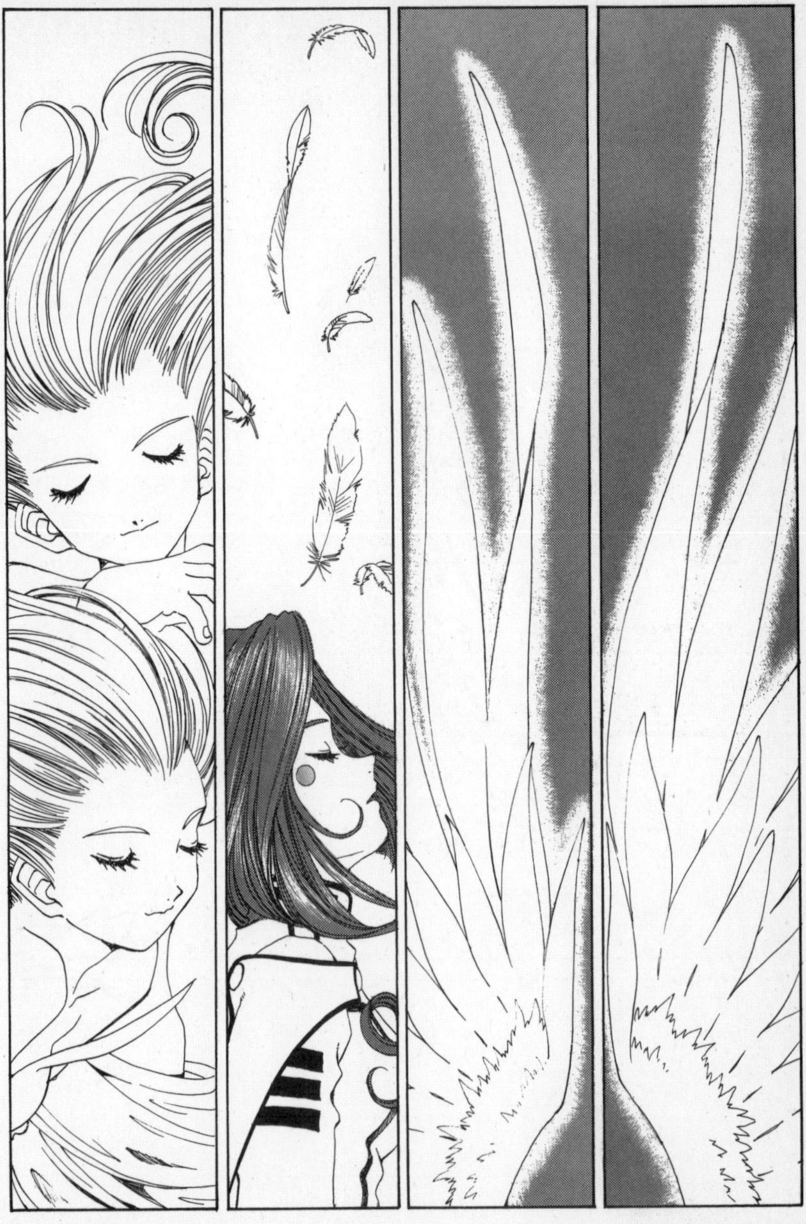

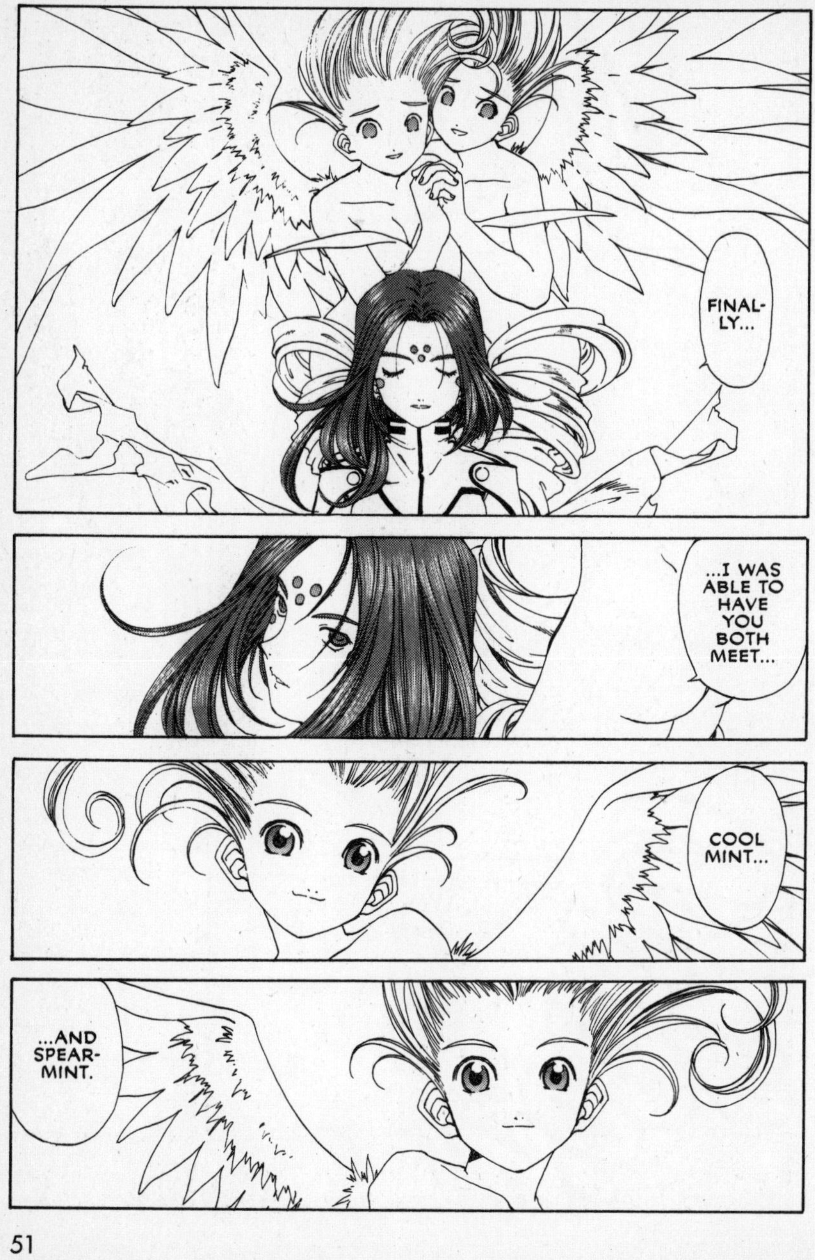
FINAL-
LY...
...I WAS ABLE TO HAVE YOU BOTH MEET...
COOL MINT...
...AND SPEAR-
MINT.

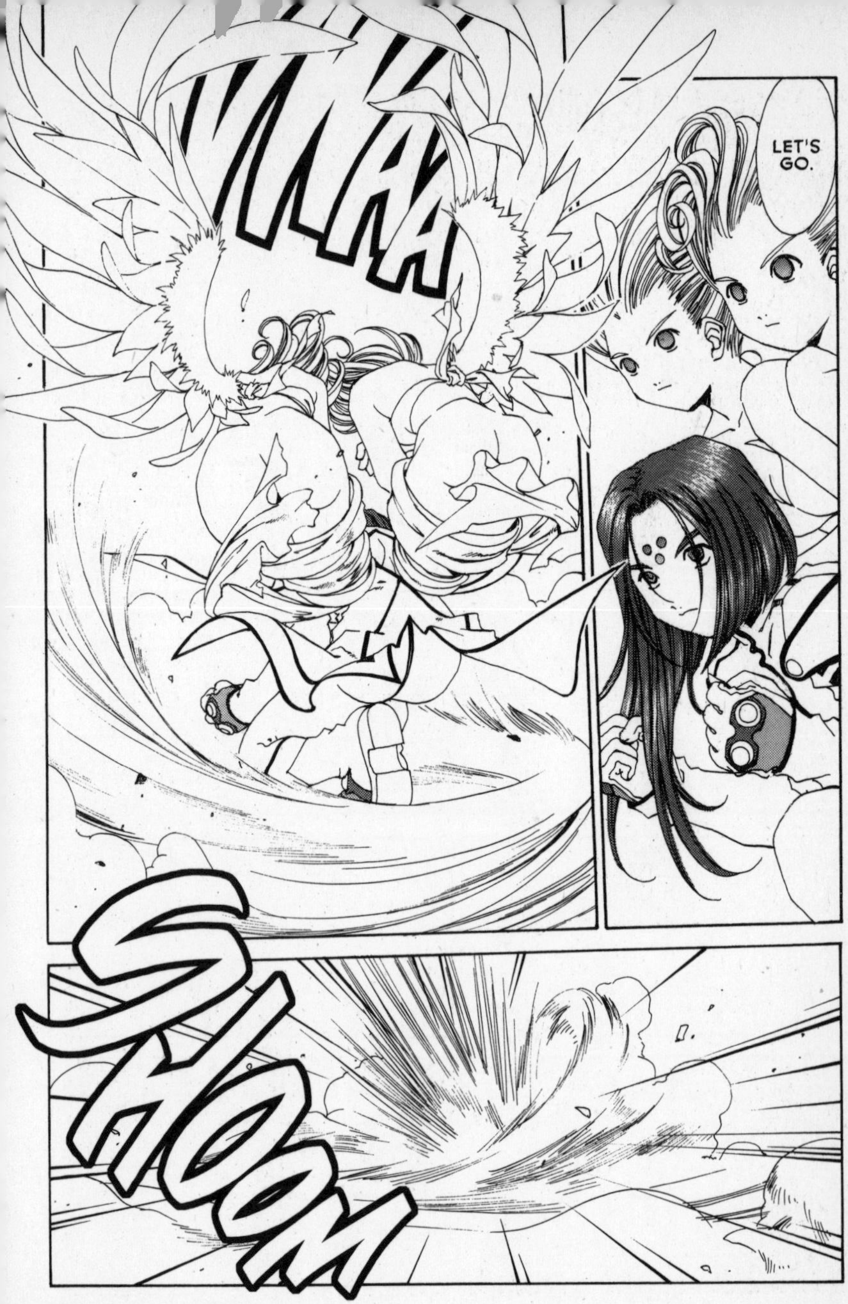
LET'S GO.
SHOOM

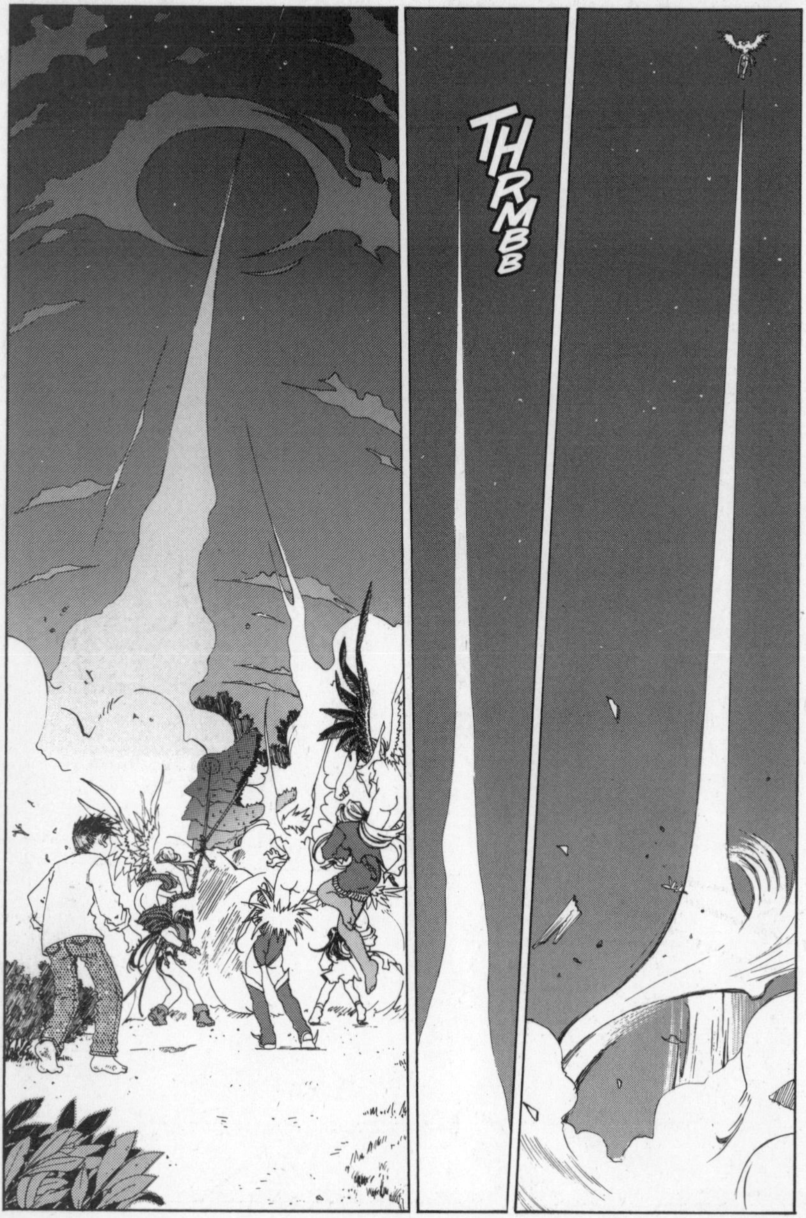
THRMBB

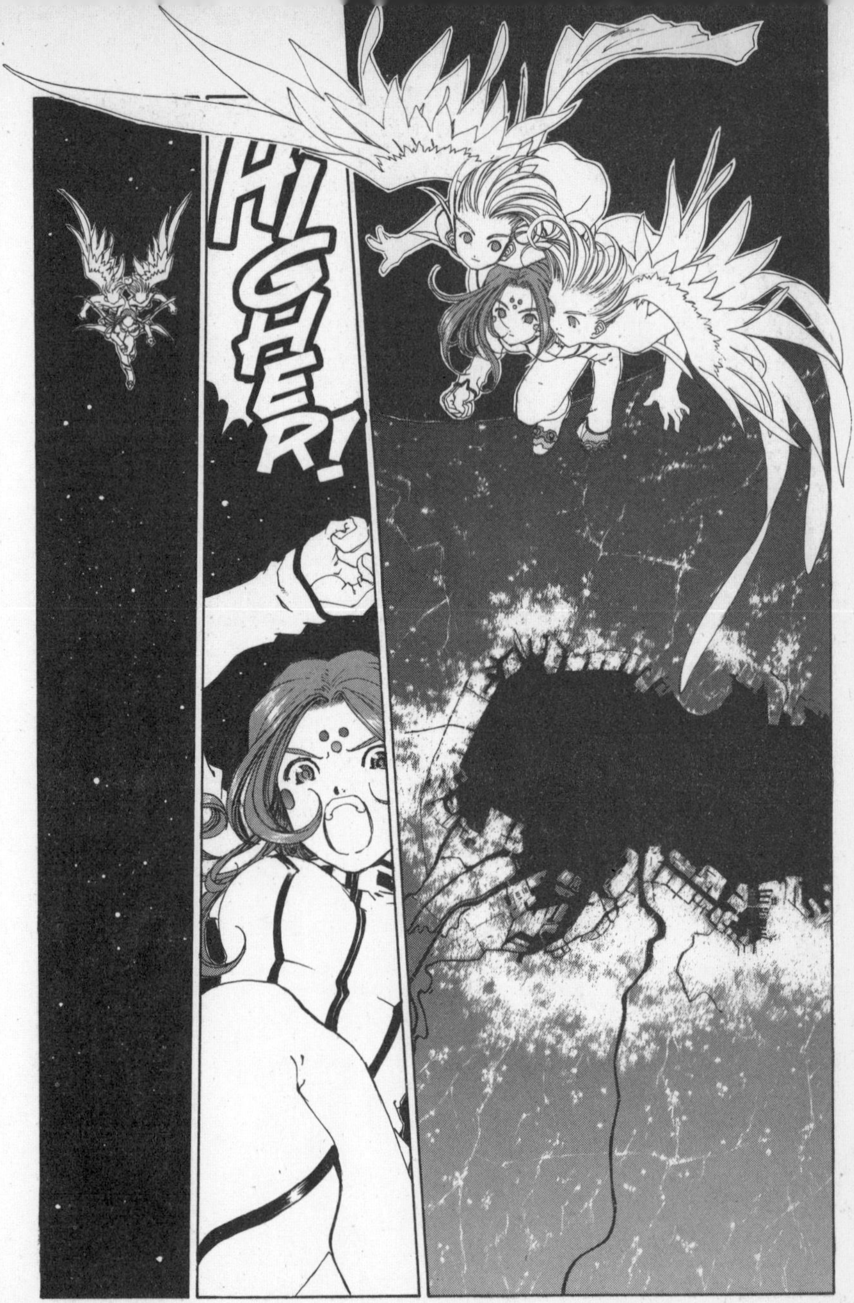
HIGHER!

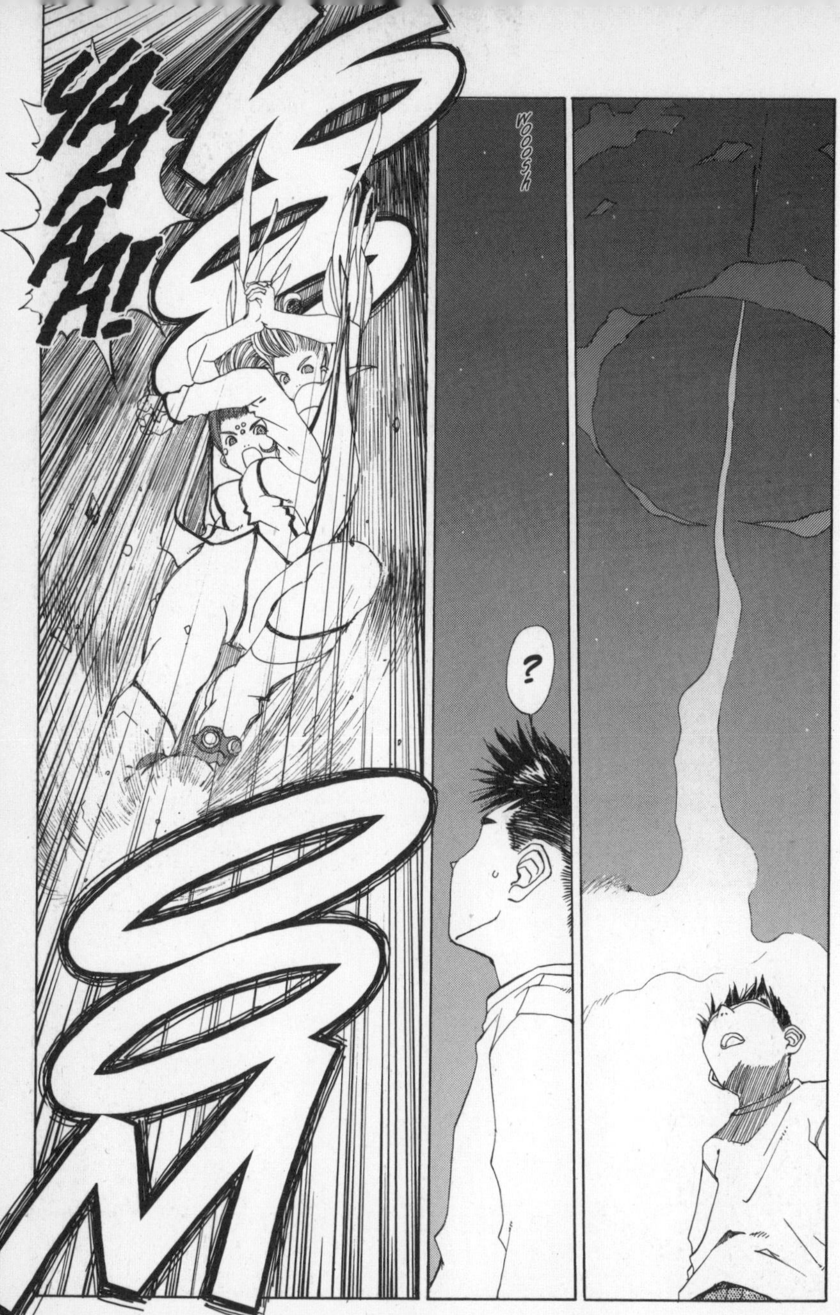
WOOOSH
?
YAAAA!

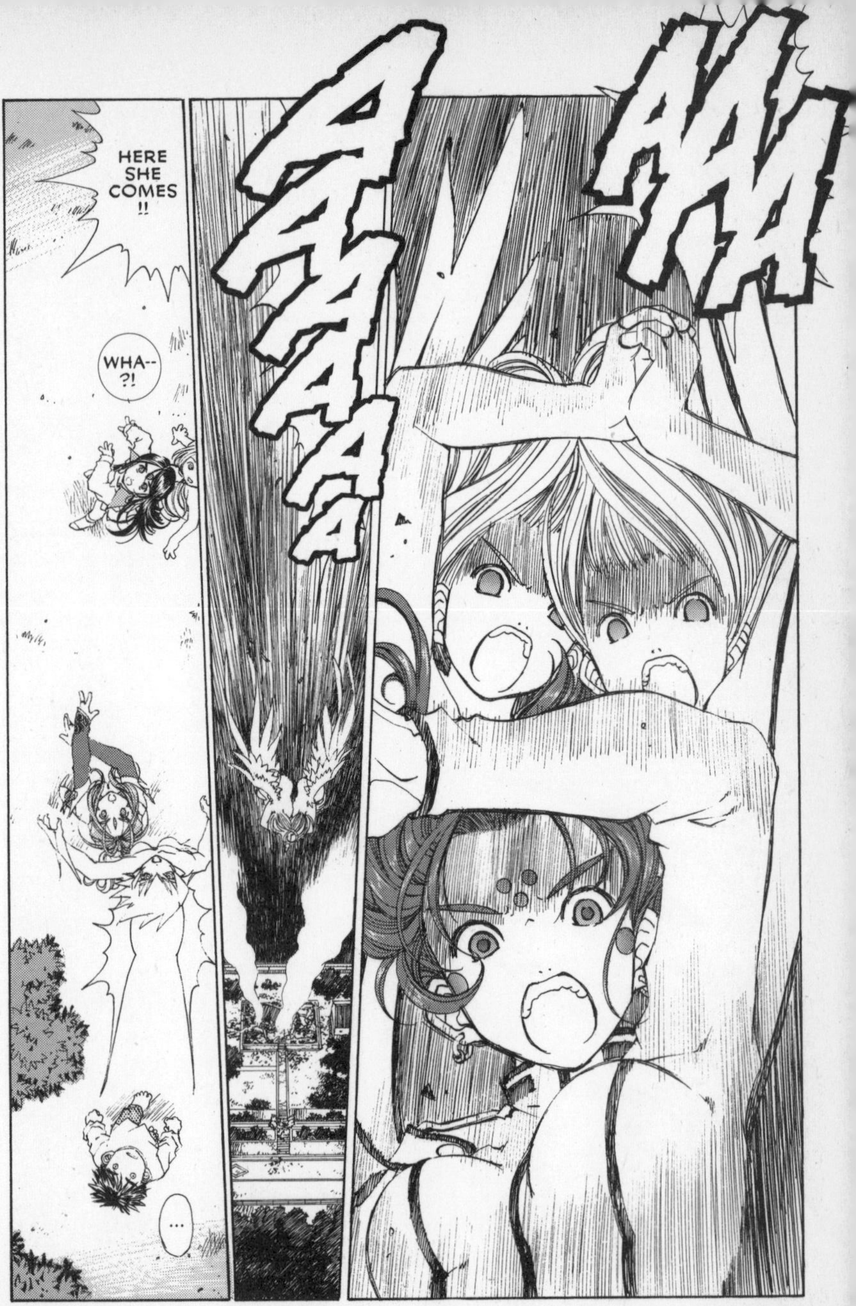
AAAAAAAAA
HERE SHE COMES !!
WHA-- ?!
...

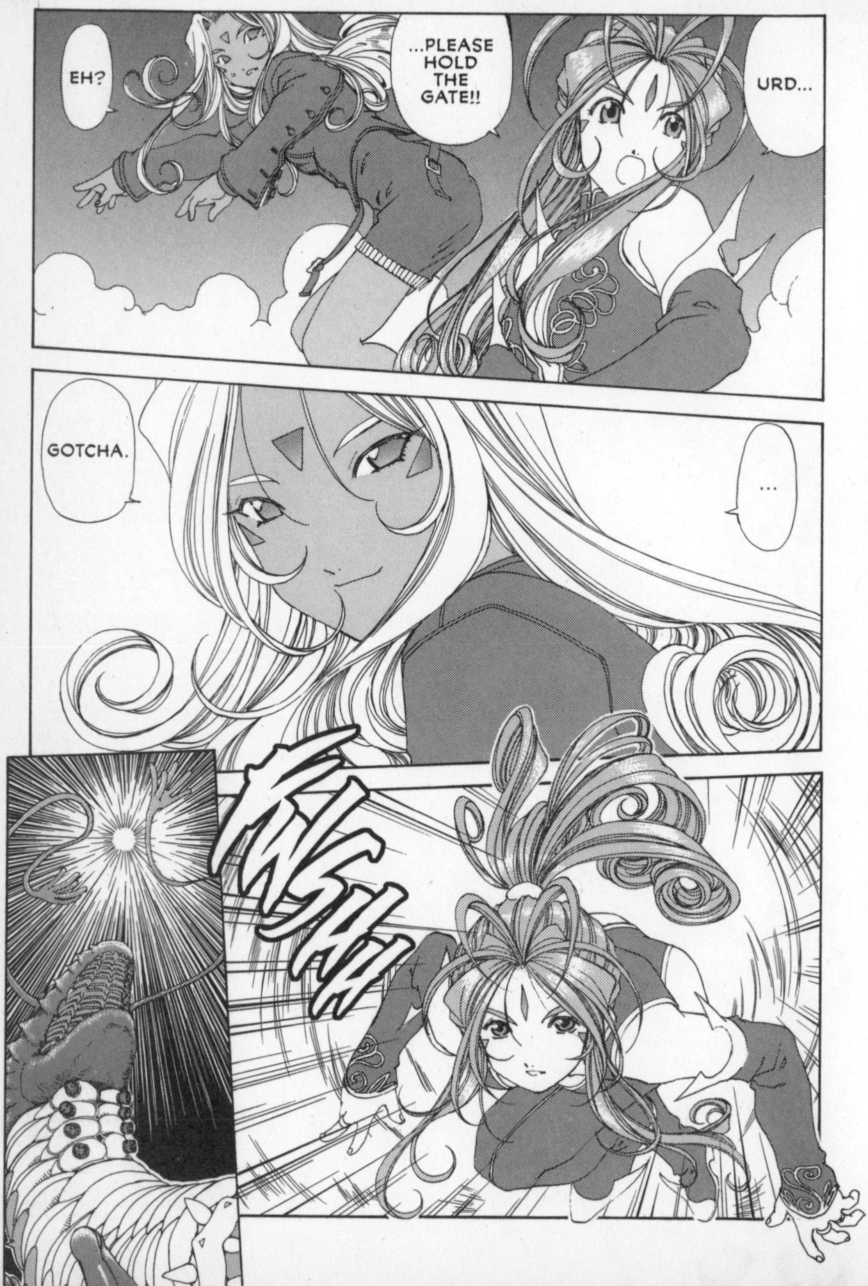
URD...
...PLEASE HOLD THE GATE!!
EH?
...
GOTCHA.

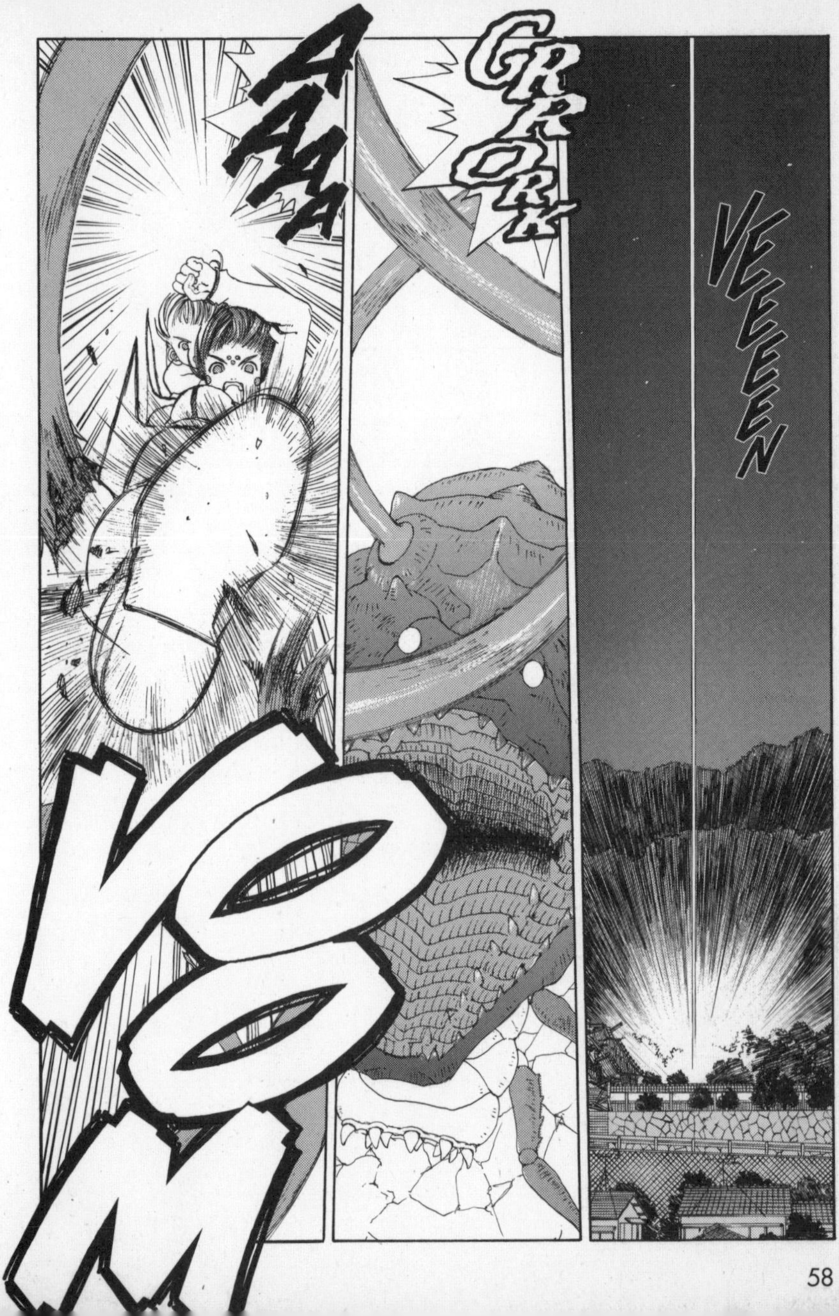
VEEEEEN
GRRORK
AAAA
VOOM

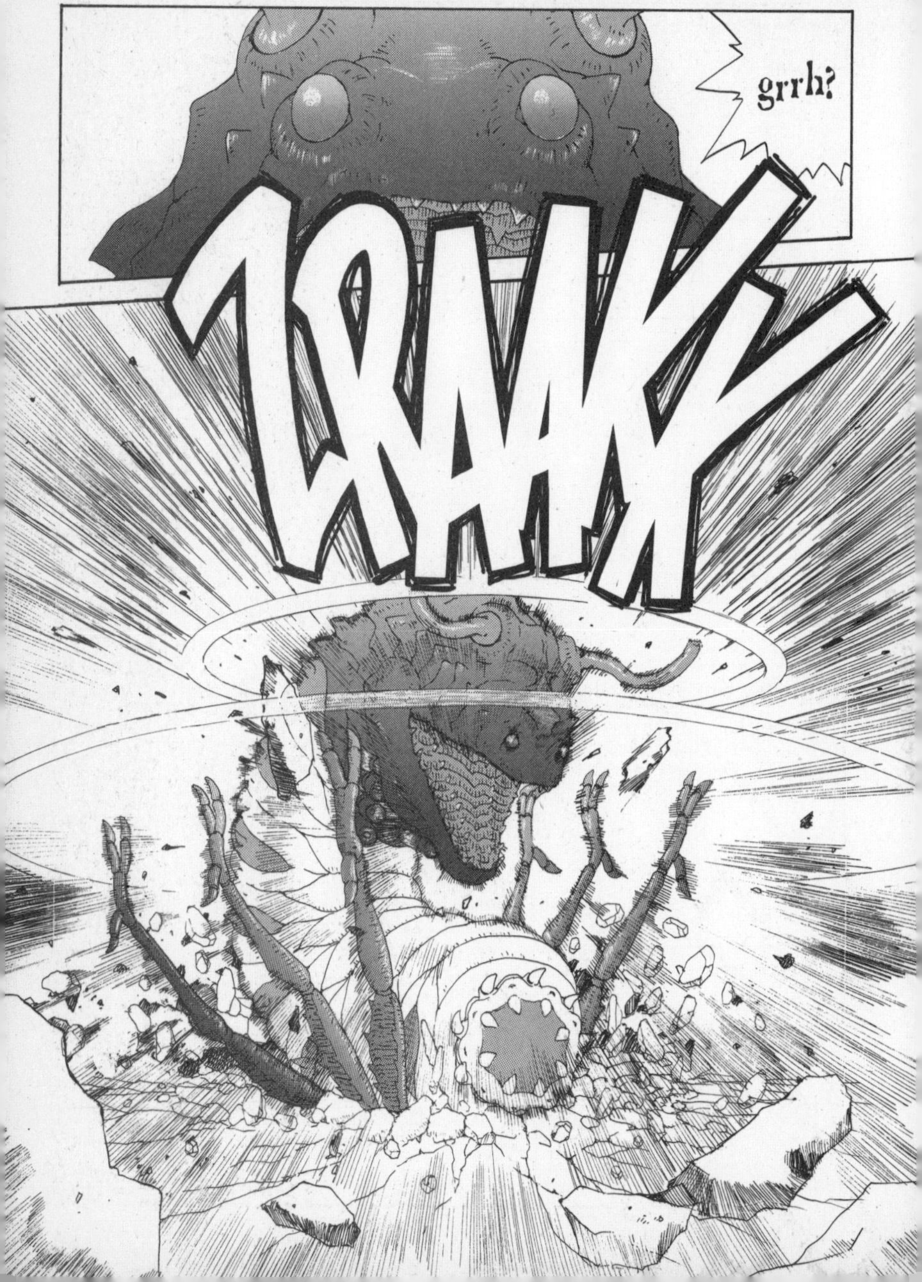
grrh?
KRAK

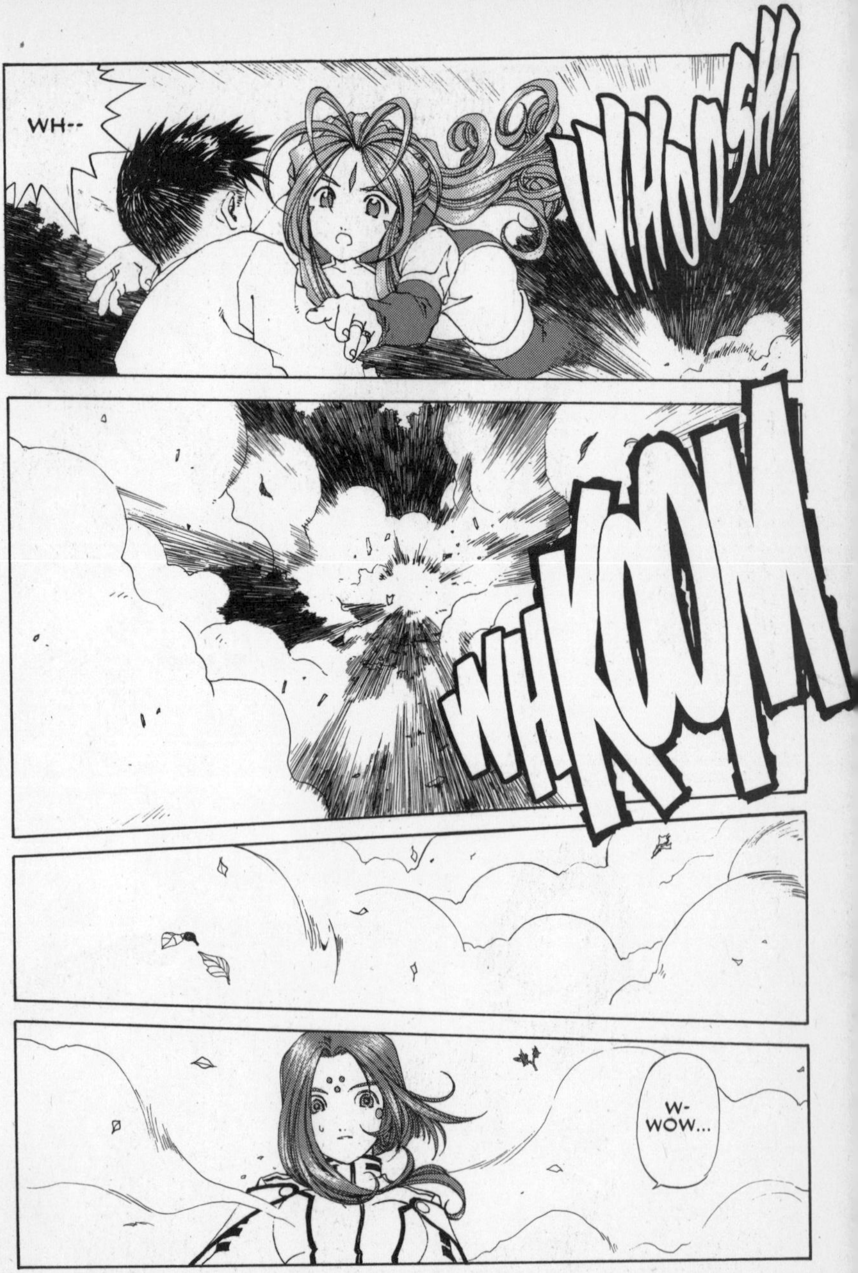
WHOOSH
WH--
WHKOOM
W-WOW...

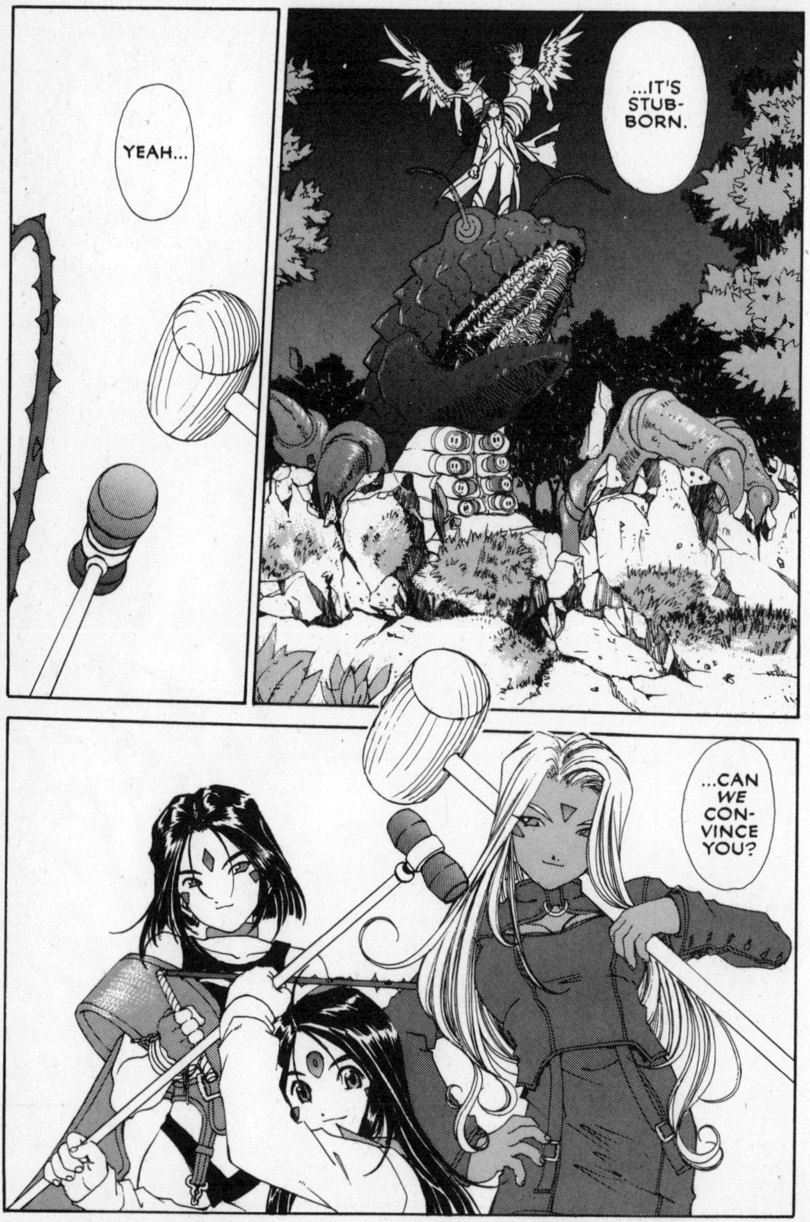
...IT'S STUB-BORN.
YEAH...
...CAN *WE* CONVINCE YOU?

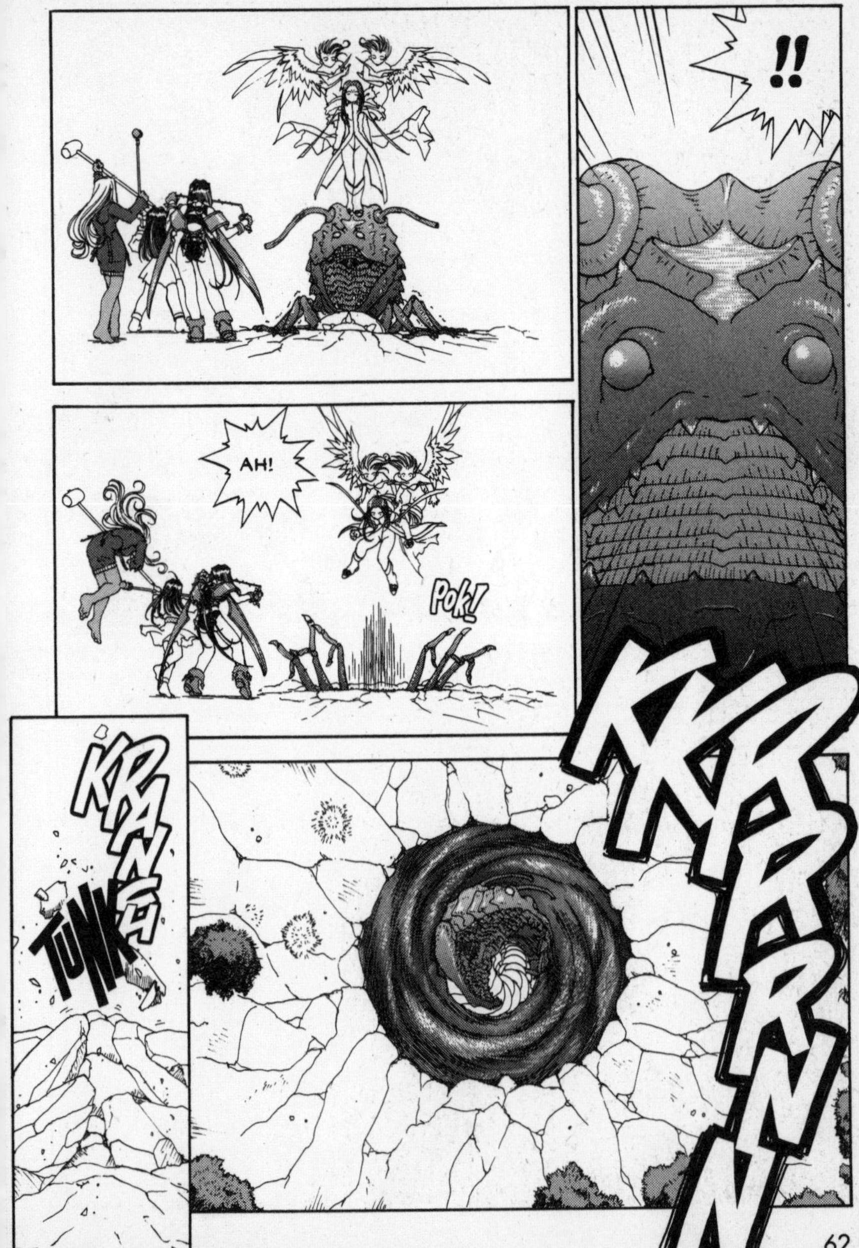
!!
KABARNN
AH!
POK!
KRANG
TUNK

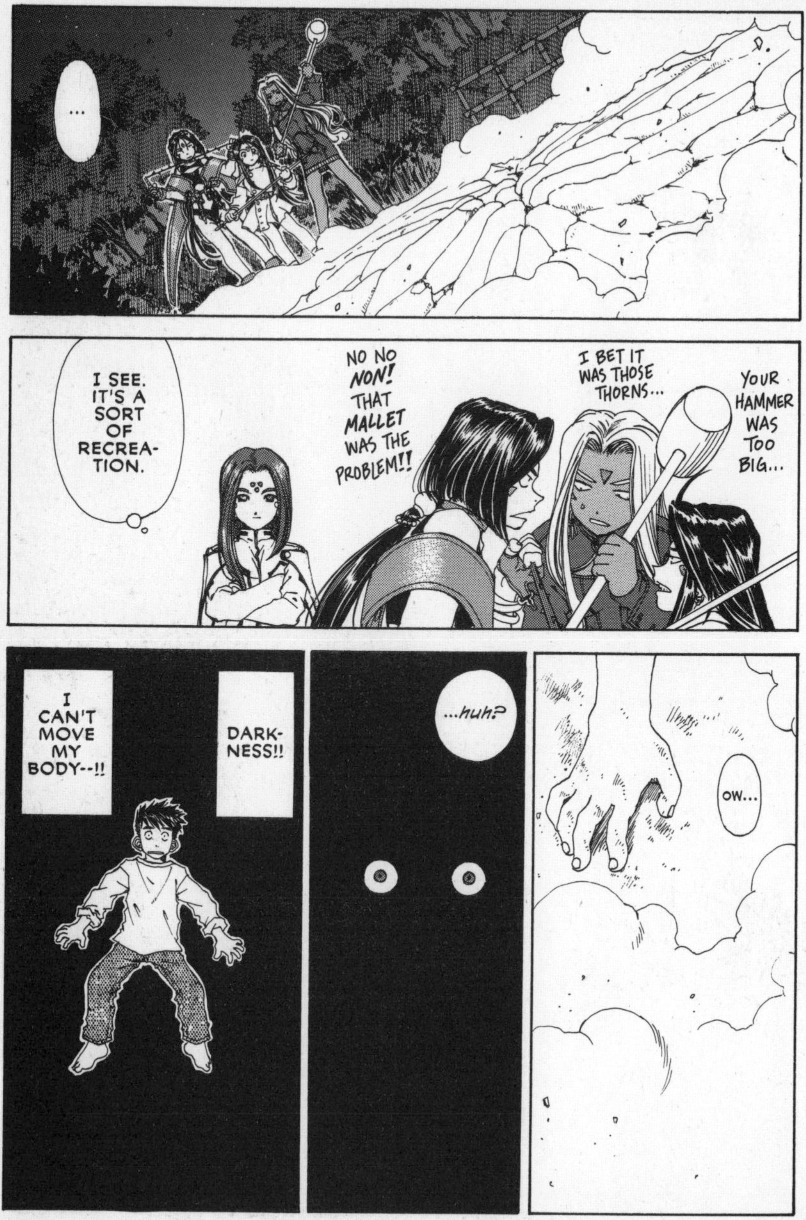
...
YOUR HAMMER WAS TOO BIG...
I BET IT WAS THOSE THORNS...
NO NO NON! THAT MALLET WAS THE PROBLEM!!
I SEE. IT'S A SORT OF RECREATION.
OW...
...huh?
DARKNESS!!
I CAN'T MOVE MY BODY--!!

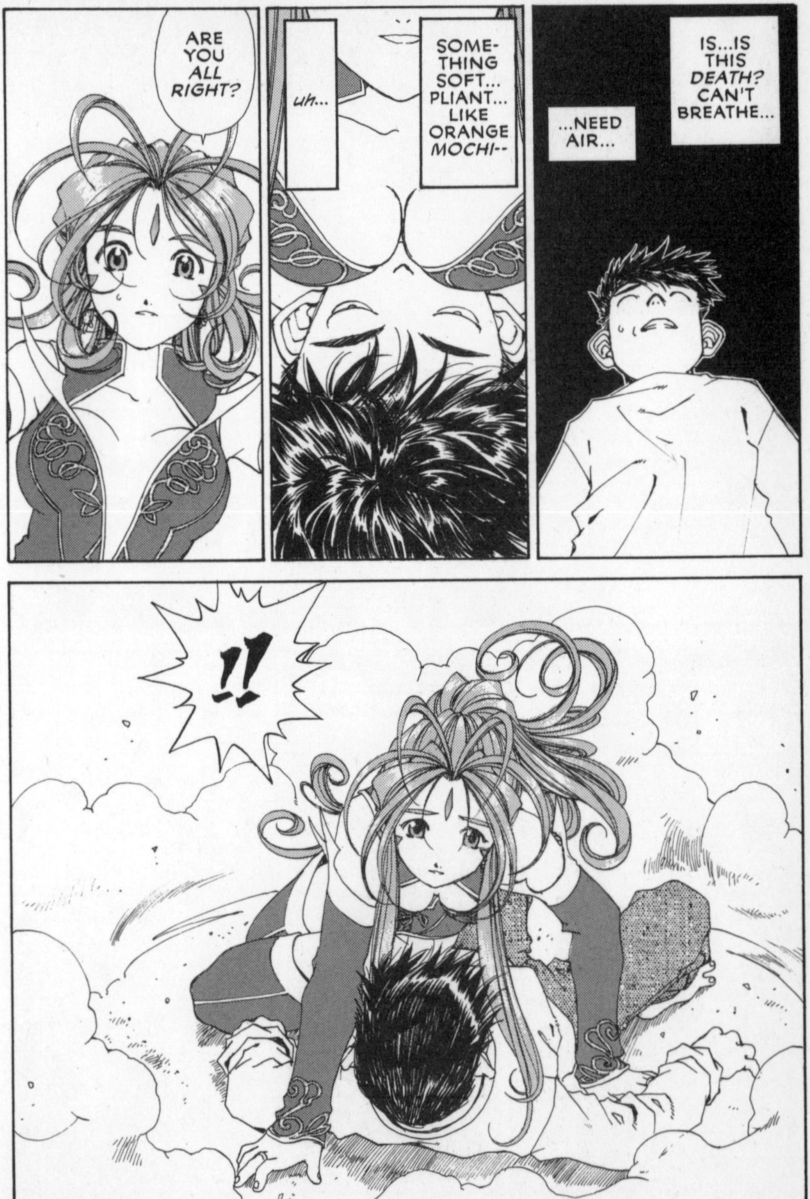
IS...IS THIS DEATH? CAN'T BREATHE...
...NEED AIR...
SOME-THING SOFT... PLIANT... LIKE ORANGE MOCHI--
uh...
ARE YOU ALL RIGHT?
!!

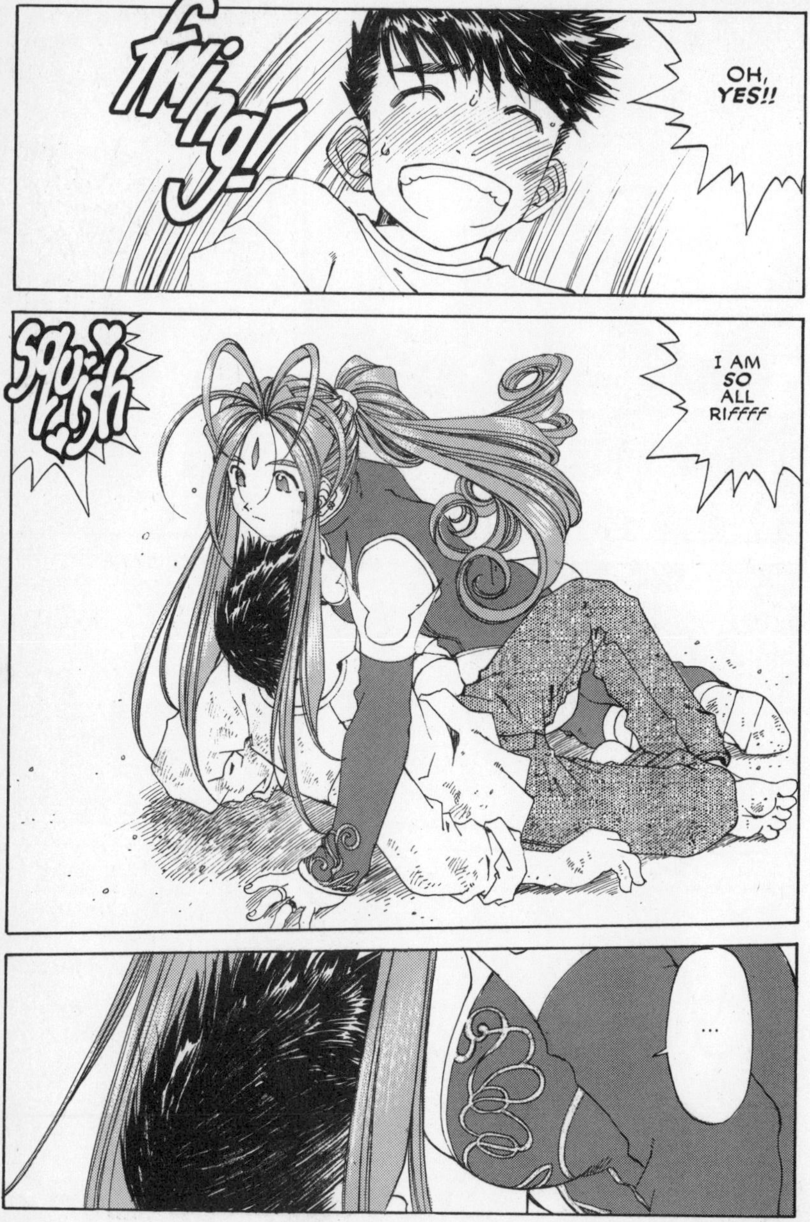
OH, YES!!
fwing!
I AM SO ALL RIffff
squish
...

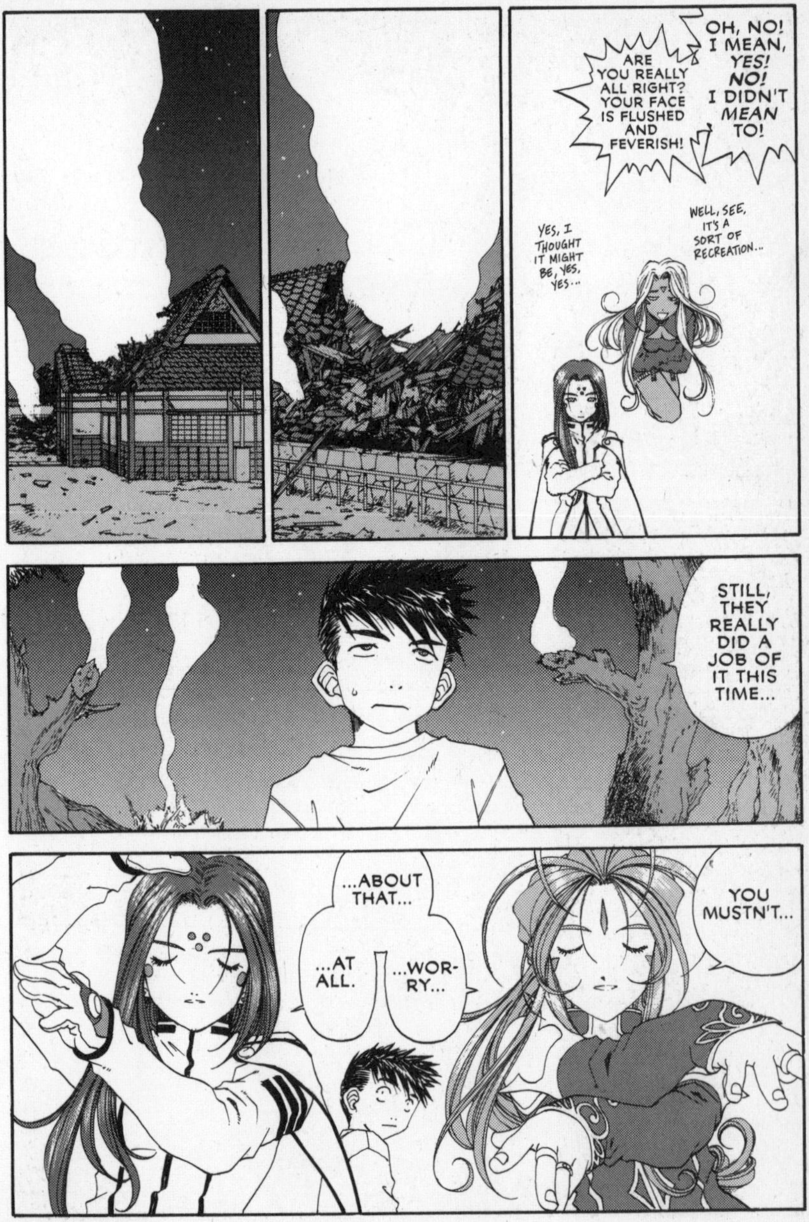
OH, NO! I MEAN, YES! NO! I DIDN'T MEAN TO!
ARE YOU REALLY ALL RIGHT? YOUR FACE IS FLUSHED AND FEVERISH!
WELL, SEE, IT'S A SORT OF RECREATION...
YES, I THOUGHT IT MIGHT BE, YES, YES...
STILL, THEY REALLY DID A JOB OF IT THIS TIME...
YOU MUSTN'T...
...WOR-RY...
...ABOUT THAT...
...AT ALL.

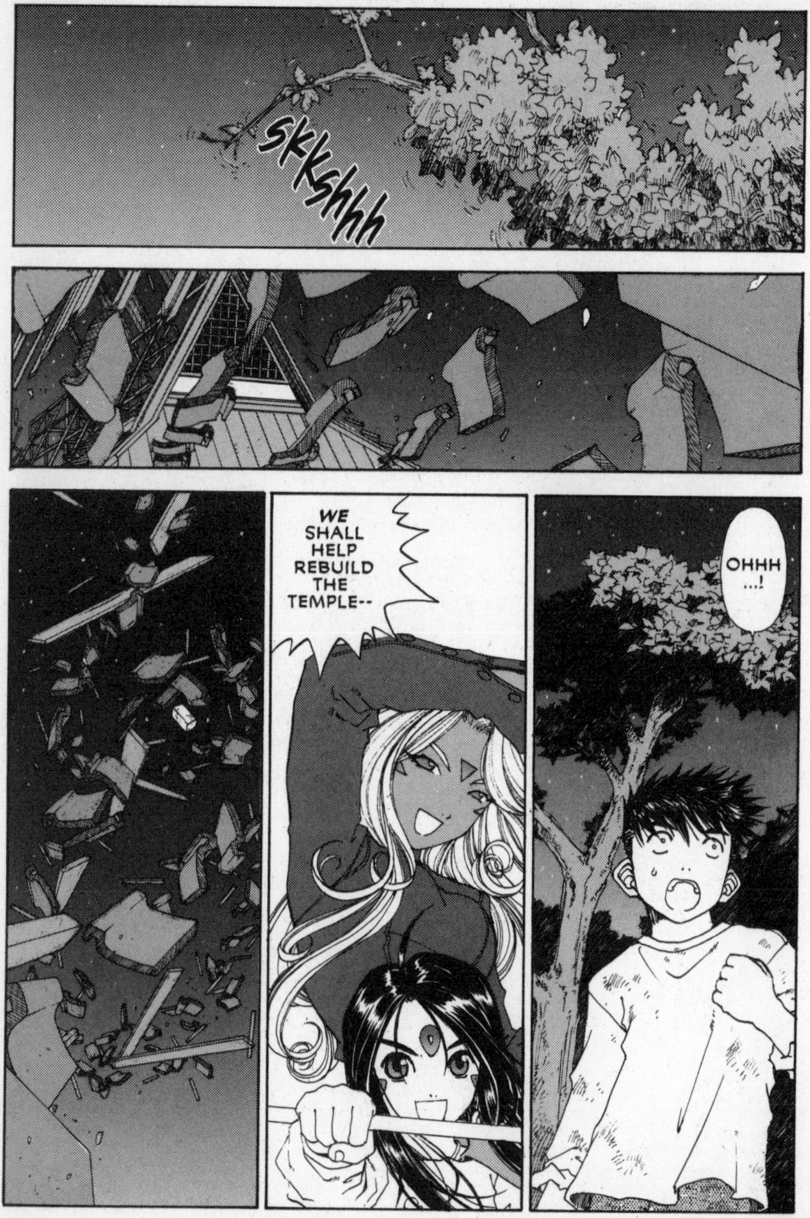
SKKSHHH
OHHH ...!
WE SHALL HELP REBUILD THE TEMPLE--

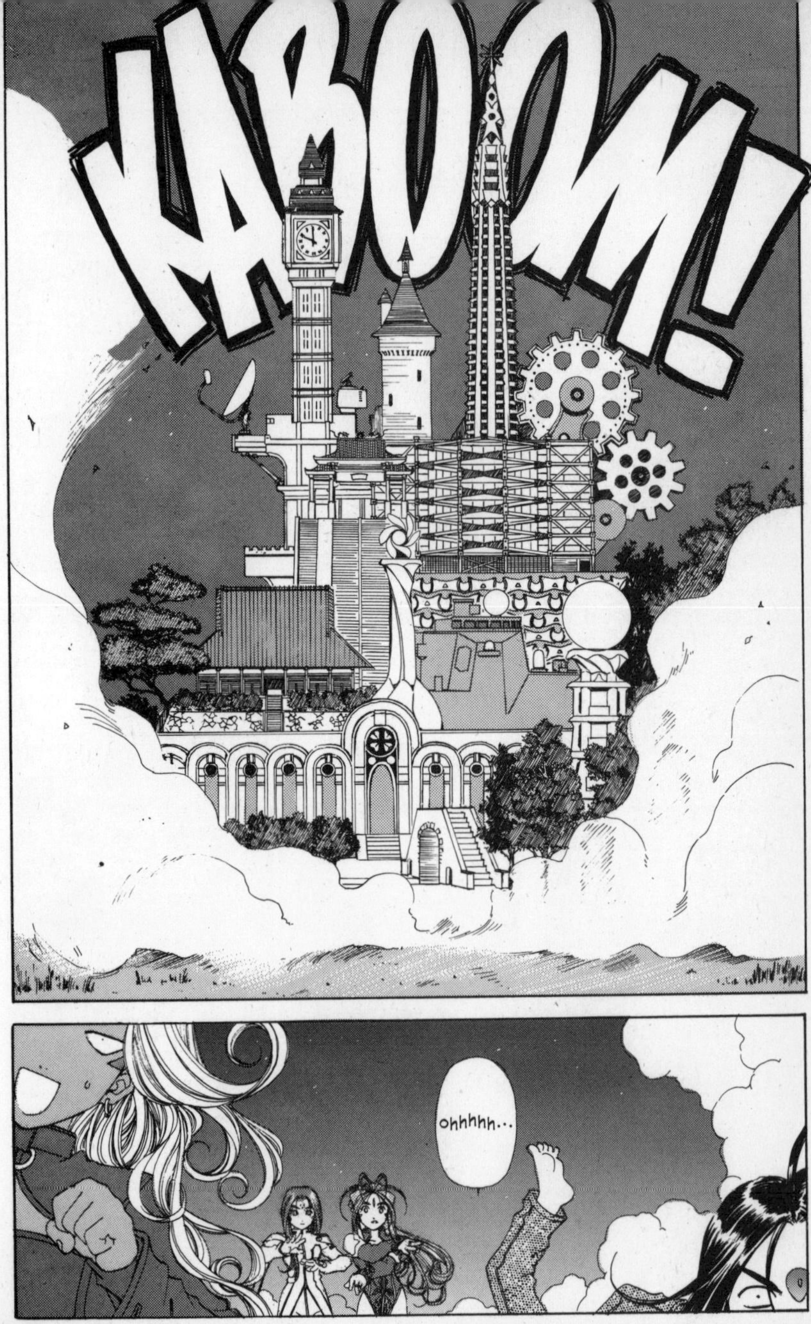
KABOOM!
ohhhhh...

CHAPTER 166

To Call You Friend

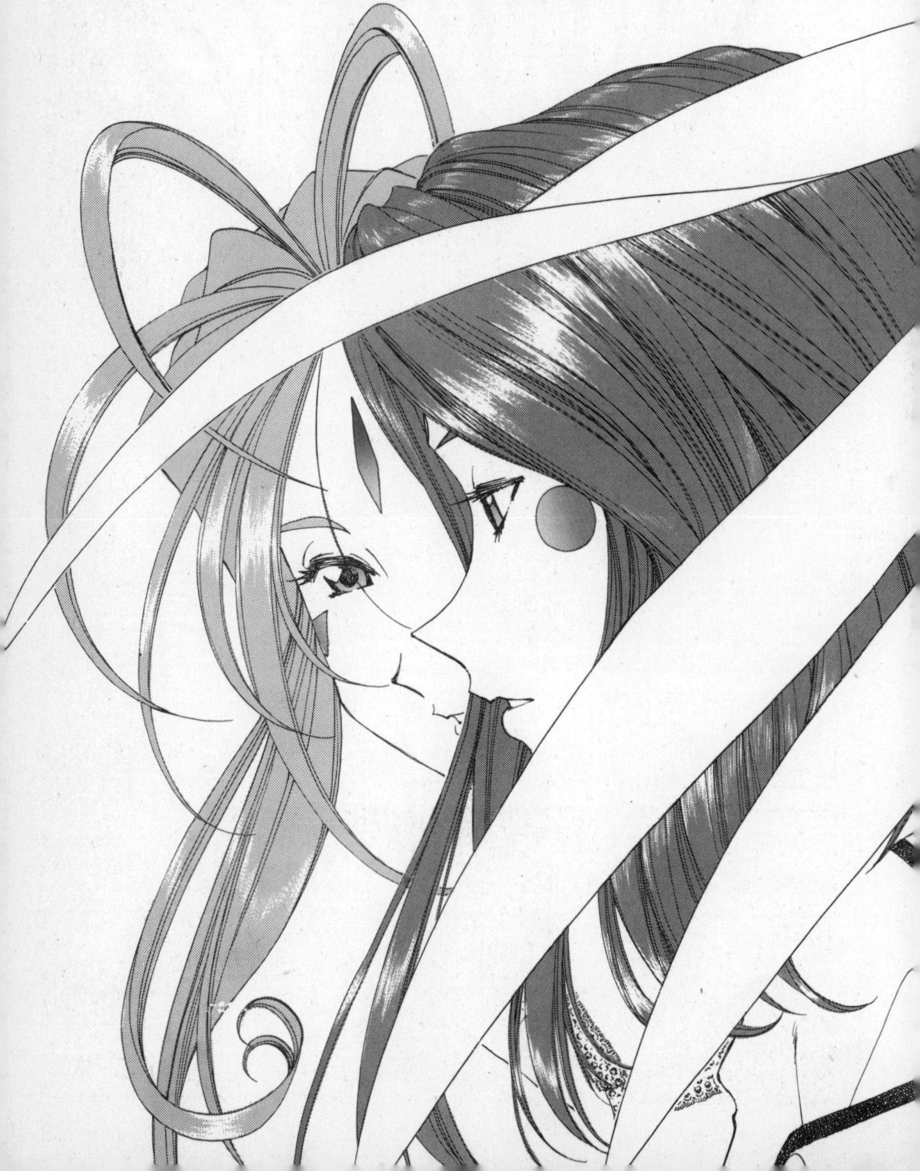

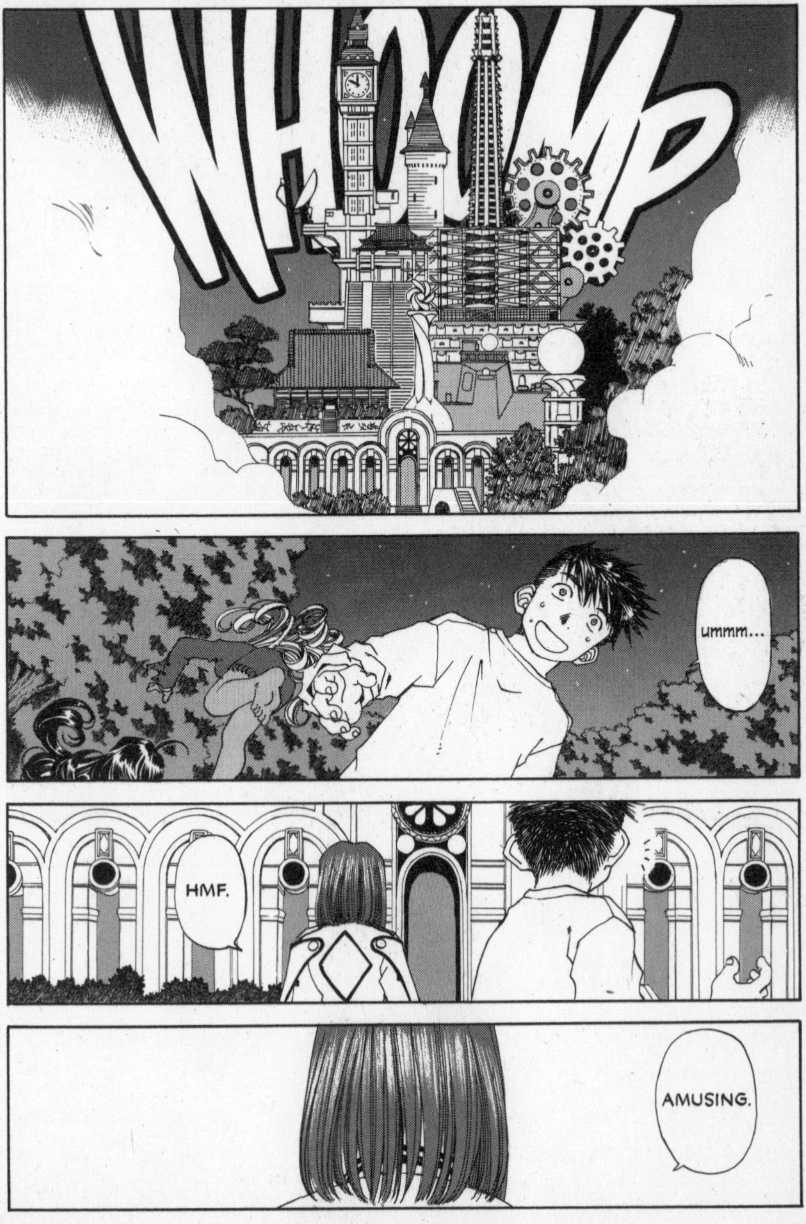
WHOOMP
ummm...
HMF.
AMUSING.

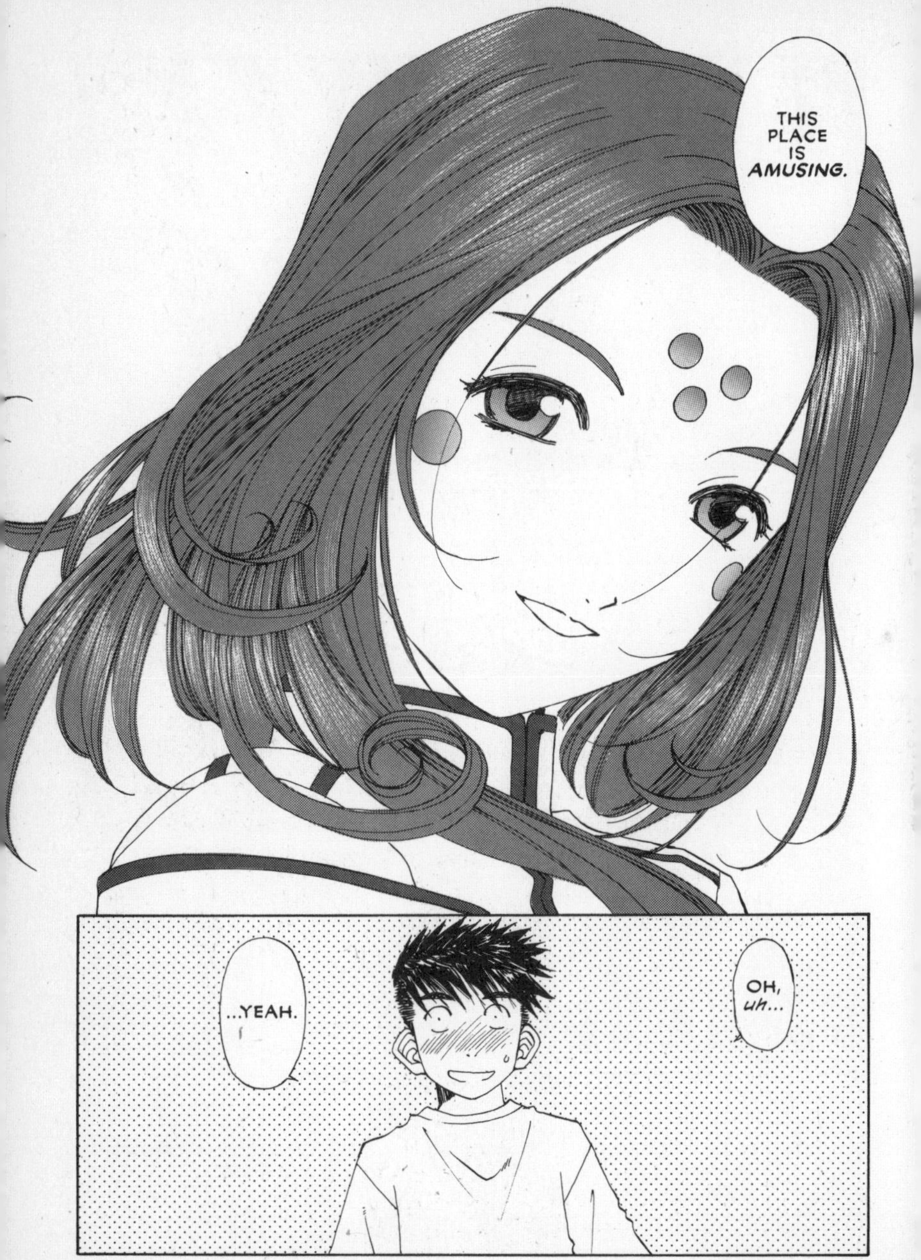
THIS PLACE IS *AMUSING.*
OH, *uh...*
...YEAH.

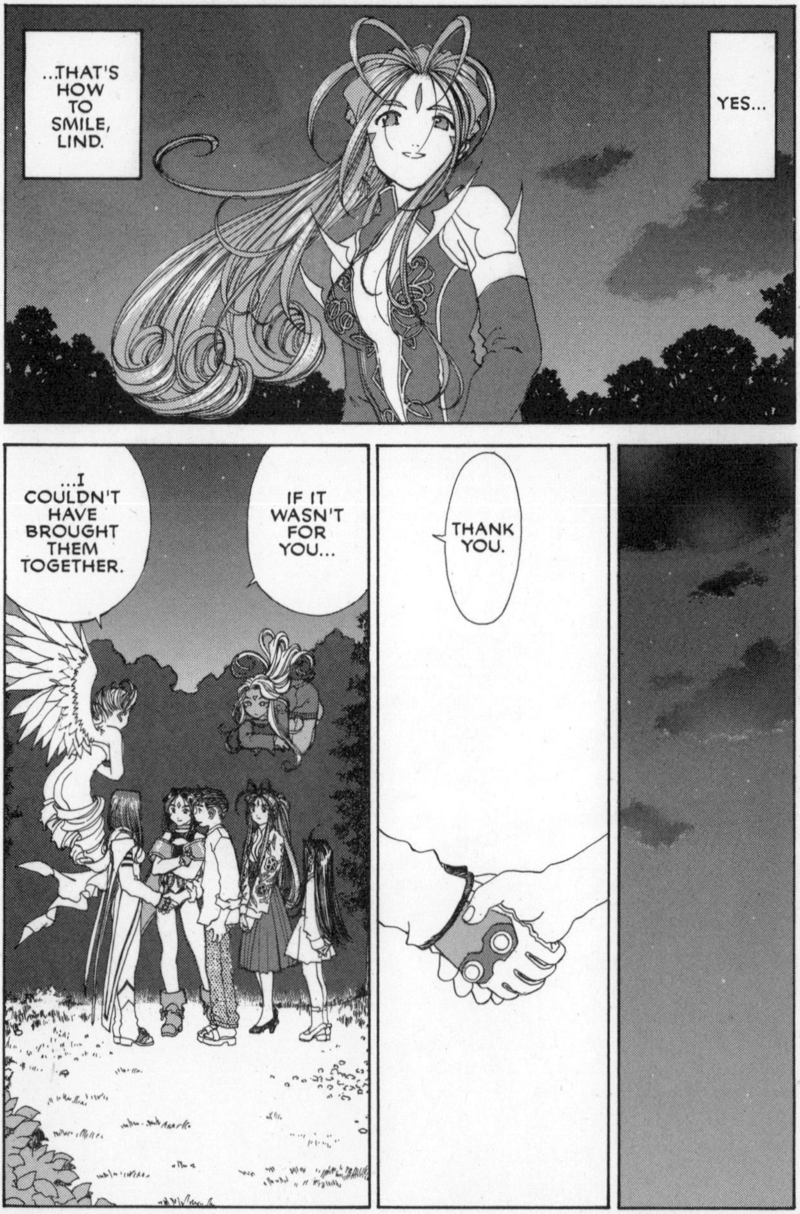
YES...
...THAT'S HOW TO SMILE, LIND.
THANK YOU.
IF IT WASN'T FOR YOU...
...I COULDN'T HAVE BROUGHT THEM TOGETHER.

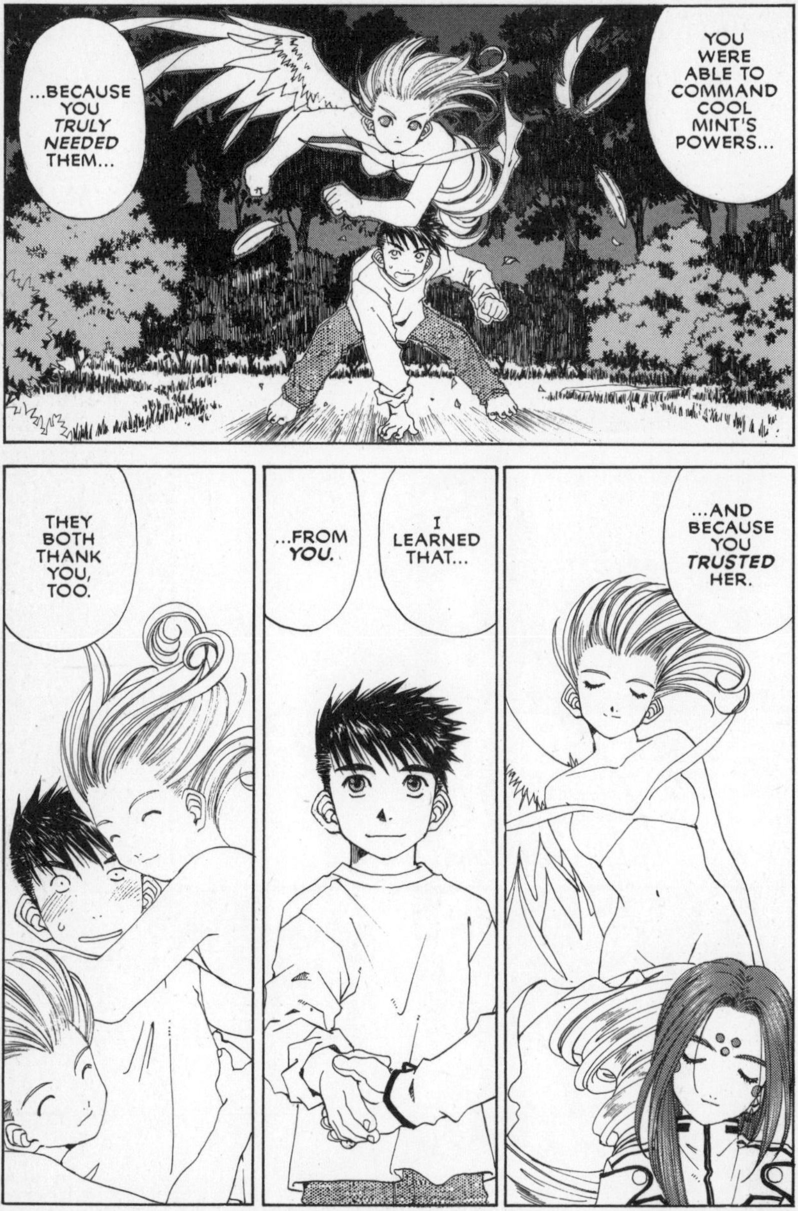
YOU WERE ABLE TO COMMAND COOL MINT'S POWERS...
...BECAUSE YOU *TRULY NEEDED* THEM...
...AND BECAUSE YOU *TRUSTED* HER.
I LEARNED THAT...
...FROM ***YOU.***
THEY BOTH THANK YOU, TOO.

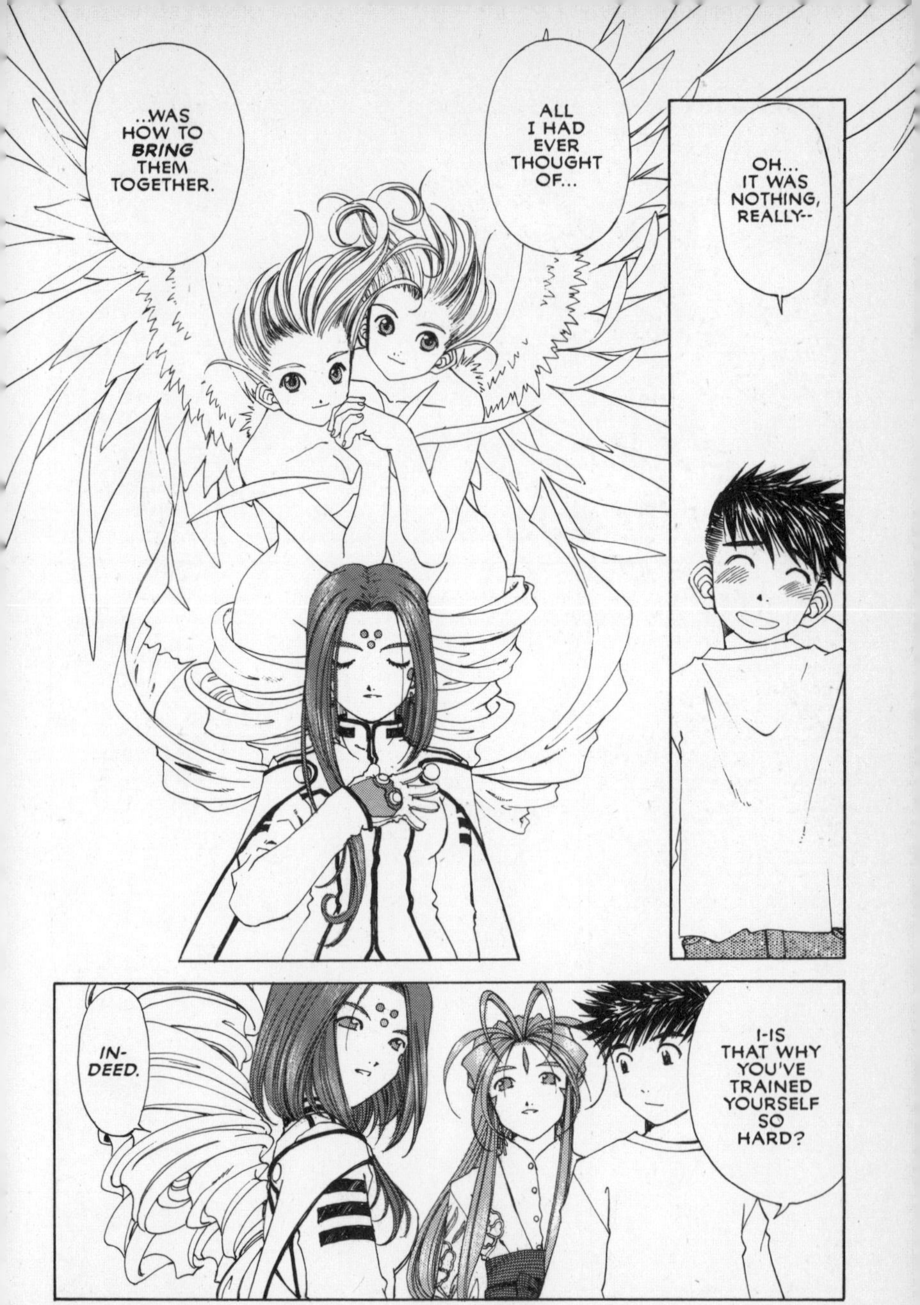
OH... IT WAS NOTHING, REALLY--
ALL I HAD EVER THOUGHT OF...
...WAS HOW TO *BRING* THEM TOGETHER.
I-IS THAT WHY YOU'VE TRAINED YOURSELF SO HARD?
IN-DEED.

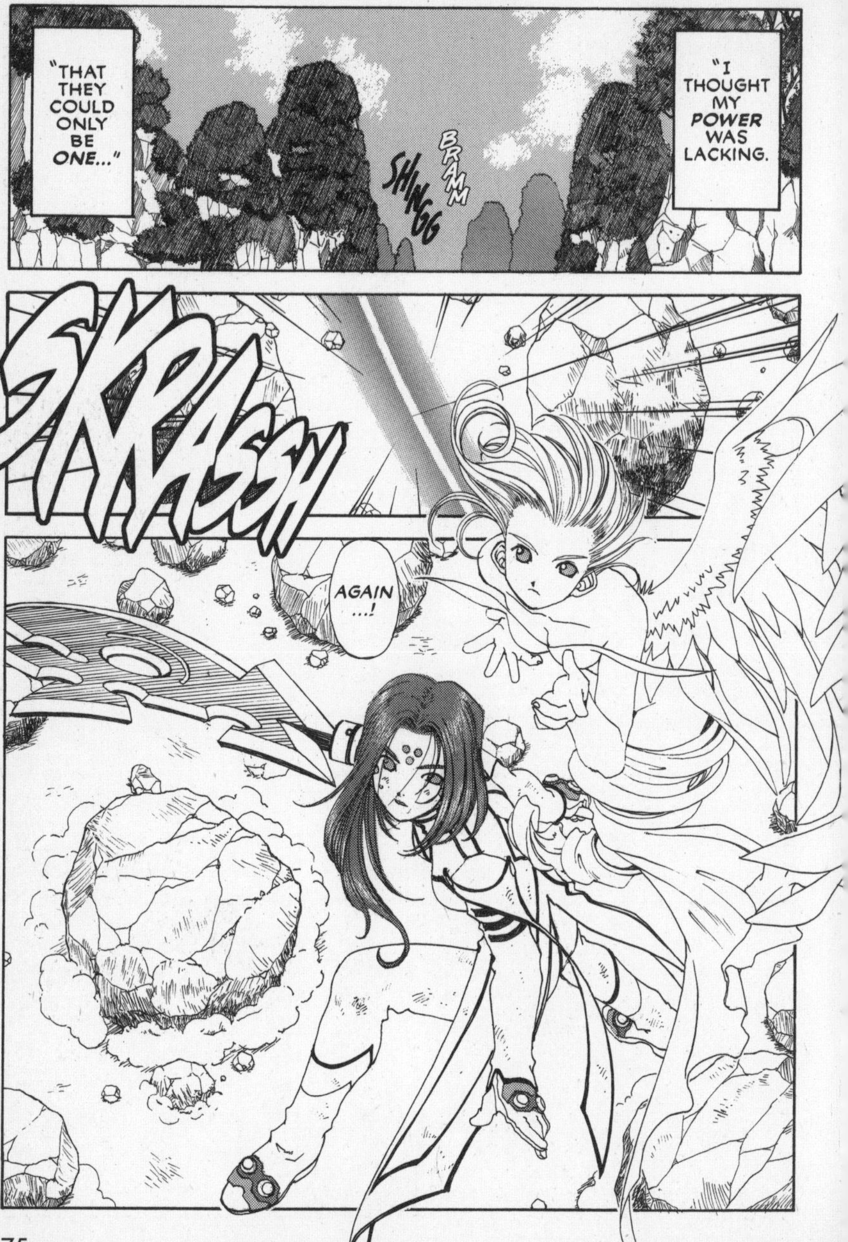
"I THOUGHT MY *POWER* WAS LACKING.
BRAMM
SHINGG
"THAT THEY COULD ONLY BE *ONE...*"
SKRASSH
AGAIN ...!

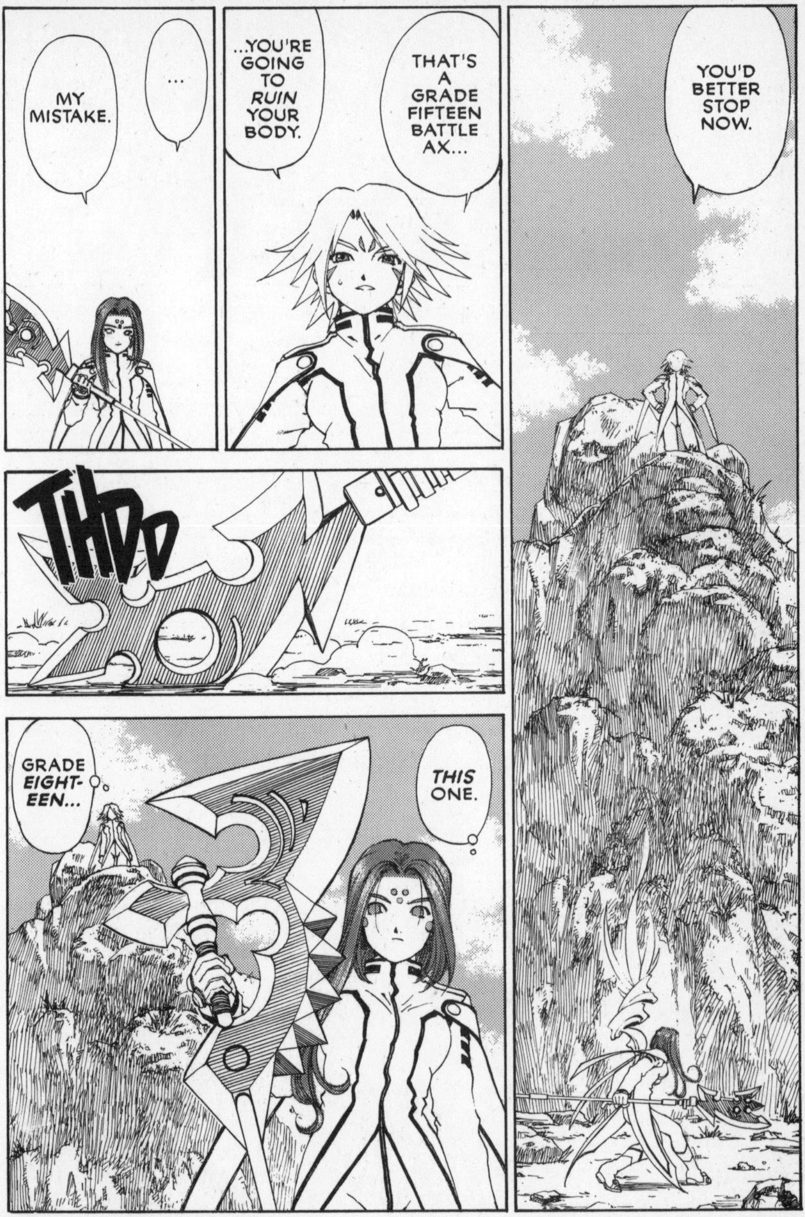
YOU'D BETTER STOP NOW.
THAT'S A GRADE FIFTEEN BATTLE AX...
...YOU'RE GOING TO *RUIN* YOUR BODY.
...
MY MISTAKE.
THDD
THIS ONE.
GRADE *EIGHT-EEN*...

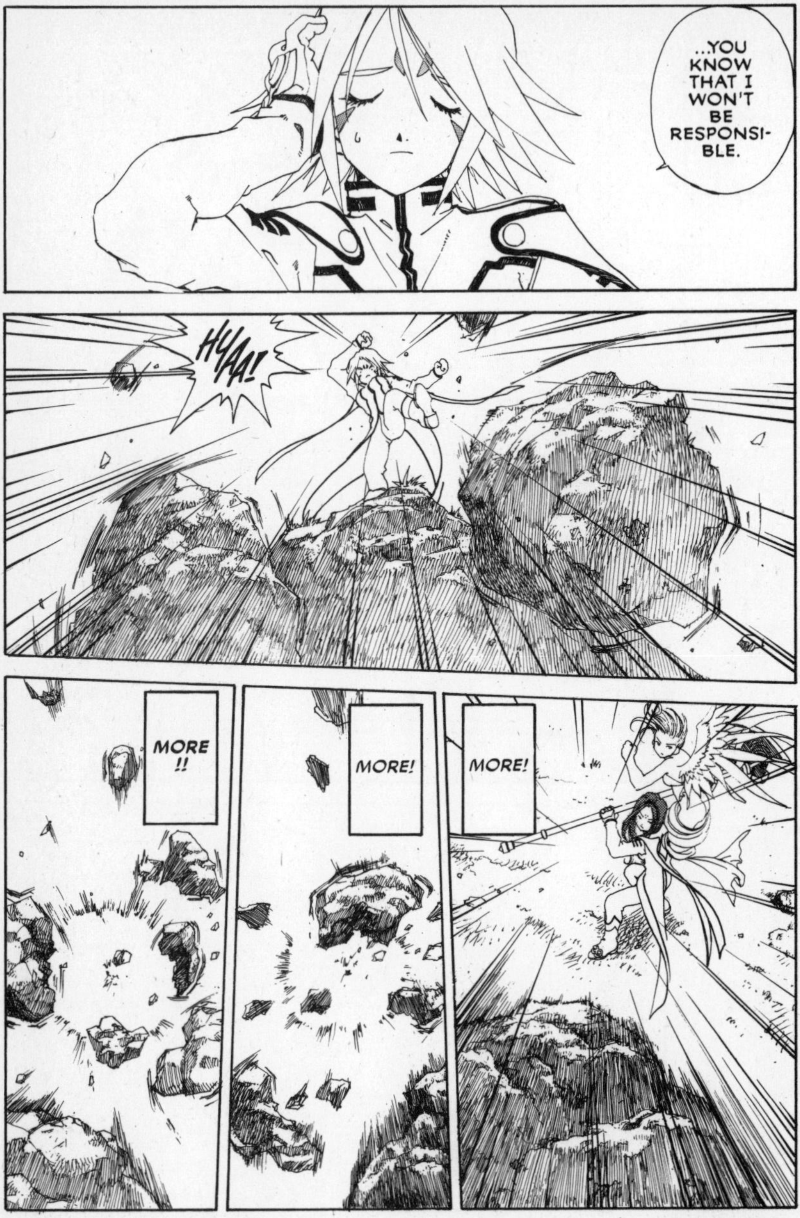
...YOU KNOW THAT I WON'T BE RESPONSIBLE.
HYAA!
MORE!
MORE!
MORE !!

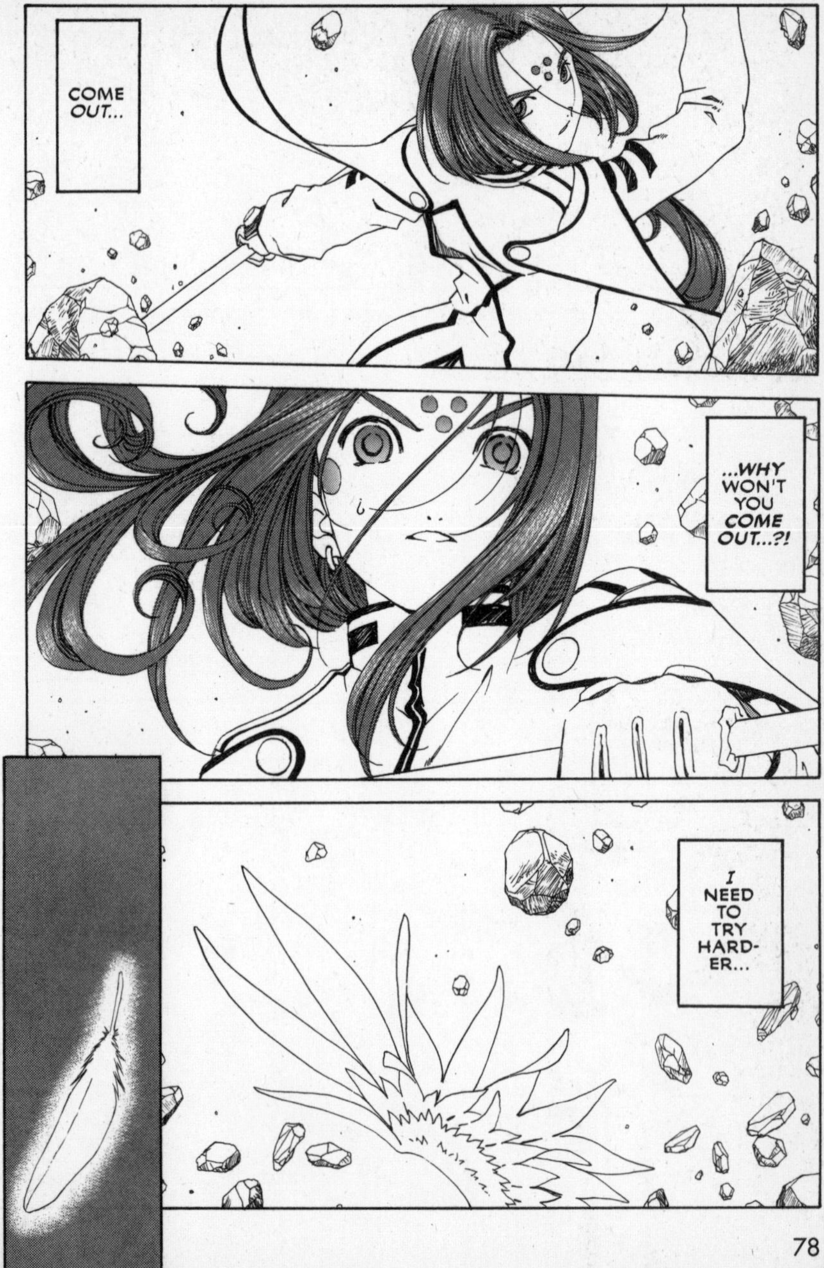
COME OUT...
...WHY WON'T YOU COME OUT...?!
I NEED TO TRY HARDER...

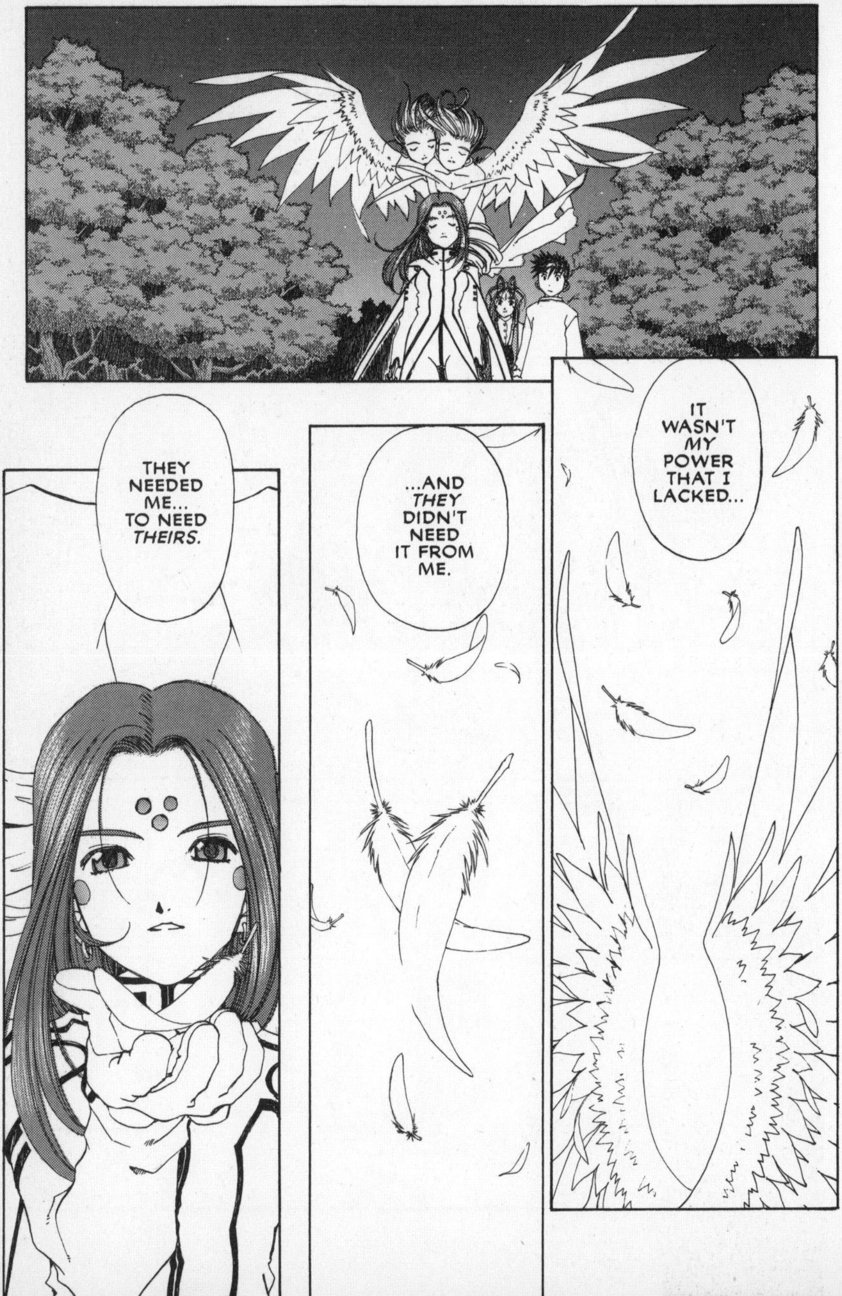
IT WASN'T *MY* POWER THAT I LACKED...
...AND *THEY* DIDN'T NEED IT FROM ME.
THEY NEEDED ME... TO NEED *THEIRS.*

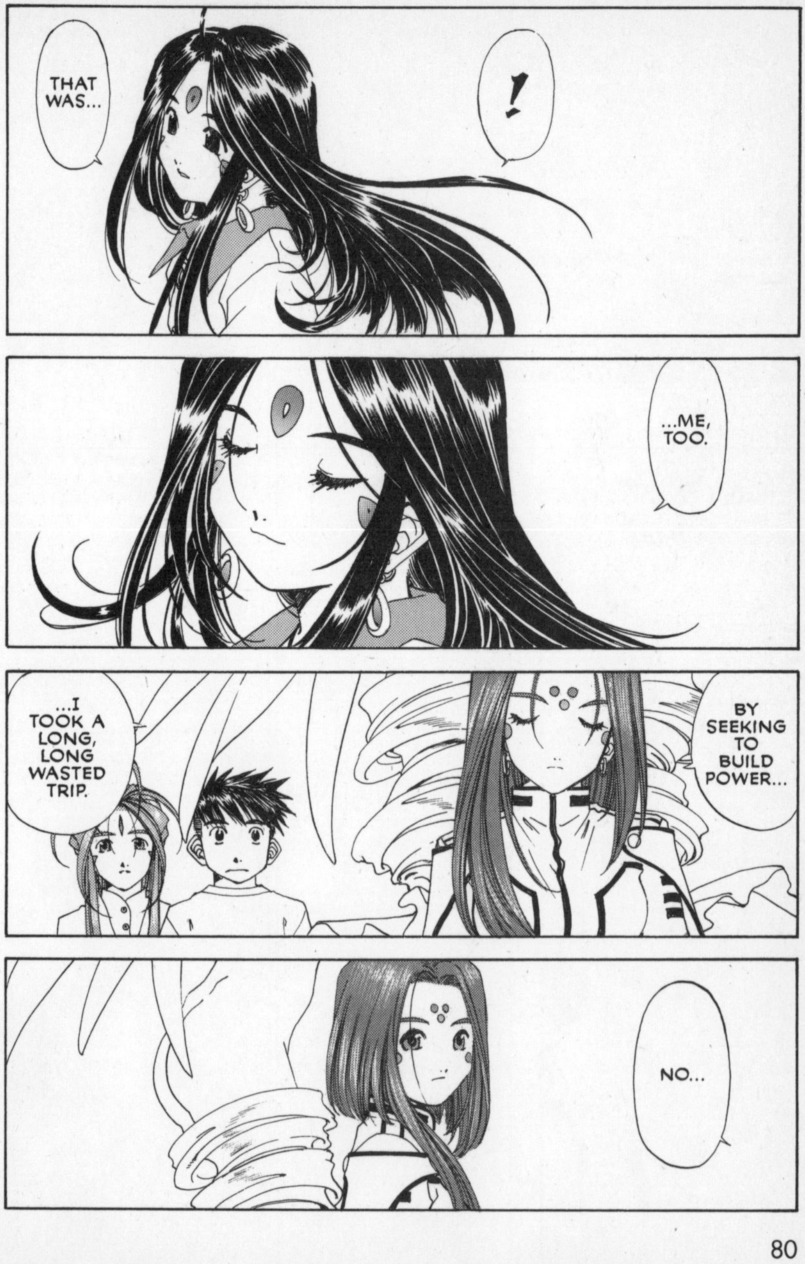
!
THAT WAS...
...ME, TOO.
BY SEEKING TO BUILD POWER...
...I TOOK A LONG, LONG WASTED TRIP.
NO...

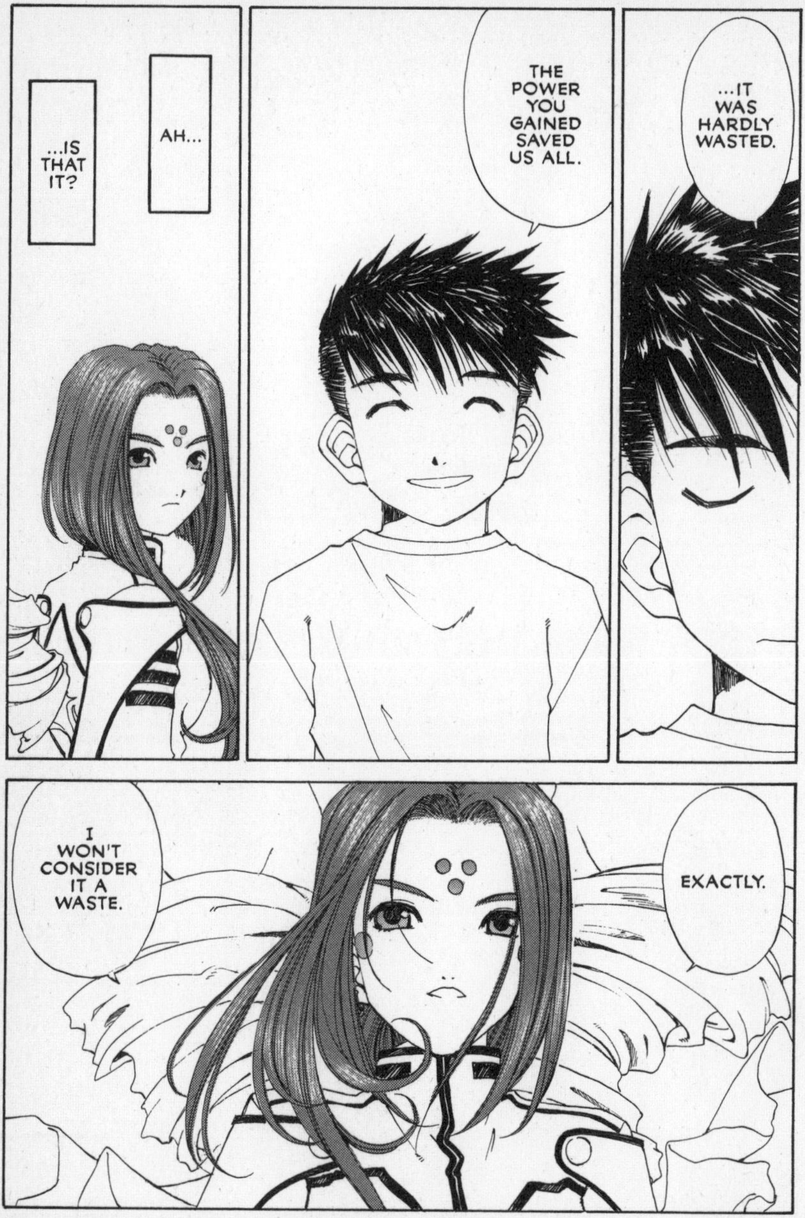
...IT WAS HARDLY WASTED.
THE POWER YOU GAINED SAVED US ALL.
AH...
...IS THAT IT?
EXACTLY.
I WON'T CONSIDER IT A WASTE.

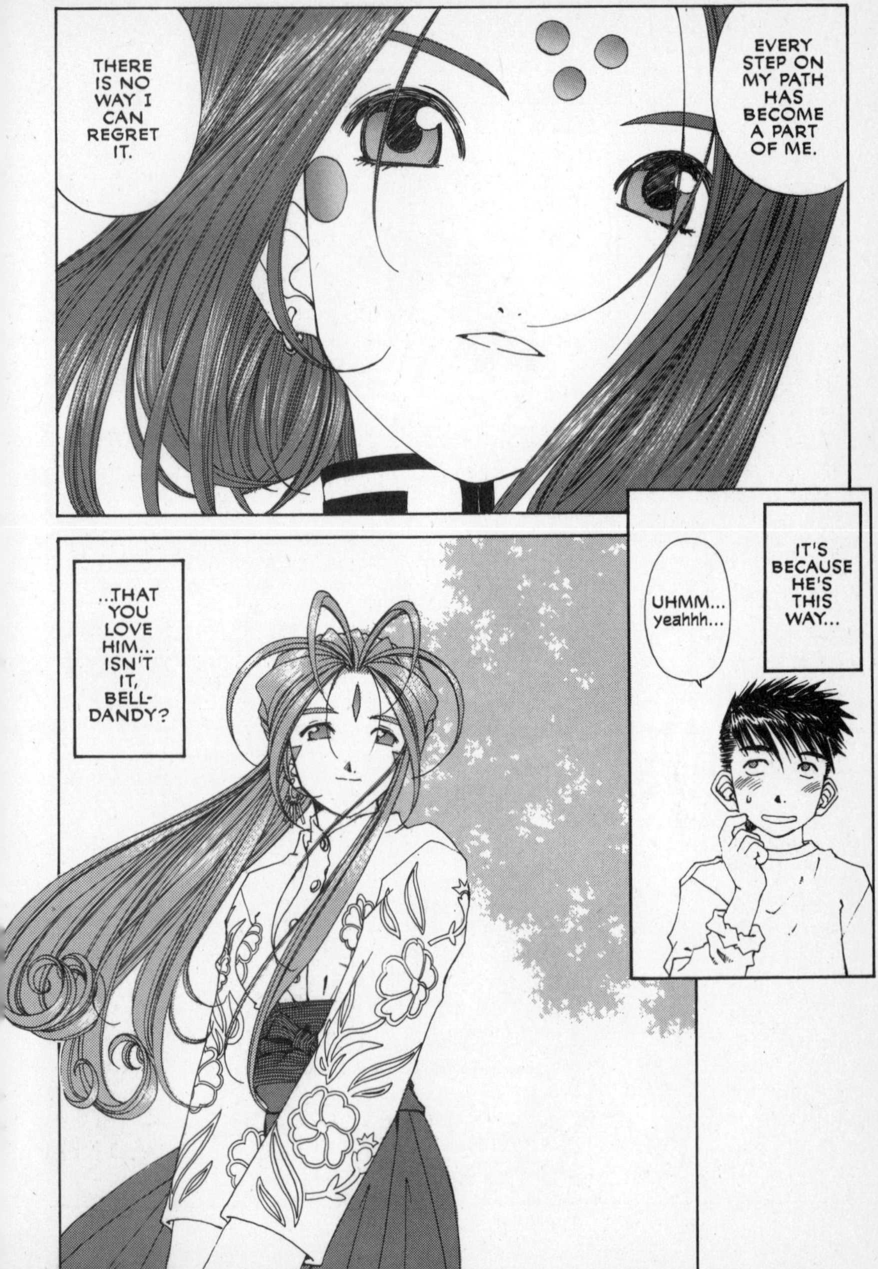
EVERY STEP ON MY PATH HAS BECOME A PART OF ME.
THERE IS NO WAY I CAN REGRET IT.
IT'S BECAUSE HE'S THIS WAY...
UHMM... yeahhh...
...THAT YOU LOVE HIM... ISN'T IT, BELL-DANDY?

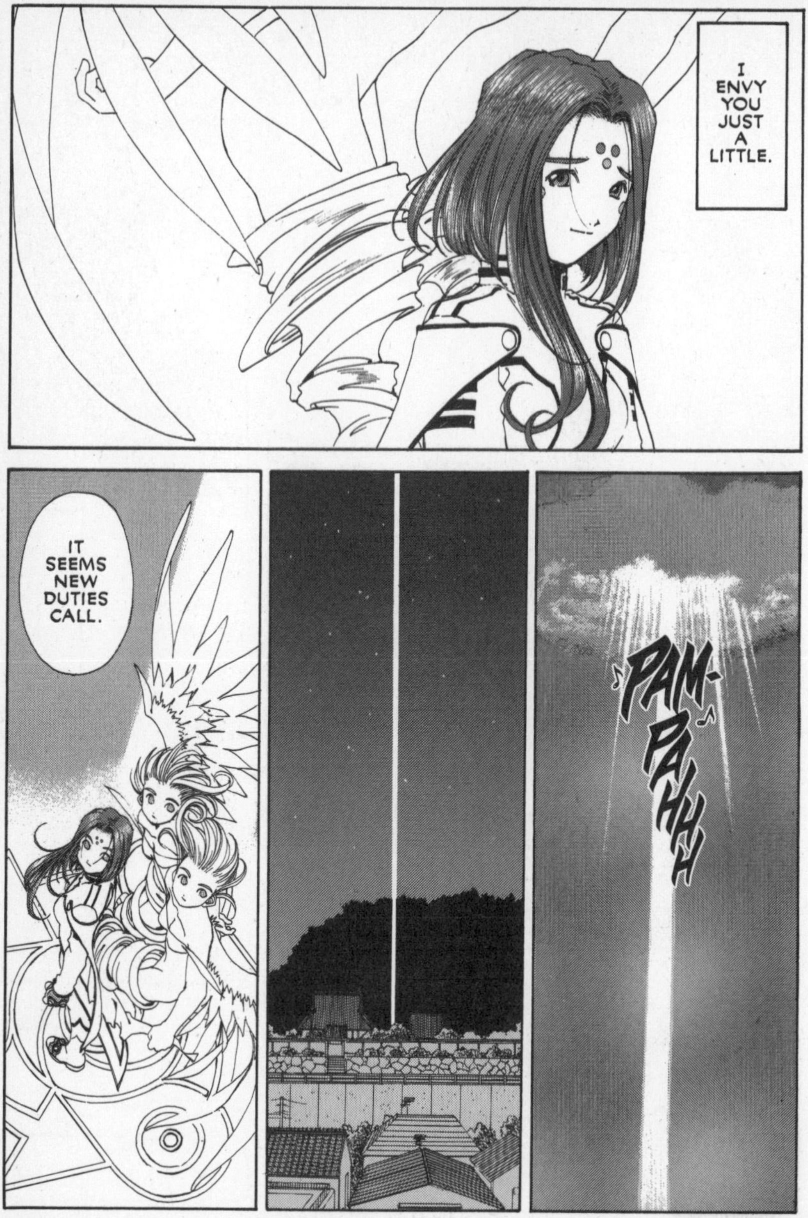
I ENVY YOU JUST A LITTLE.
PAM-PAHHH
IT SEEMS NEW DUTIES CALL.

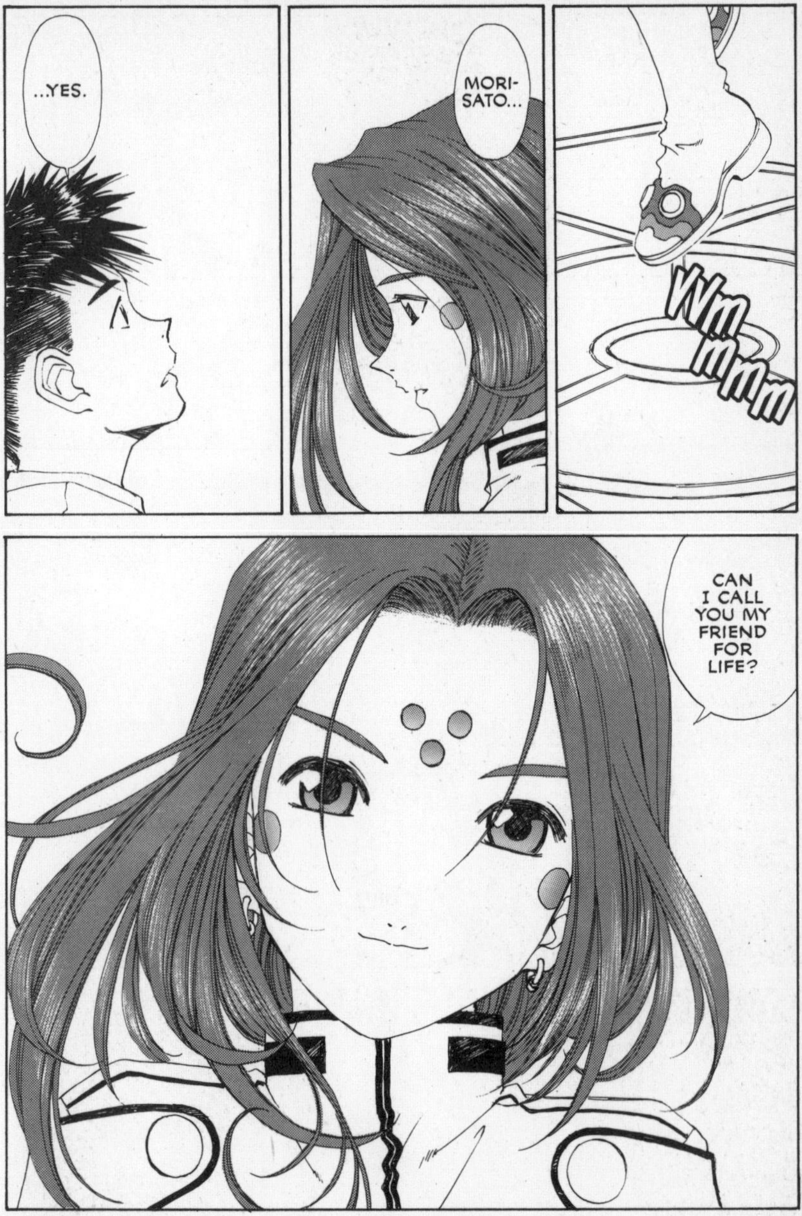
VVm MMMm
MORI-SATO...
...YES.
CAN I CALL YOU MY FRIEND FOR LIFE?

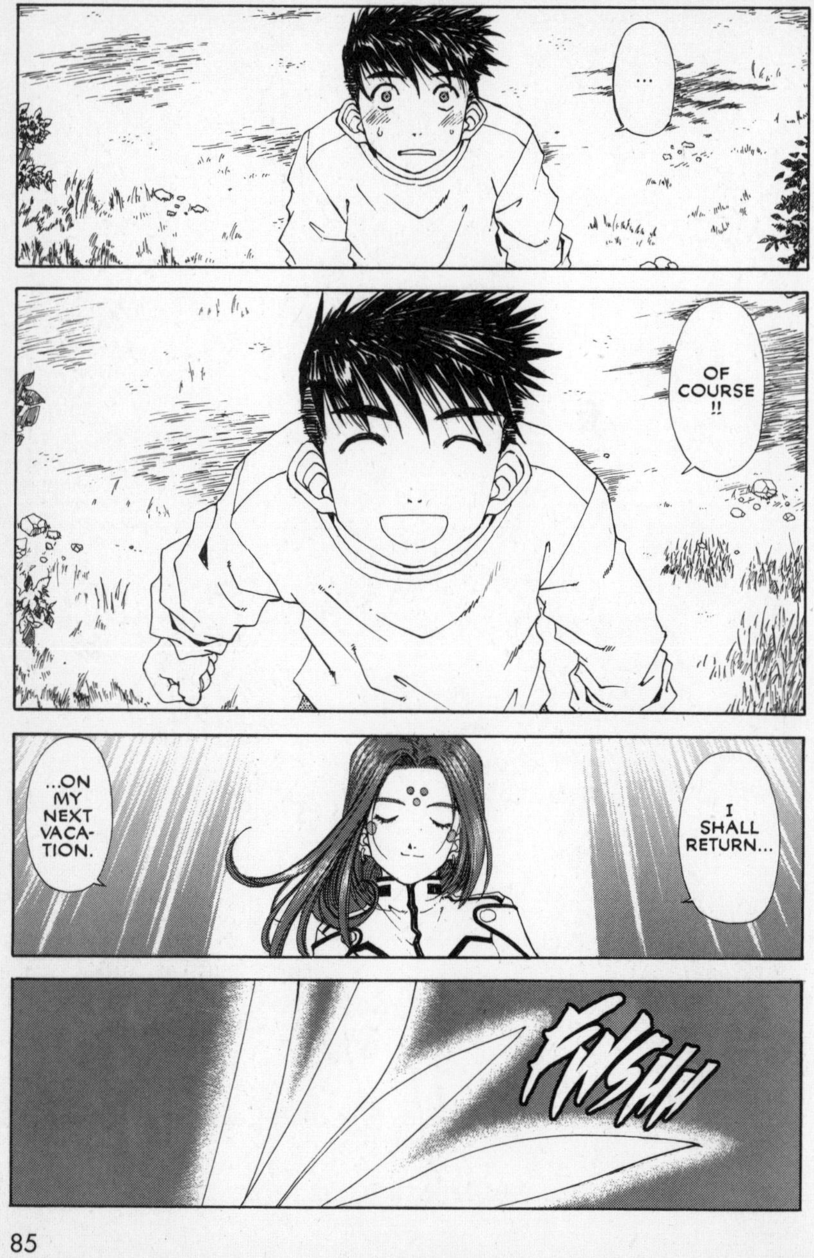
...
OF COURSE !!
I SHALL RETURN...
...ON MY NEXT VACA-TION.
FWSHH

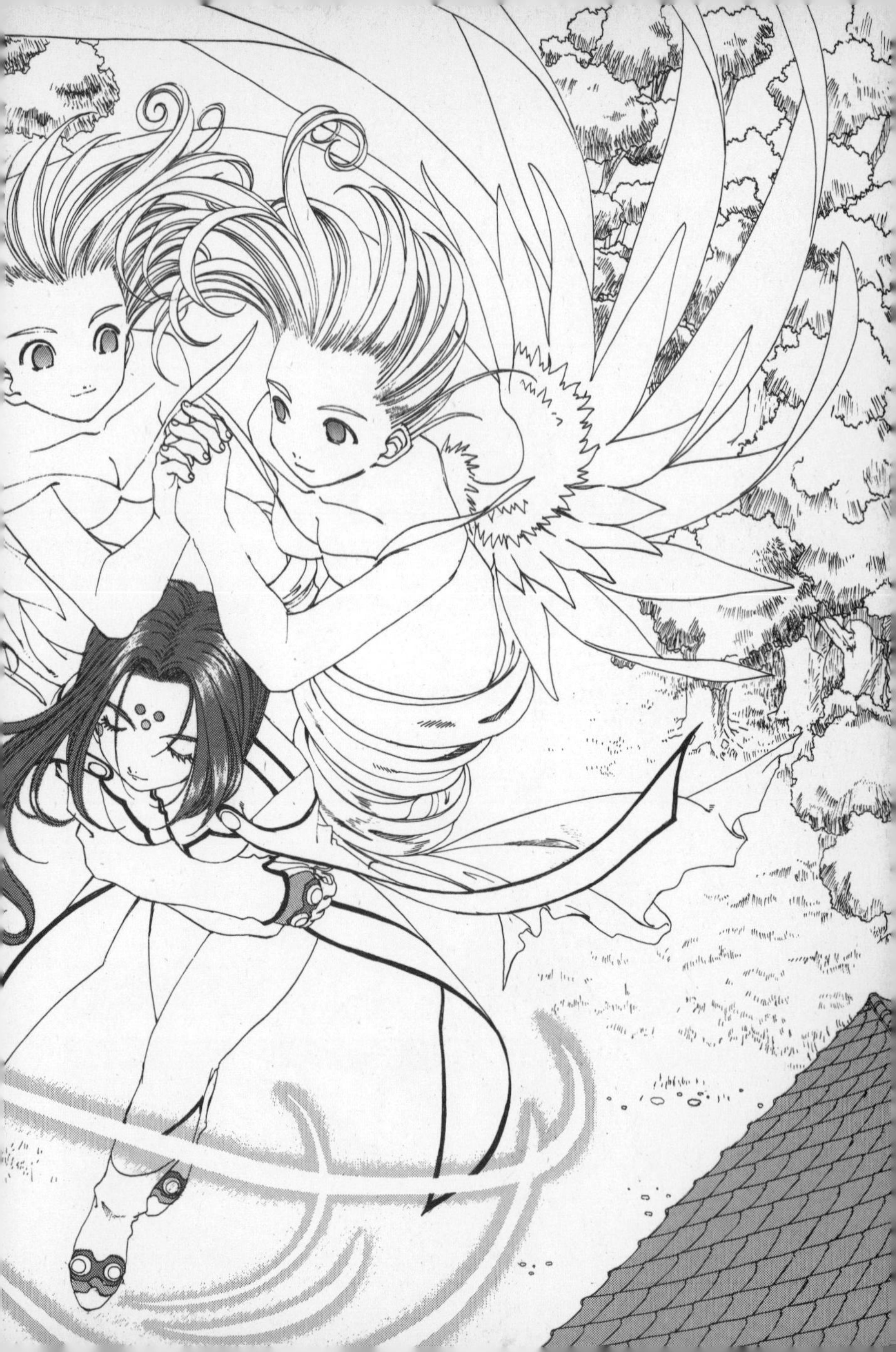

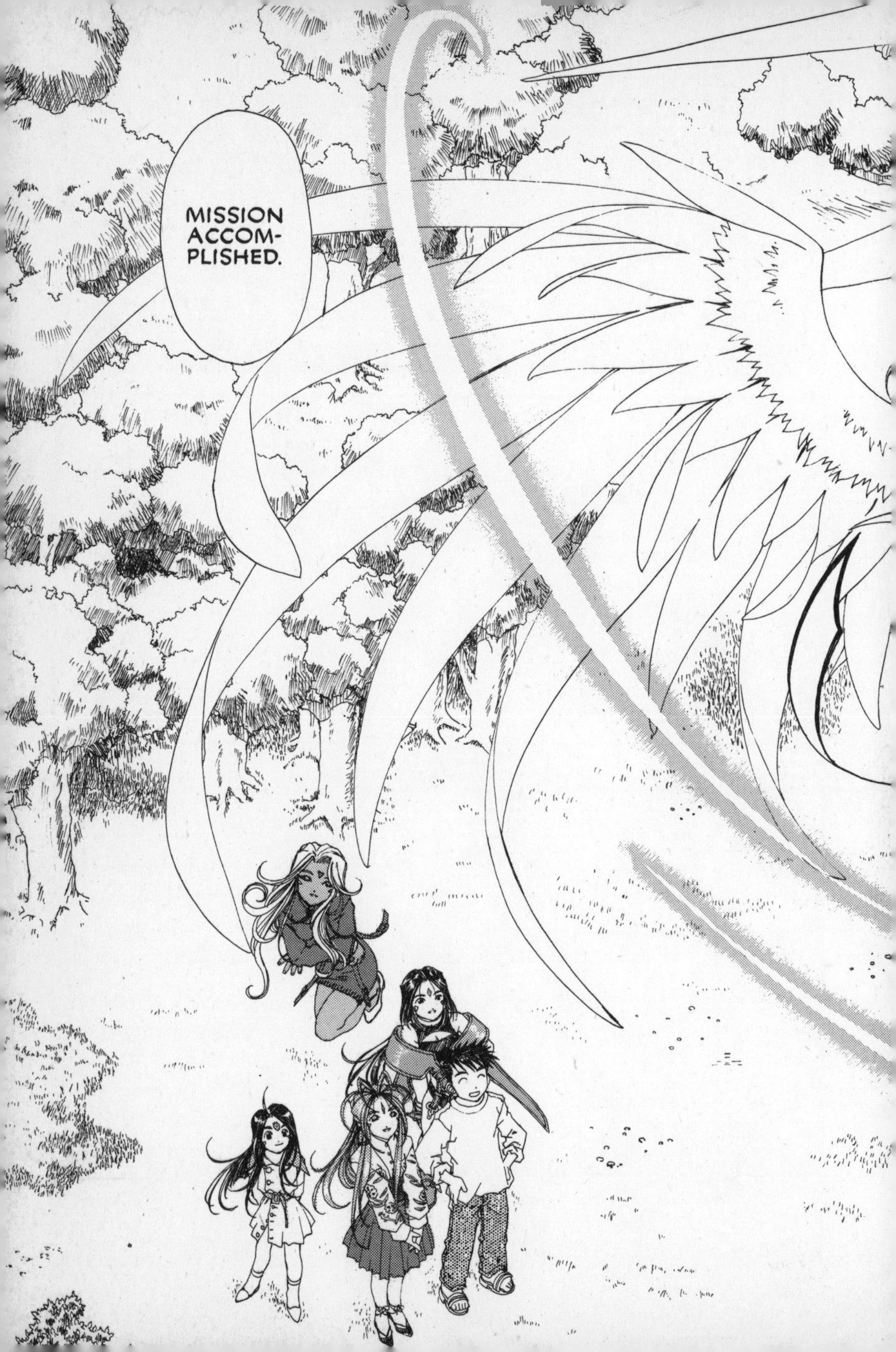
MISSION ACCOM-PLISHED.

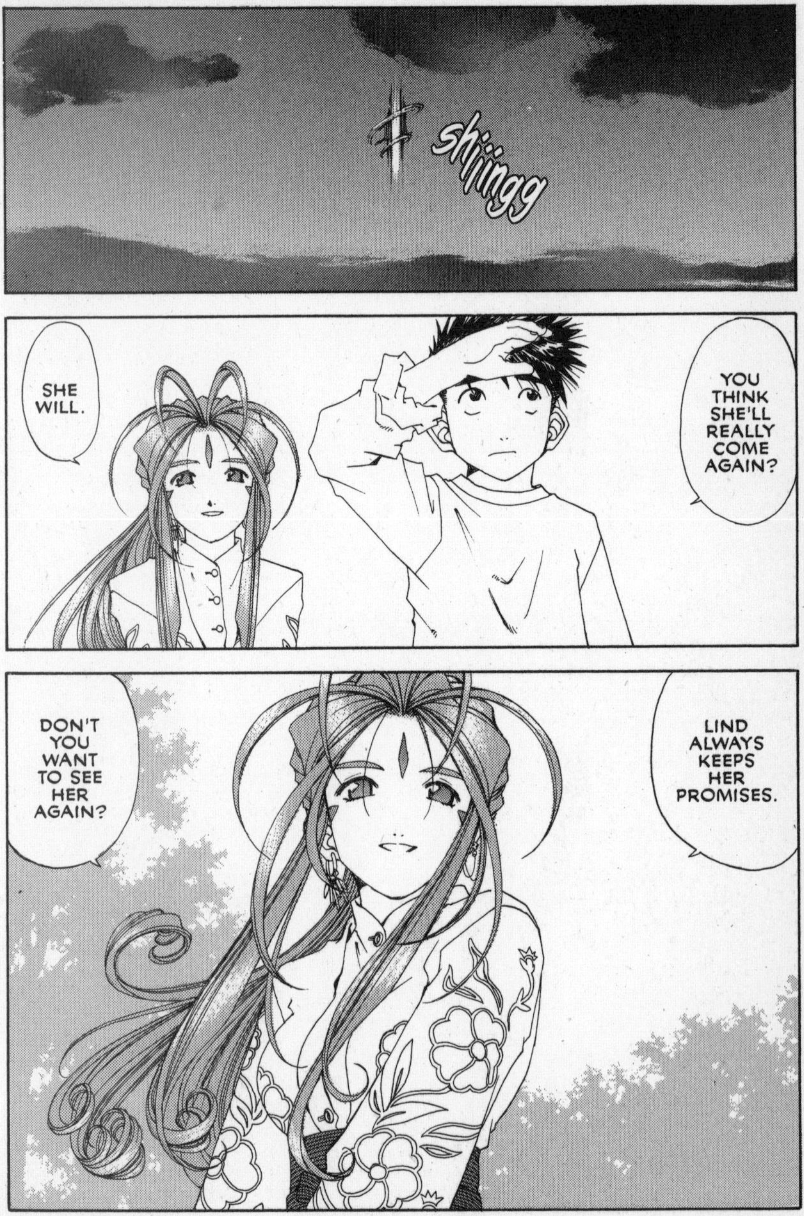
shiiingg
YOU THINK SHE'LL REALLY COME AGAIN?
SHE WILL.
LIND ALWAYS KEEPS HER PROMISES.
DON'T YOU WANT TO SEE HER AGAIN?

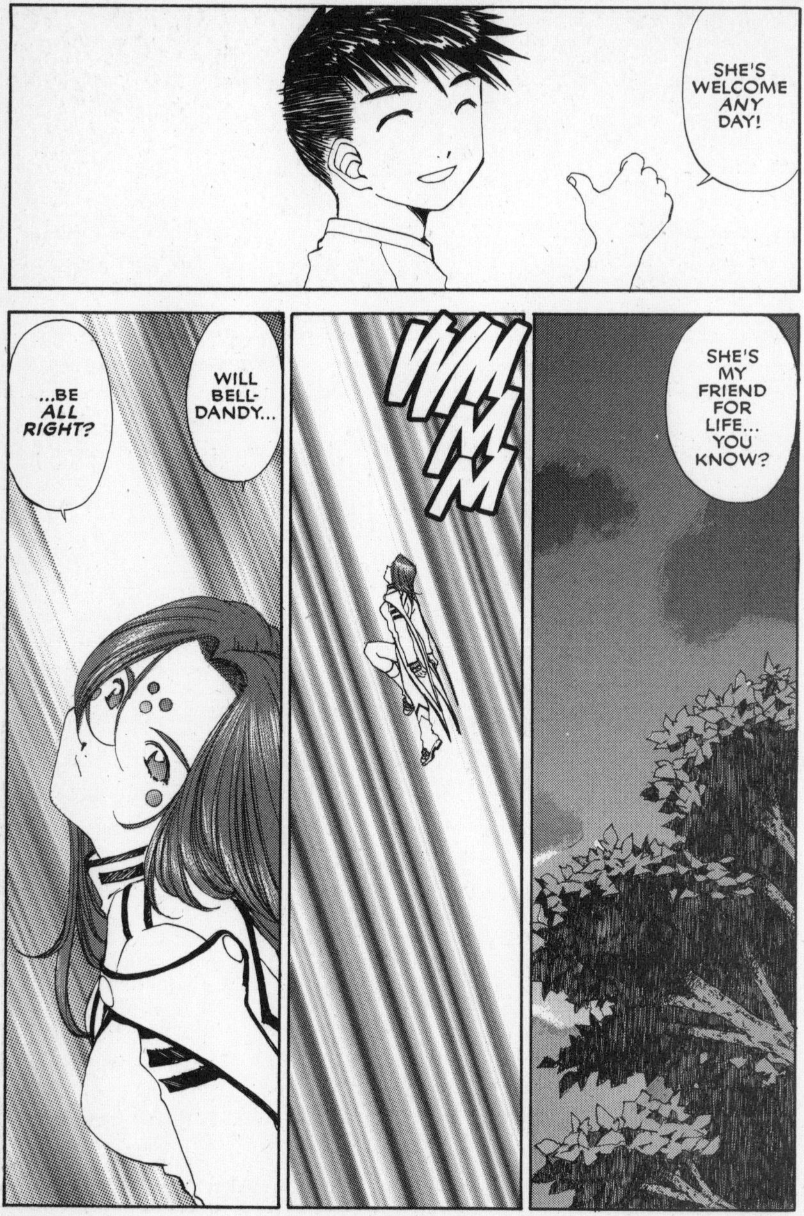
SHE'S WELCOME *ANY* DAY!
SHE'S MY FRIEND FOR LIFE... YOU KNOW?
WMMMM
WILL BELL-DANDY...
...BE *ALL* RIGHT?

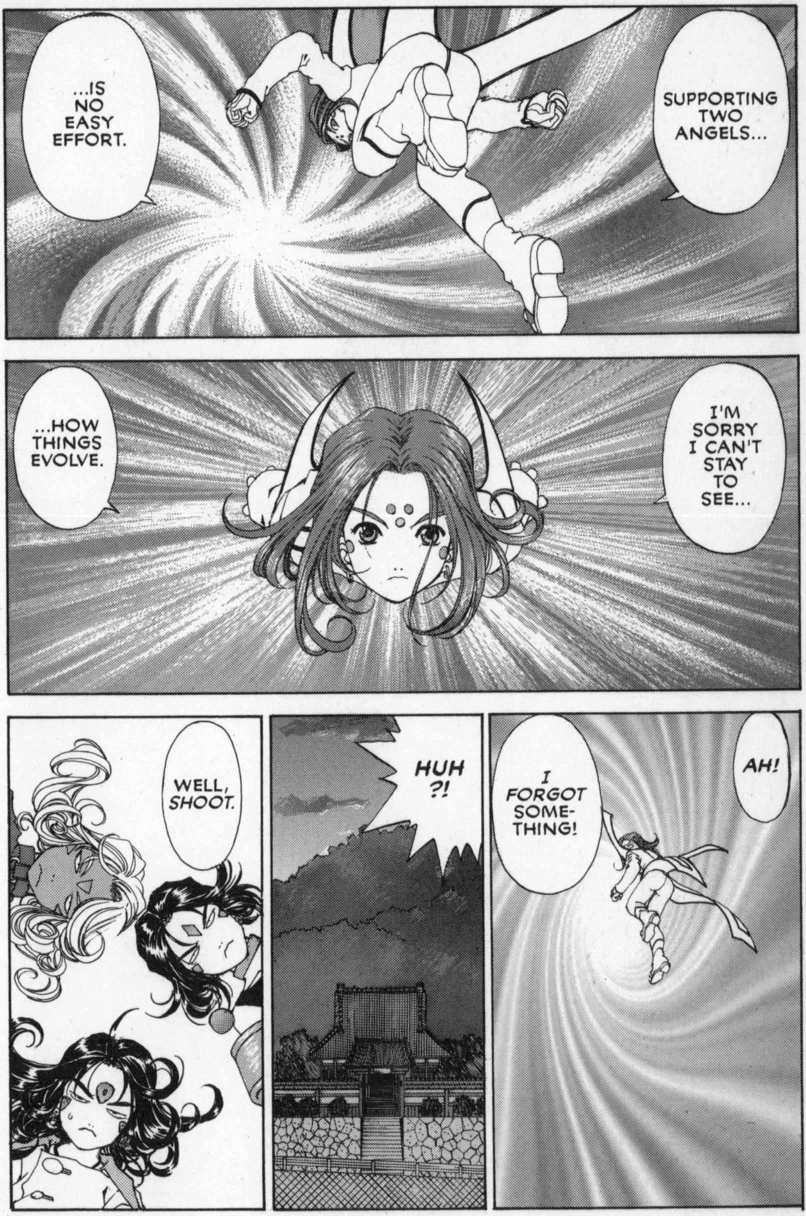
SUPPORTING TWO ANGELS...
...IS NO EASY EFFORT.
I'M SORRY I CAN'T STAY TO SEE...
...HOW THINGS EVOLVE.
AH!
I FORGOT SOME-THING!
HUH ?!
WELL, SHOOT.

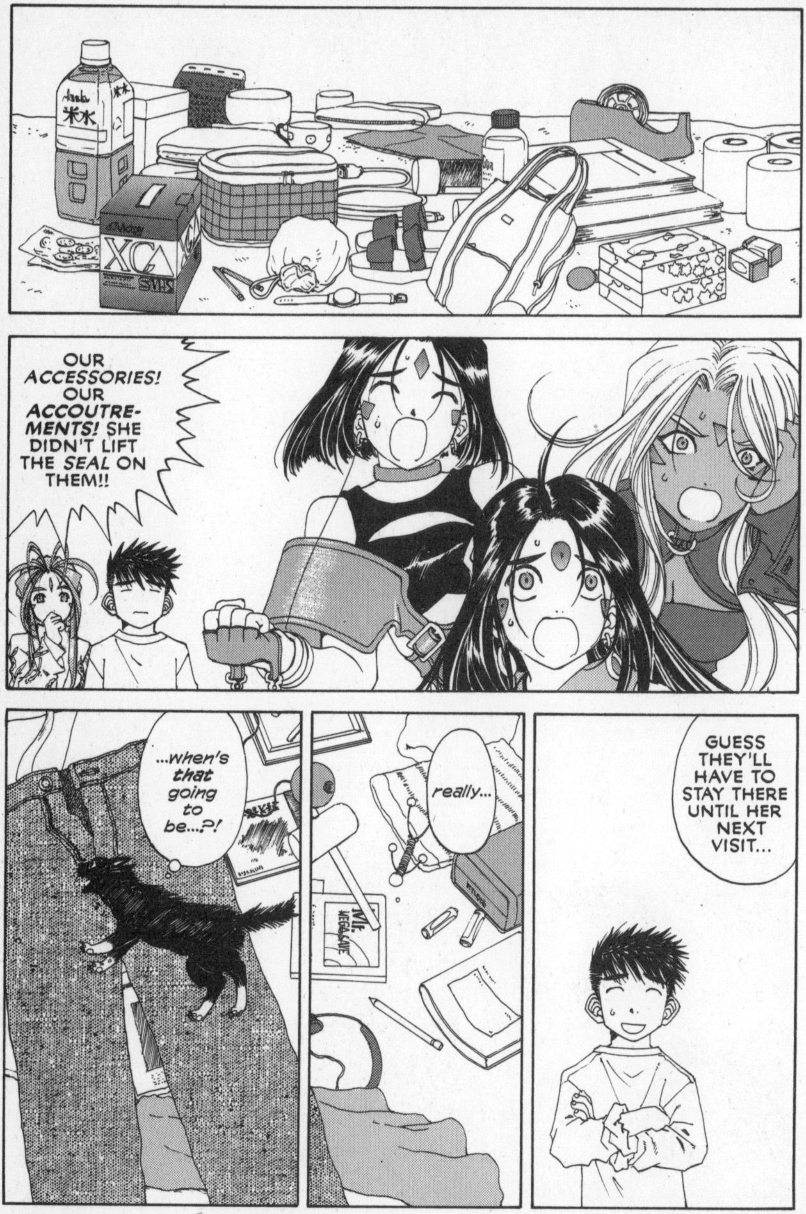
OUR ACCESSORIES! OUR ACCOUTREMENTS! SHE DIDN'T LIFT THE SEAL ON THEM!!
GUESS THEY'LL HAVE TO STAY THERE UNTIL HER NEXT VISIT...
really...
...when's that going to be...?!

OH MY GODDESS!
CHIHIRO

CHAPTER 167

Inside Belldandy

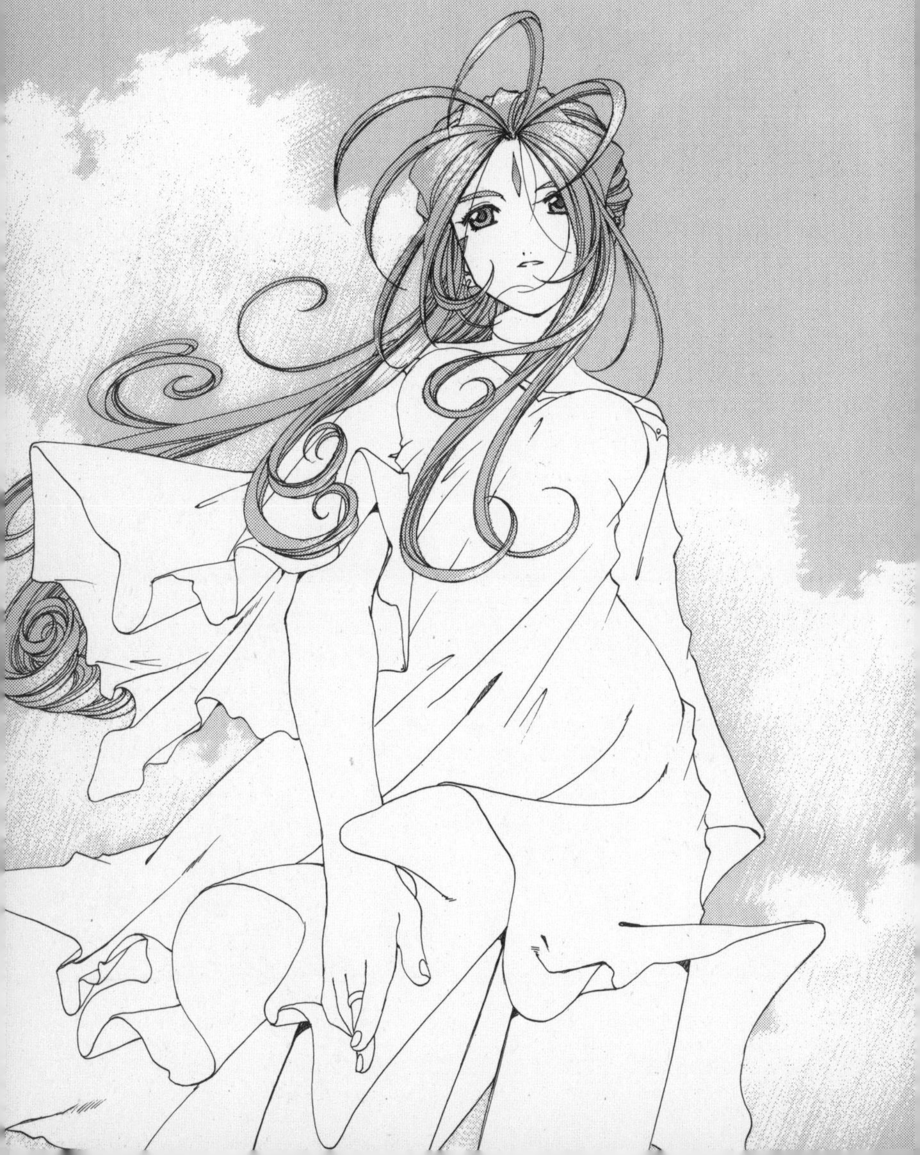

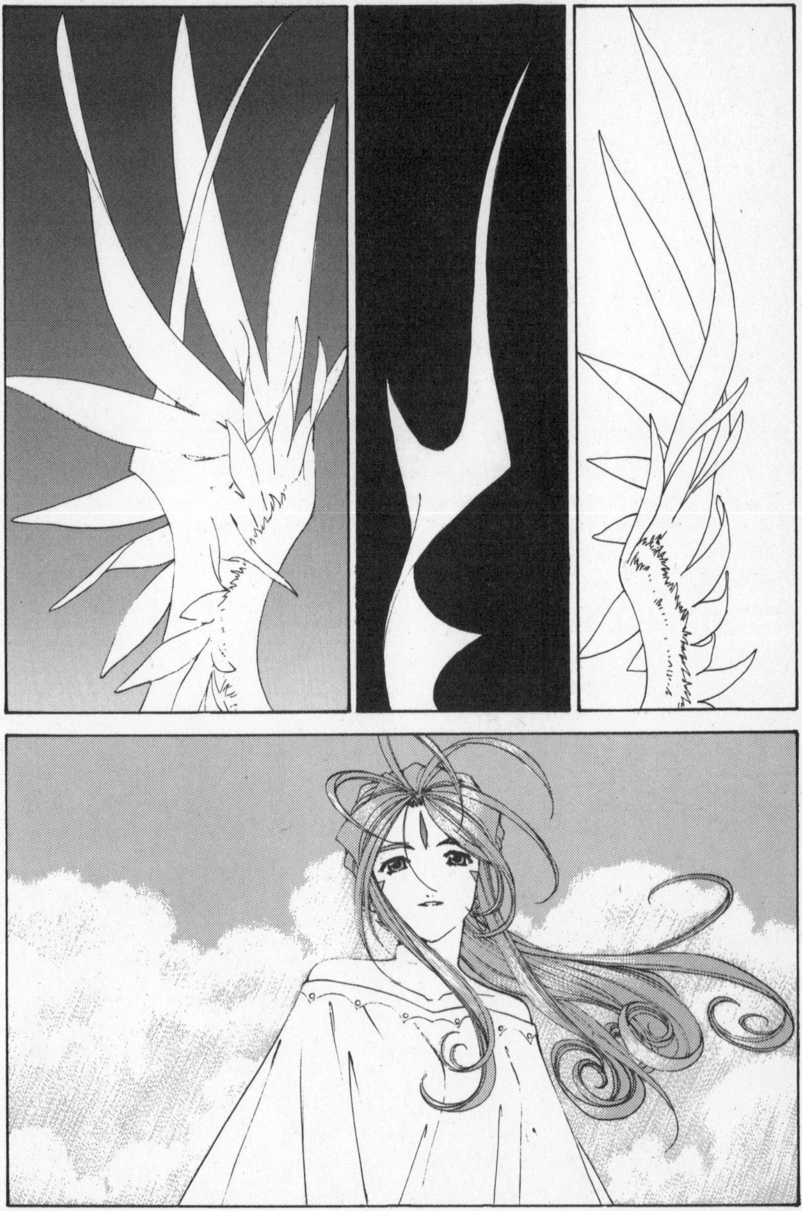

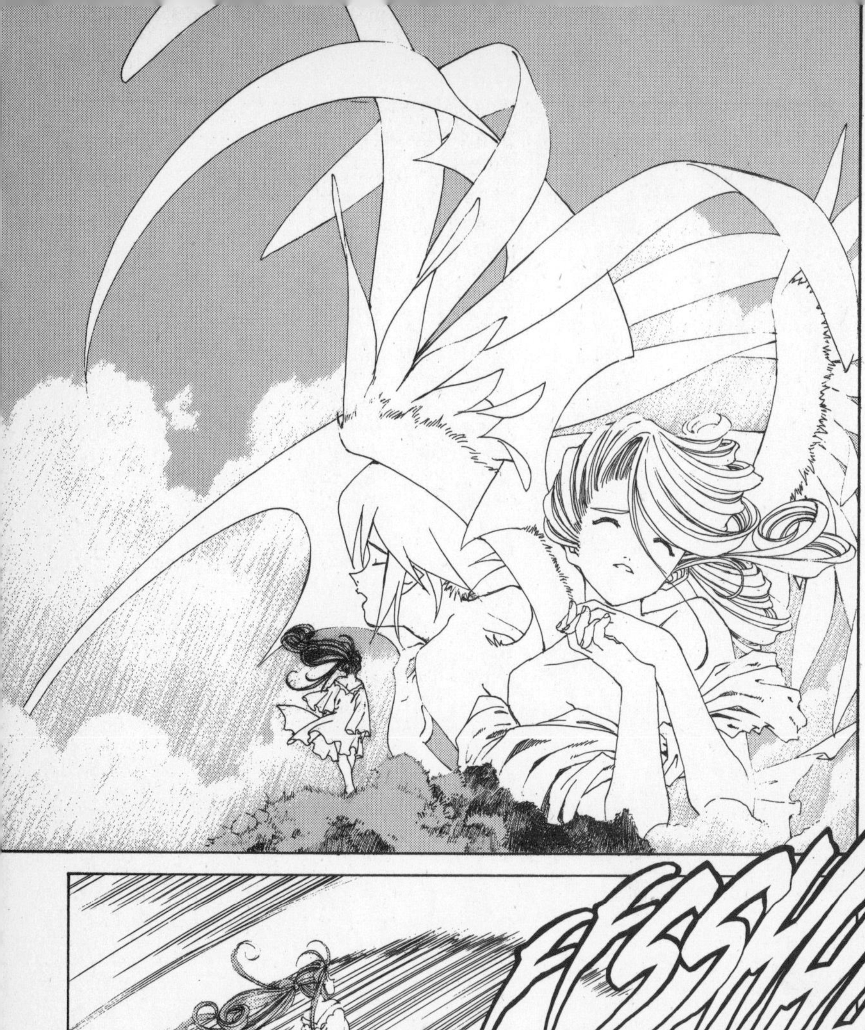

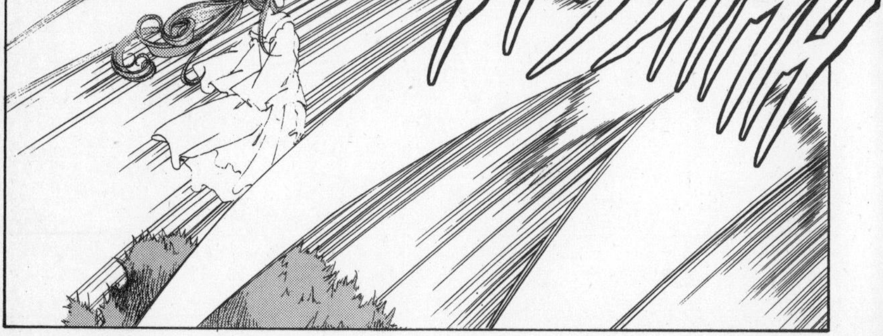
FSSHH

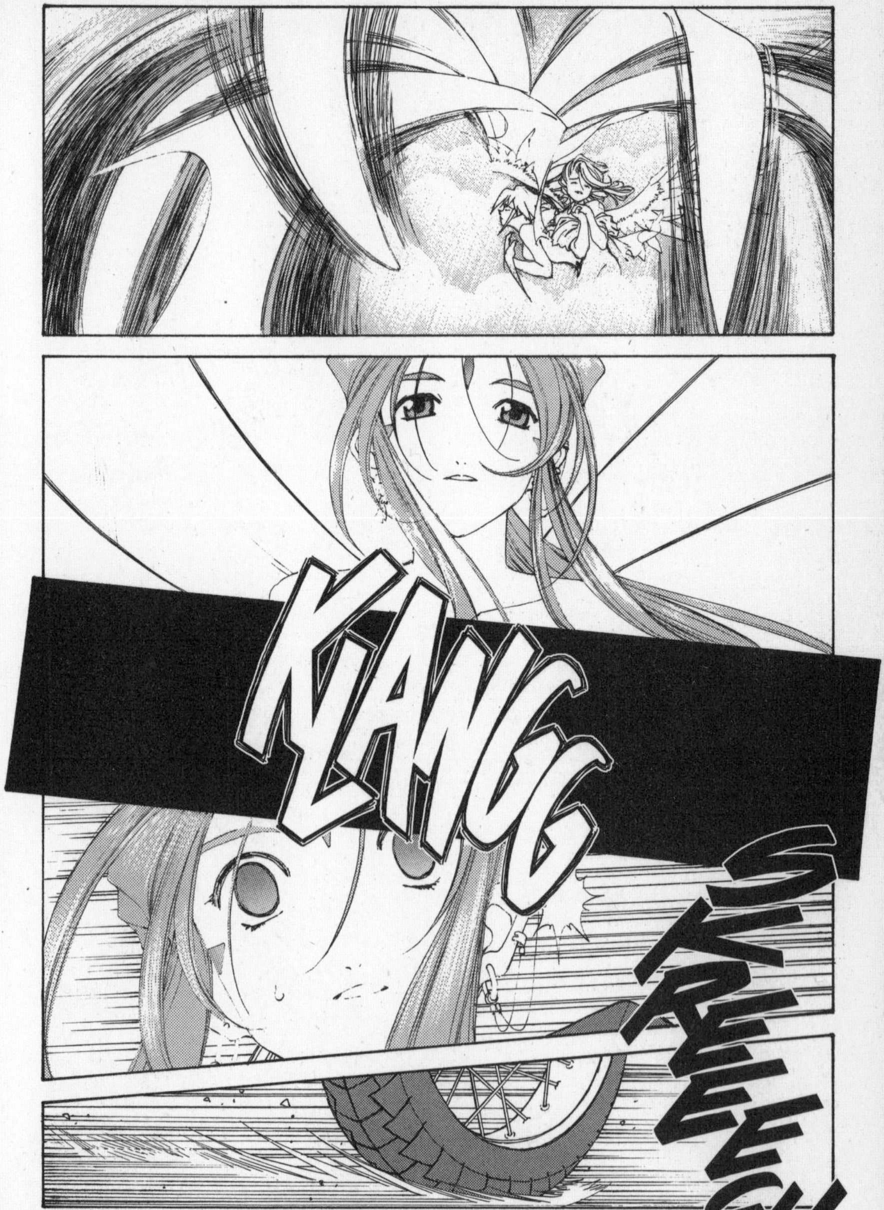
KLANG
SKREEECH

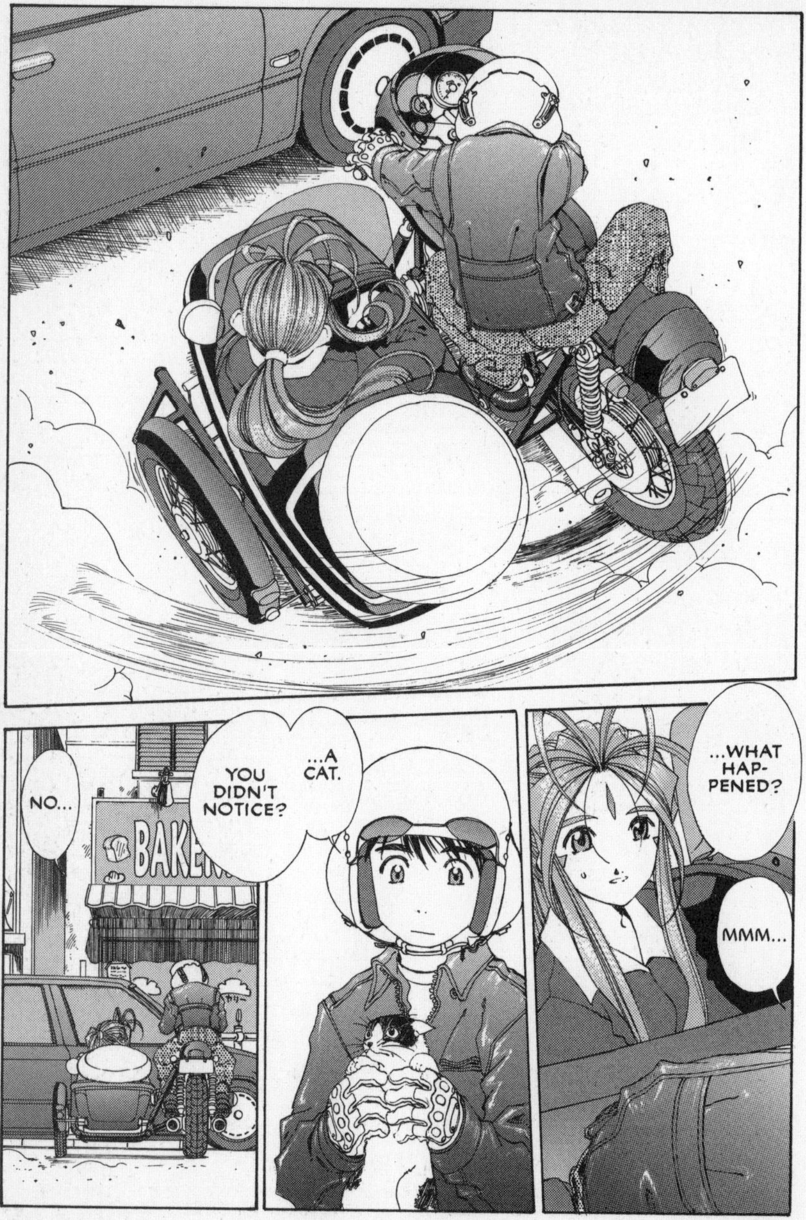
...WHAT HAP-PENED?
MMM...
...A CAT.
YOU DIDN'T NOTICE?
NO...

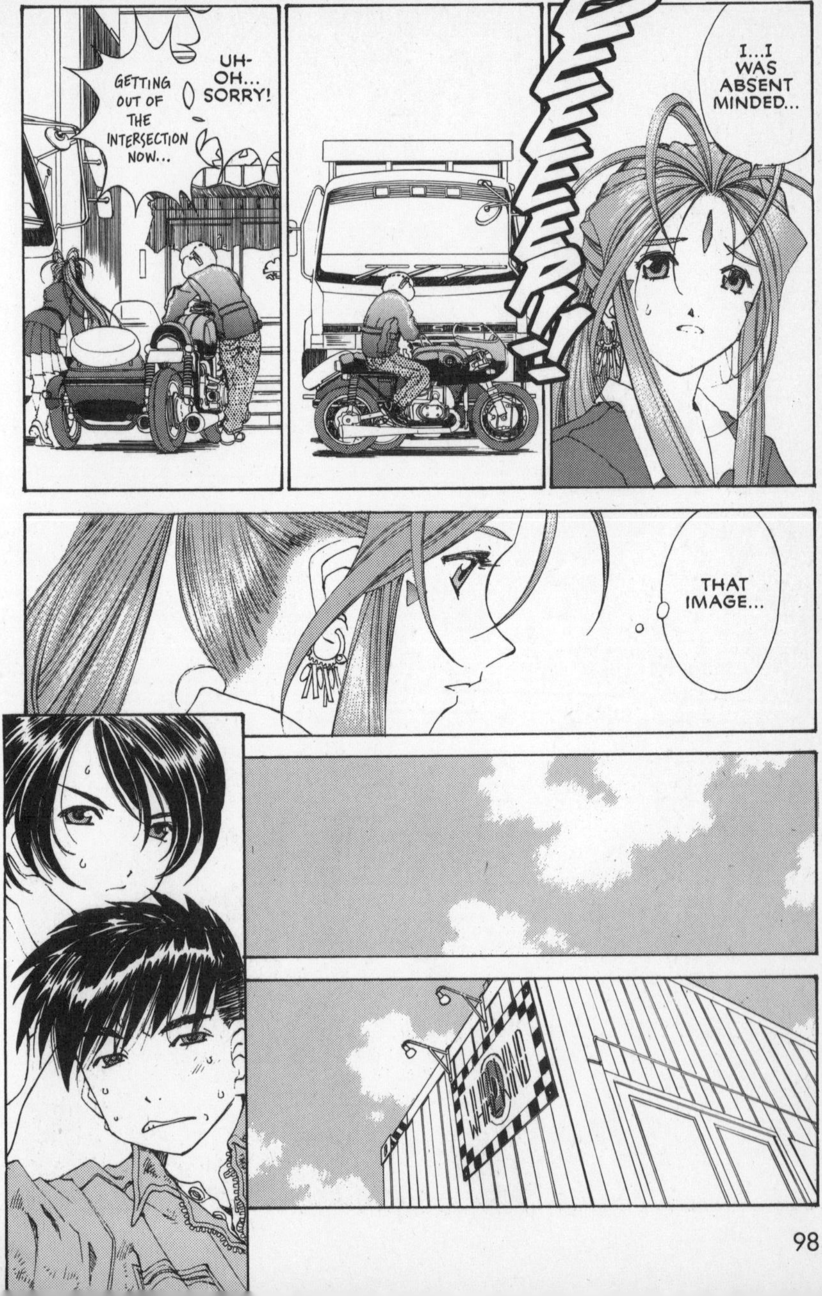
BEEEEP!!!
I...I WAS ABSENT MINDED...
UH-OH... SORRY!
GETTING OUT OF THE INTERSECTION NOW...
THAT IMAGE...

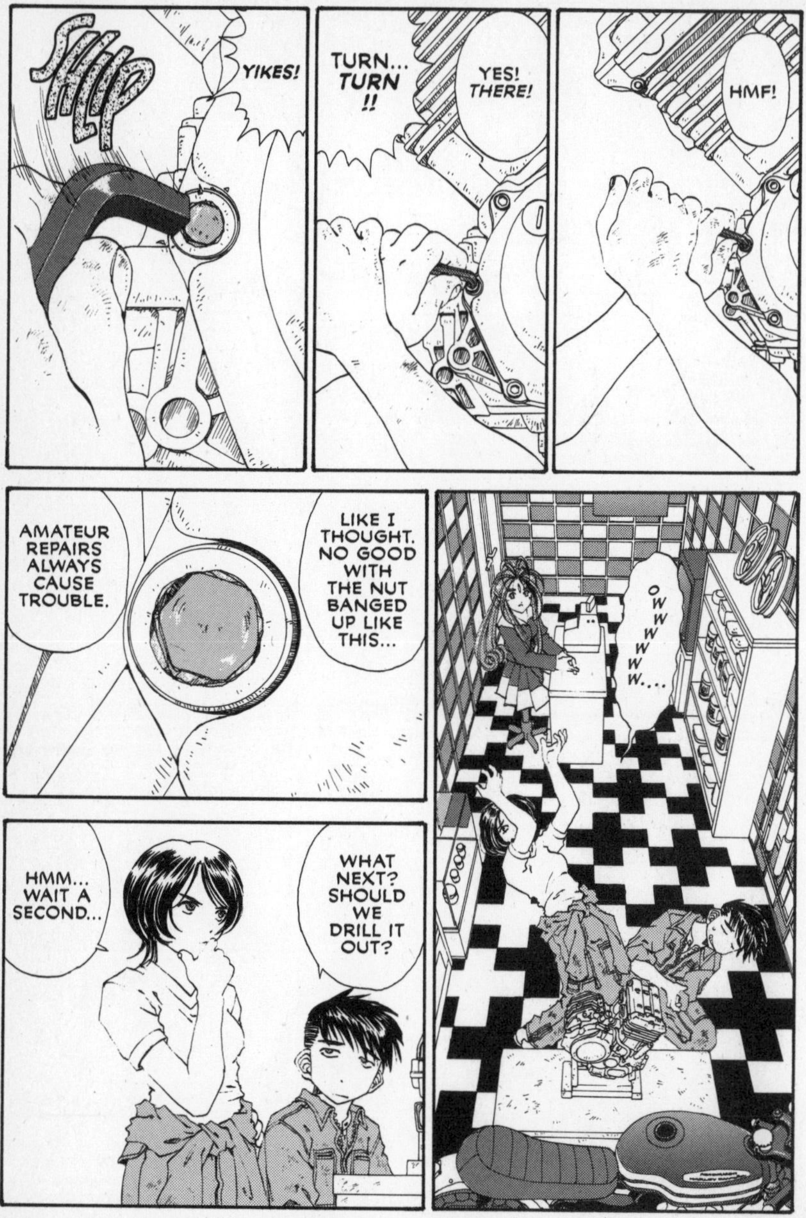
HMF!
YES! THERE!
TURN... TURN !!
YIKES!
SHLIP
OWWWWWWW...
LIKE I THOUGHT. NO GOOD WITH THE NUT BANGED UP LIKE THIS...
AMATEUR REPAIRS ALWAYS CAUSE TROUBLE.
WHAT NEXT? SHOULD WE DRILL IT OUT?
HMM... WAIT A SECOND...

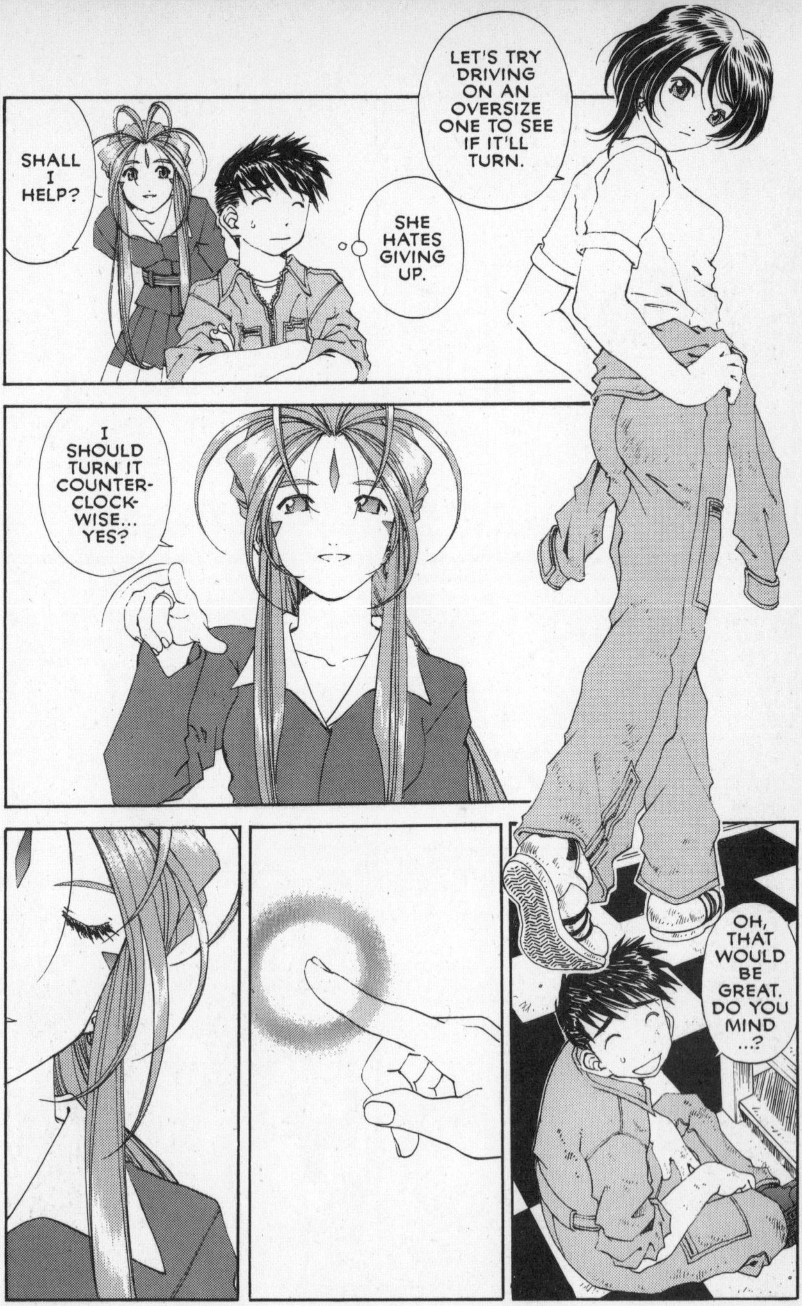
LET'S TRY DRIVING ON AN OVERSIZE ONE TO SEE IF IT'LL TURN.
SHE HATES GIVING UP.
SHALL I HELP?
I SHOULD TURN IT COUNTER-CLOCKWISE... YES?
OH, THAT WOULD BE GREAT. DO YOU MIND ...?

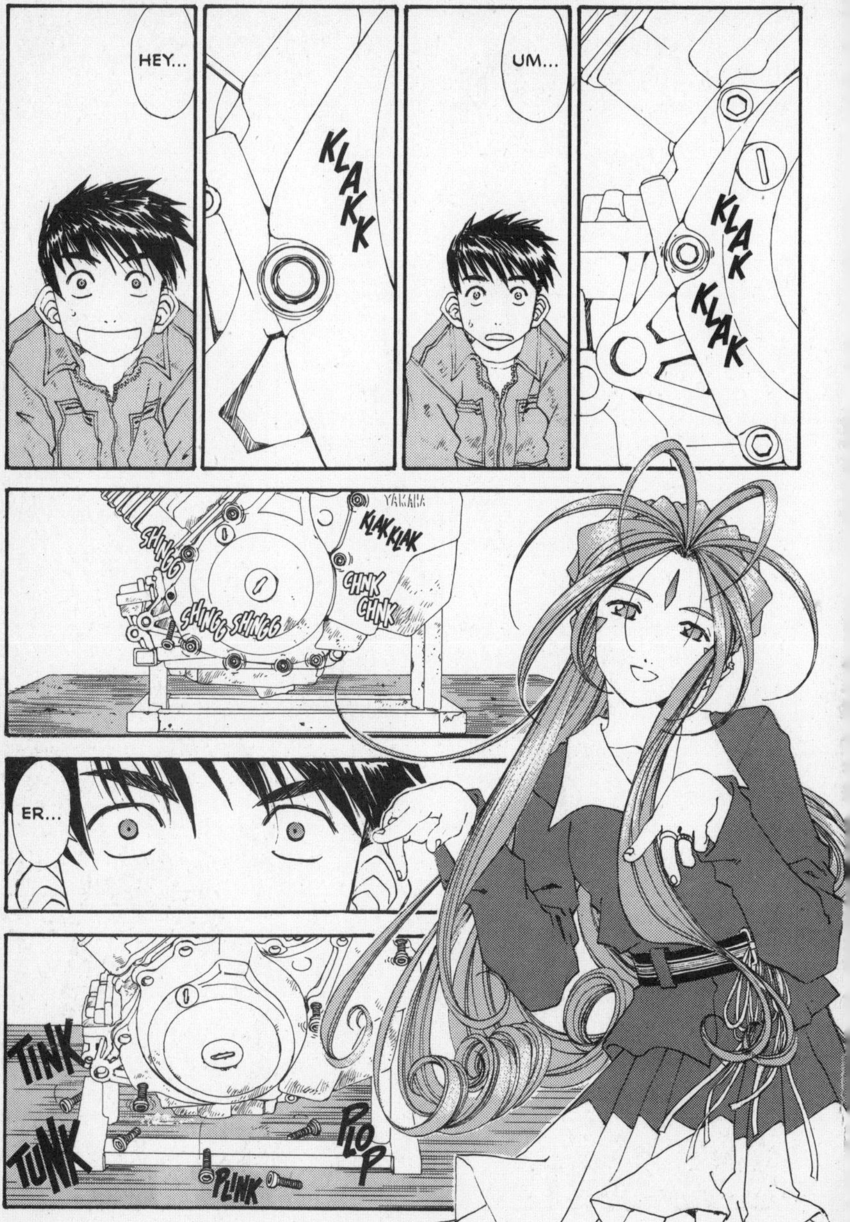
KLAK
KLAK
UM...
KLAKK
HEY...
KLAKKLAK
CHNK
CHNK
SHINGG
SHINGG SHINGG
ER...
PLOP
TINK
PLINK
TUNK

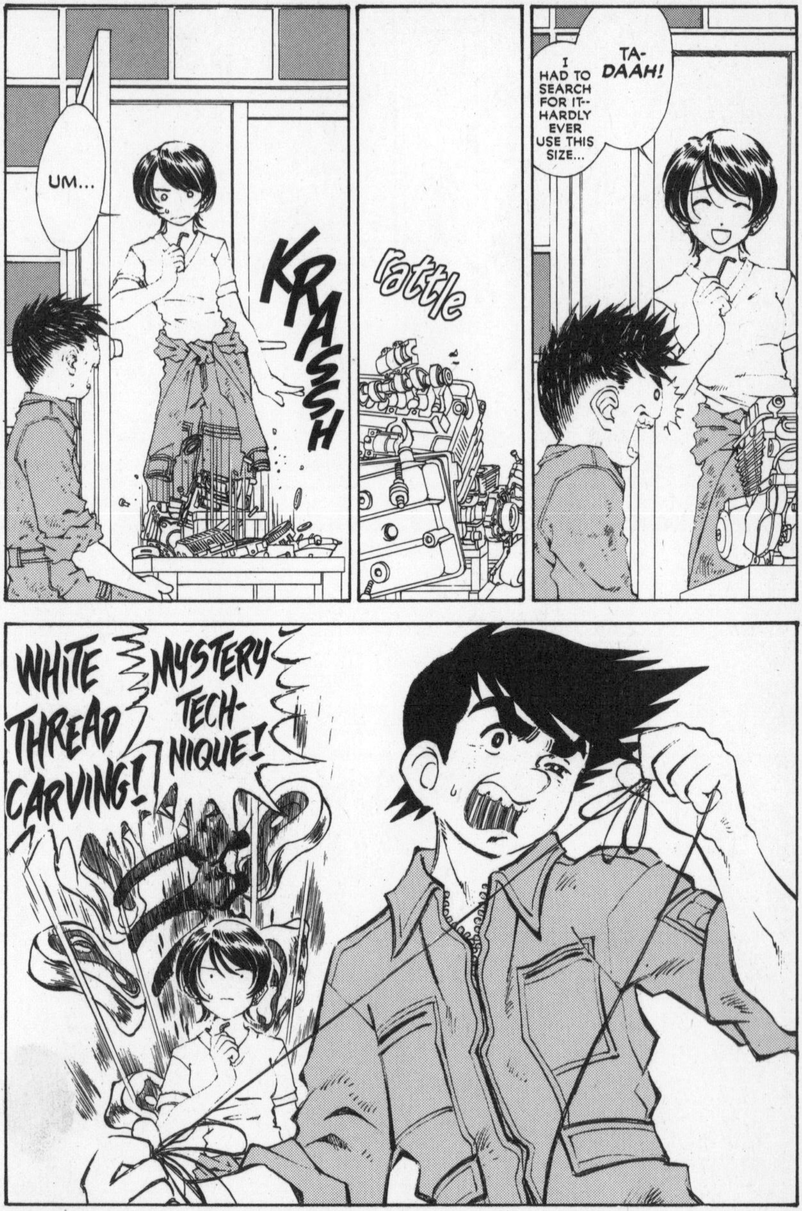
TA-DAAH!
I HAD TO SEARCH FOR IT-- HARDLY EVER USE THIS SIZE...
rattle
UM...
KRASSSH
MYSTERY TECH-NIQUE!
WHITE THREAD CARVING!

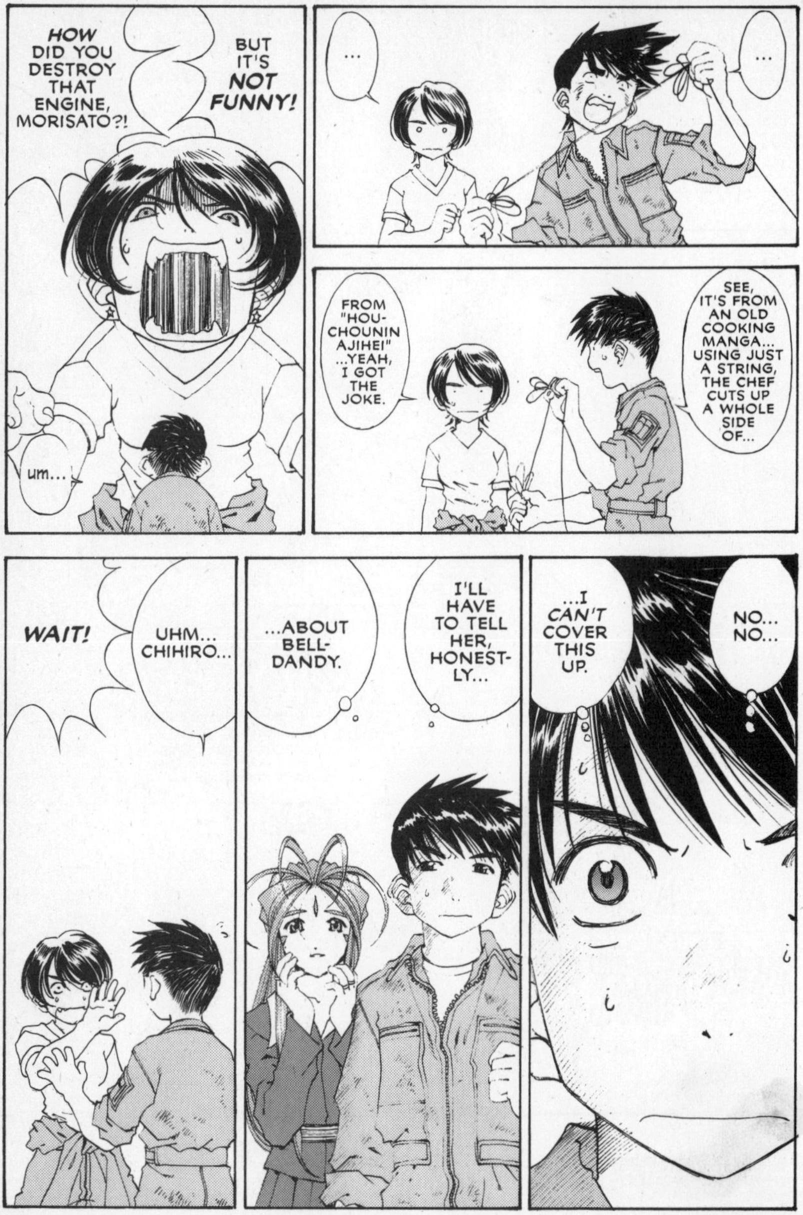
...
...
SEE, IT'S FROM AN OLD COOKING MANGA... USING JUST A STRING, THE CHEF CUTS UP A WHOLE SIDE OF...
FROM "HOU-CHOUNIN AJIHEI" ...YEAH, I GOT THE JOKE.
BUT IT'S *NOT FUNNY!*
HOW DID YOU DESTROY THAT ENGINE, MORISATO?!
um...
NO... NO...
...I *CAN'T* COVER THIS UP.
I'LL HAVE TO TELL HER, HONEST-LY...
...ABOUT BELL-DANDY.
UHM... CHIHIRO...
WAIT!

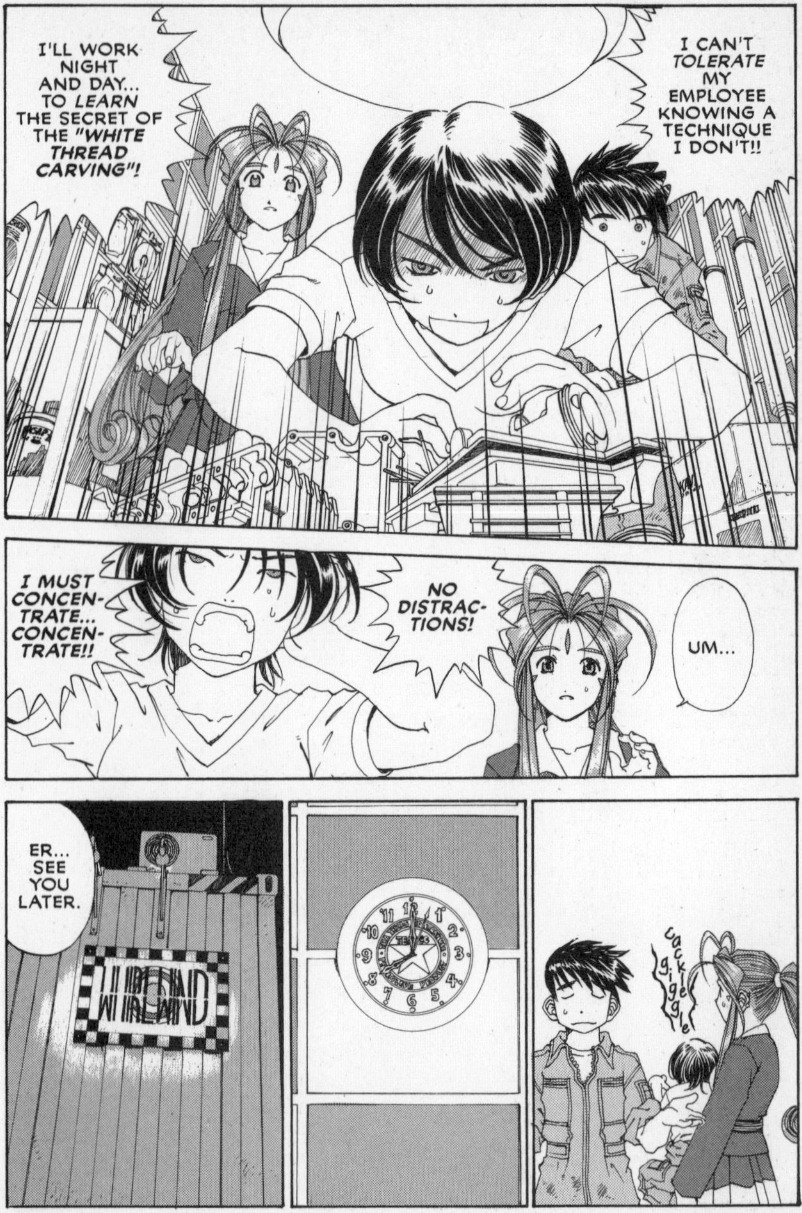
I CAN'T TOLERATE MY EMPLOYEE KNOWING A TECHNIQUE I DON'T!!
I'LL WORK NIGHT AND DAY... TO LEARN THE SECRET OF THE "WHITE THREAD CARVING"!
UM...
NO DISTRACTIONS!
I MUST CONCENTRATE... CONCENTRATE!!
cackle giggle giggle
ER... SEE YOU LATER.
WHIRLWIND

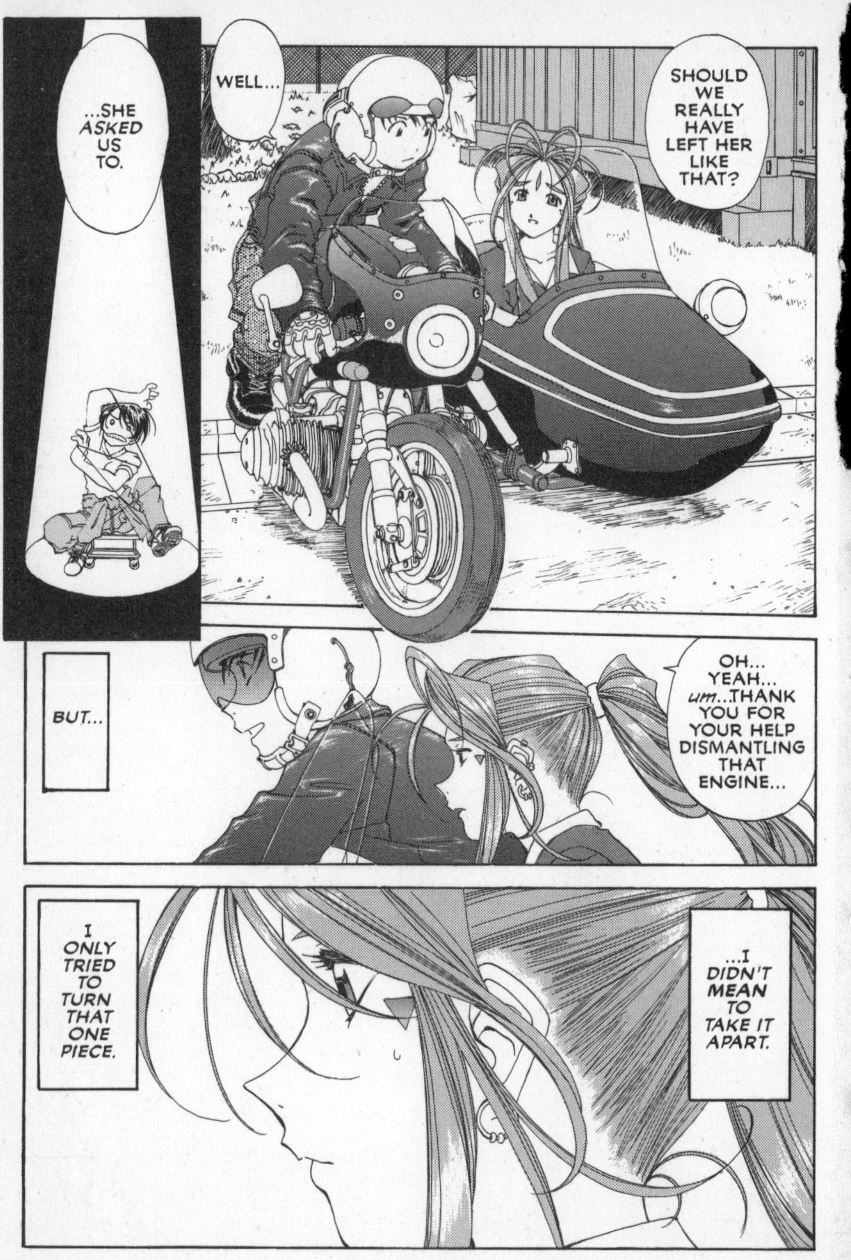
SHOULD WE REALLY HAVE LEFT HER LIKE THAT?
WELL...
...SHE *ASKED* US TO.
OH... YEAH... *um*...THANK YOU FOR YOUR HELP DISMANTLING THAT ENGINE...
BUT...
...I DIDN'T MEAN TO TAKE IT APART.
I ONLY TRIED TO TURN THAT ONE PIECE.

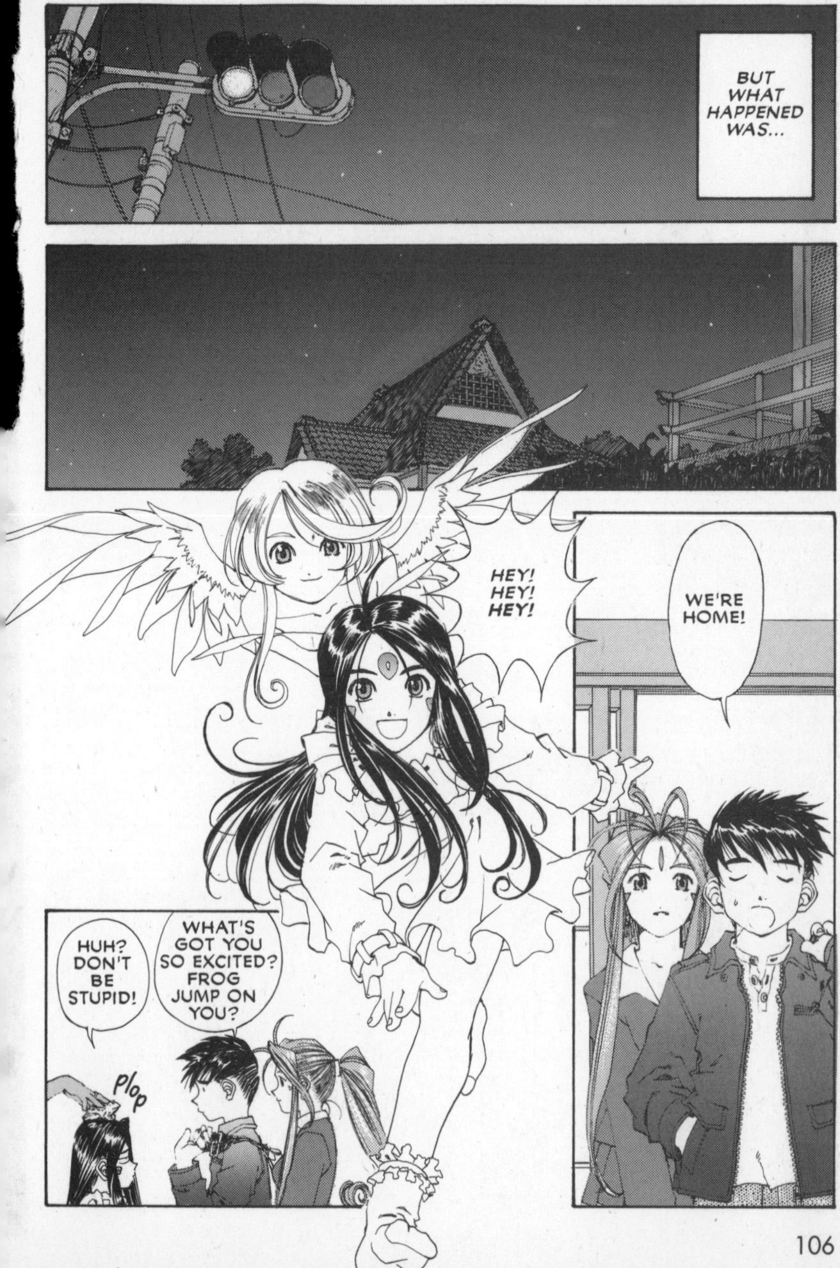
BUT WHAT HAPPENED WAS...
WE'RE HOME!
HEY! HEY! HEY!
WHAT'S GOT YOU SO EXCITED? FROG JUMP ON YOU?
HUH? DON'T BE STUPID!
plop

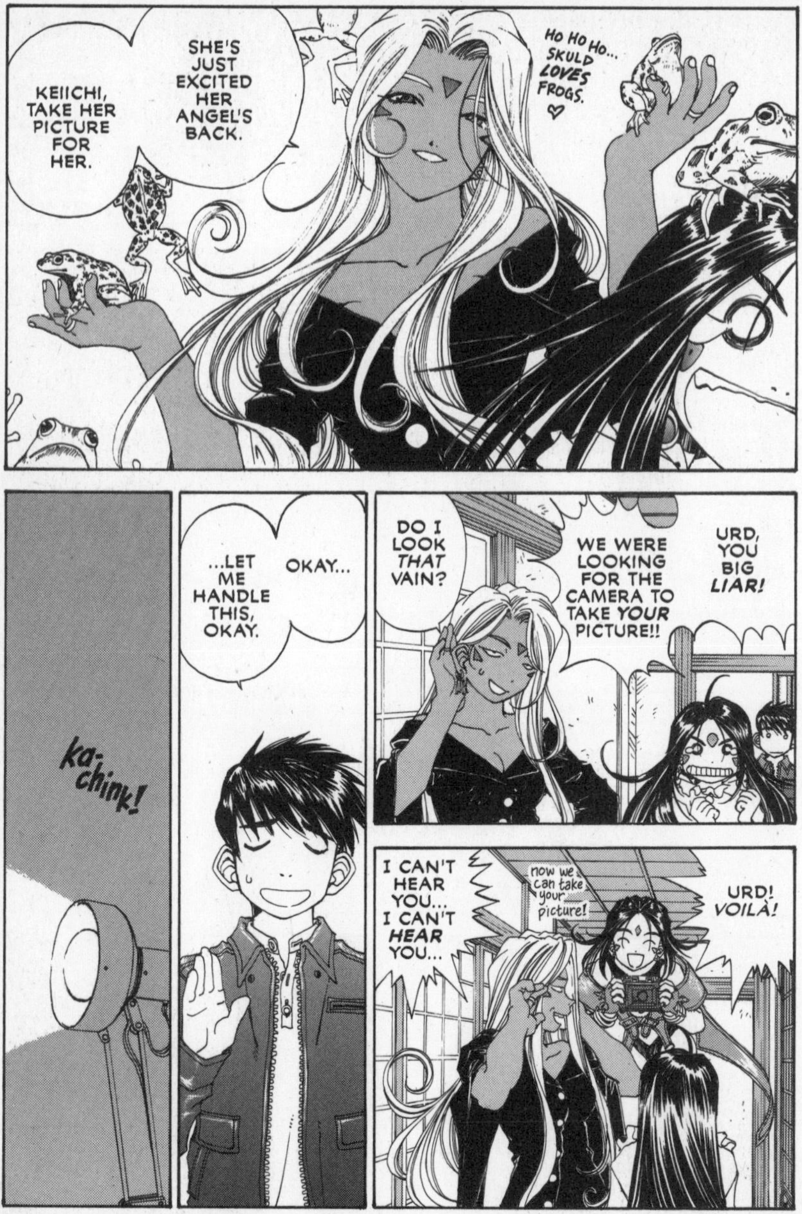
HO HO HO... SKULD LOVES FROGS. ♡
SHE'S JUST EXCITED HER ANGEL'S BACK.
KEIICHI, TAKE HER PICTURE FOR HER.
URD, YOU BIG LIAR!
WE WERE LOOKING FOR THE CAMERA TO TAKE YOUR PICTURE!!
DO I LOOK THAT VAIN?
URD! VOILÀ!
now we can take your picture!
I CAN'T HEAR YOU... I CAN'T HEAR YOU...
OKAY...
...LET ME HANDLE THIS, OKAY.
ka-chink!

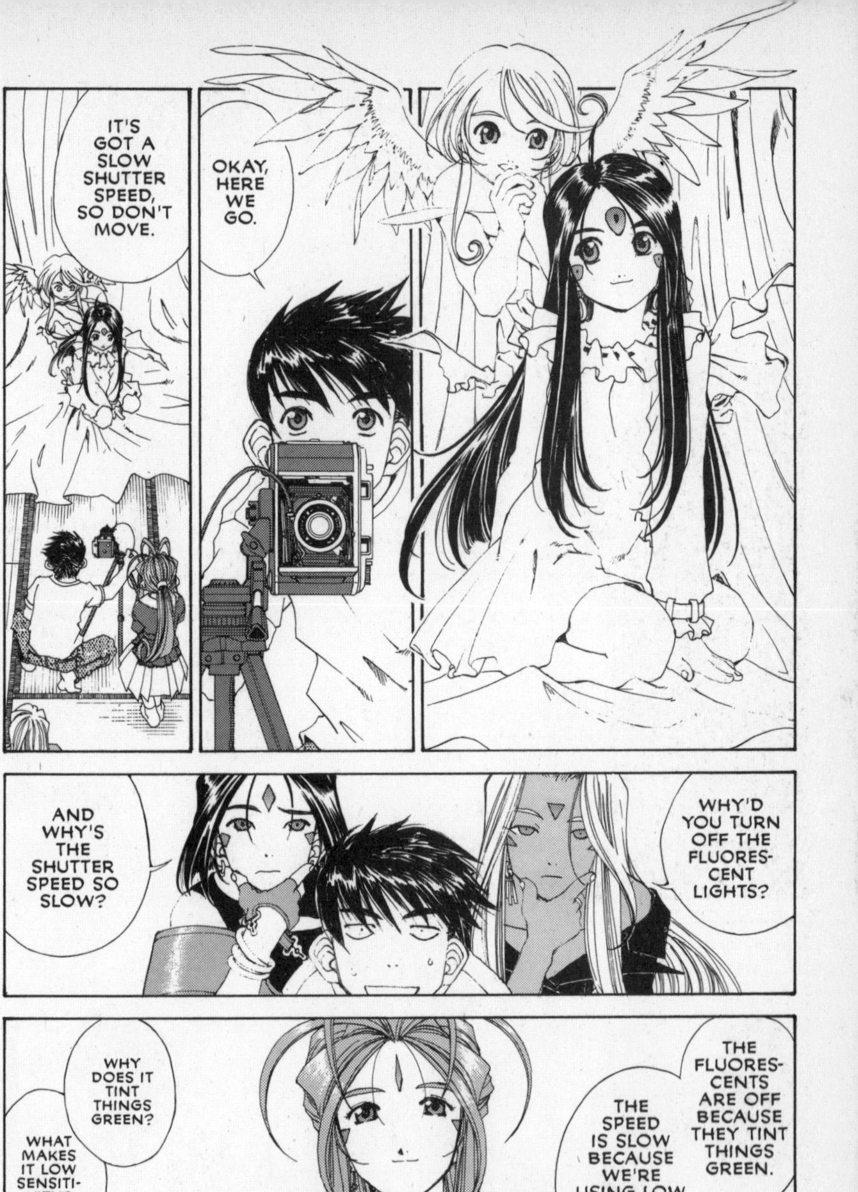
OKAY, HERE WE GO.
IT'S GOT A SLOW SHUTTER SPEED, SO DON'T MOVE.
WHY'D YOU TURN OFF THE FLUORES-CENT LIGHTS?
AND WHY'S THE SHUTTER SPEED SO SLOW?
THE FLUORES-CENTS ARE OFF BECAUSE THEY TINT THINGS GREEN.
THE SPEED IS SLOW BECAUSE WE'RE USING LOW SENSITIVITY FILM.
WHY DOES IT TINT THINGS GREEN?
WHAT MAKES IT LOW SENSITI-VITY?

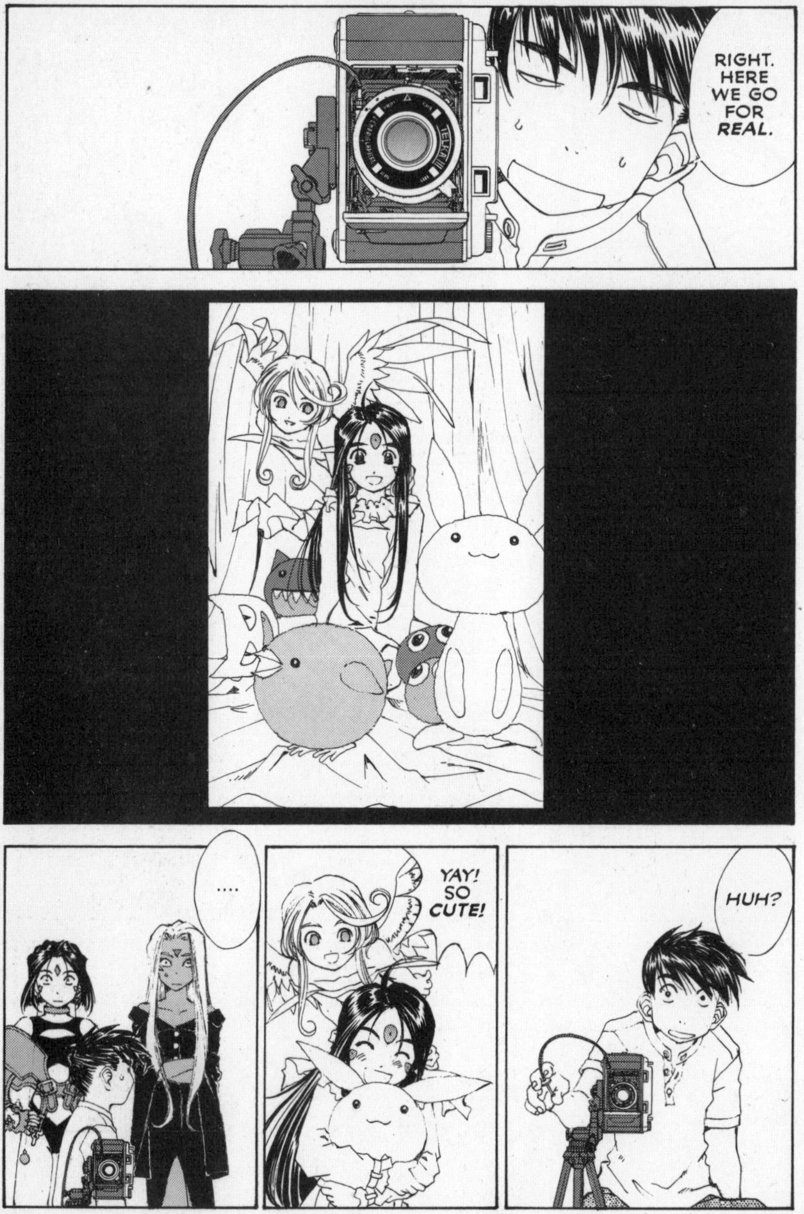
RIGHT. HERE WE GO FOR *REAL*.
HUH?
YAY! SO *CUTE!*
....

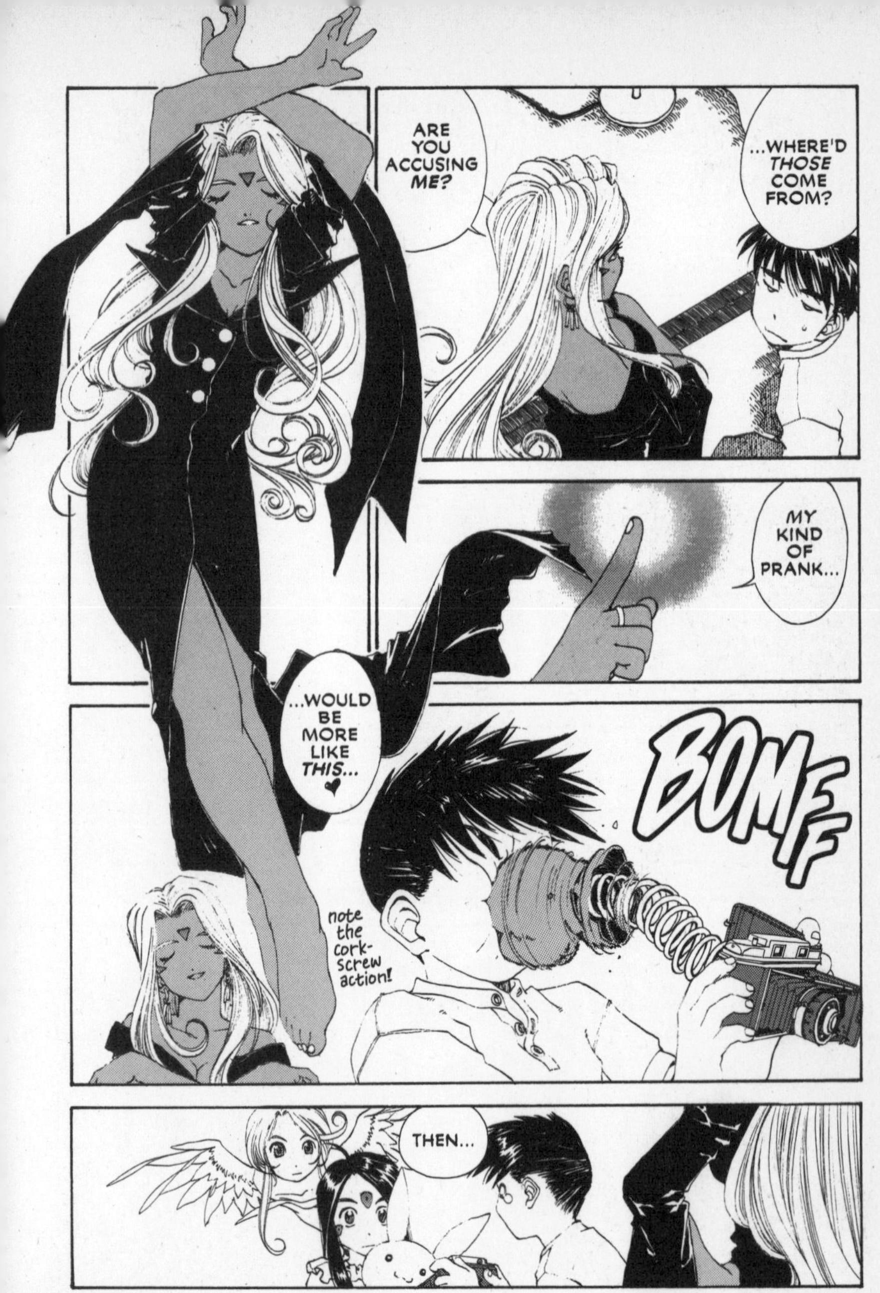
...WHERE'D *THOSE* COME FROM?
ARE YOU ACCUSING *ME*?
MY KIND OF PRANK...
...WOULD BE MORE LIKE *THIS*... ♥
BOMFF
note the cork-screw action!
THEN...

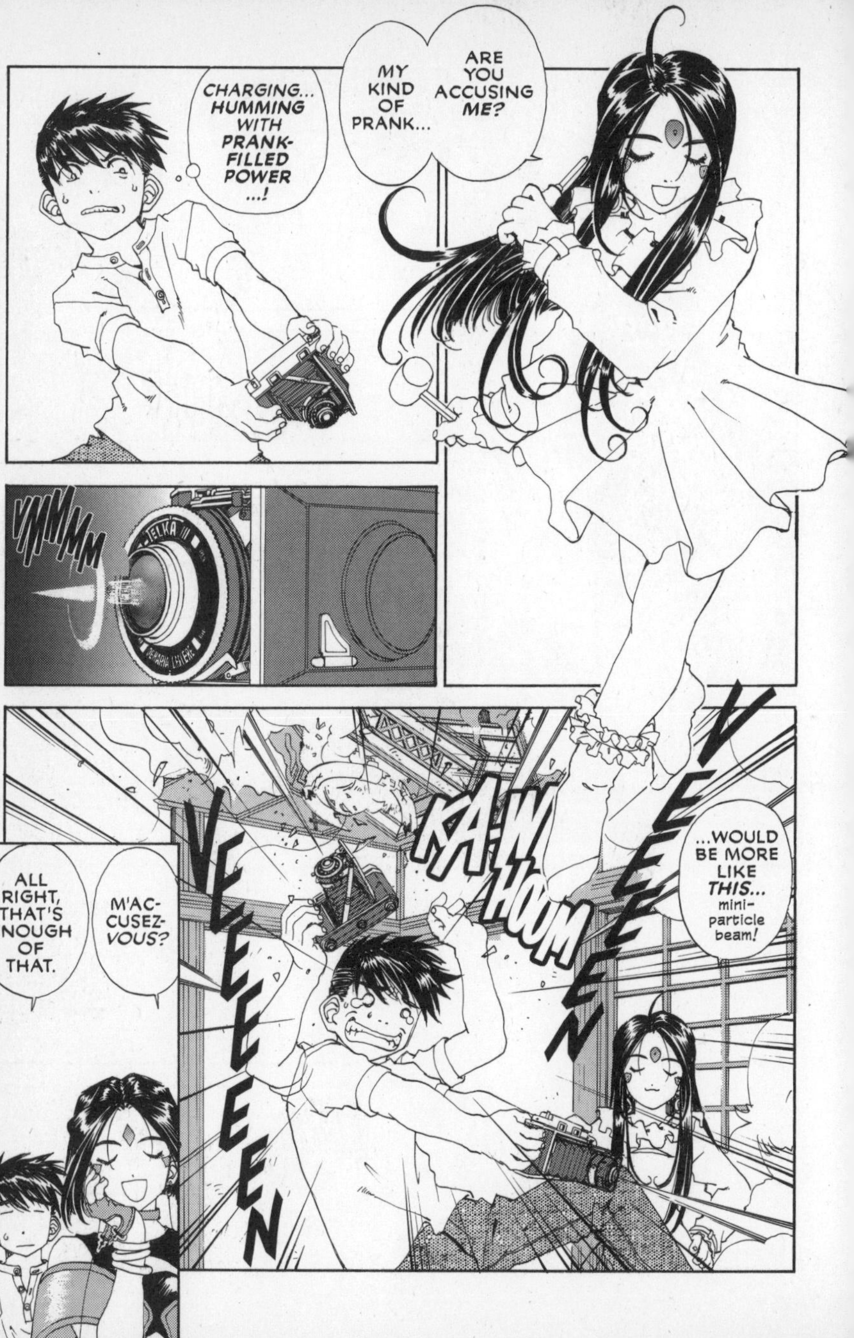
ARE YOU ACCUSING ME?
MY KIND OF PRANK...
CHARGING... HUMMING WITH PRANK-FILLED POWER ...!
VMMMMM
...WOULD BE MORE LIKE THIS... mini-particle beam!
VEEEEEEEN
KA-WHOOM
VEEEEEEN
M'AC-CUSEZ-VOUS?
ALL RIGHT, THAT'S ENOUGH OF THAT.

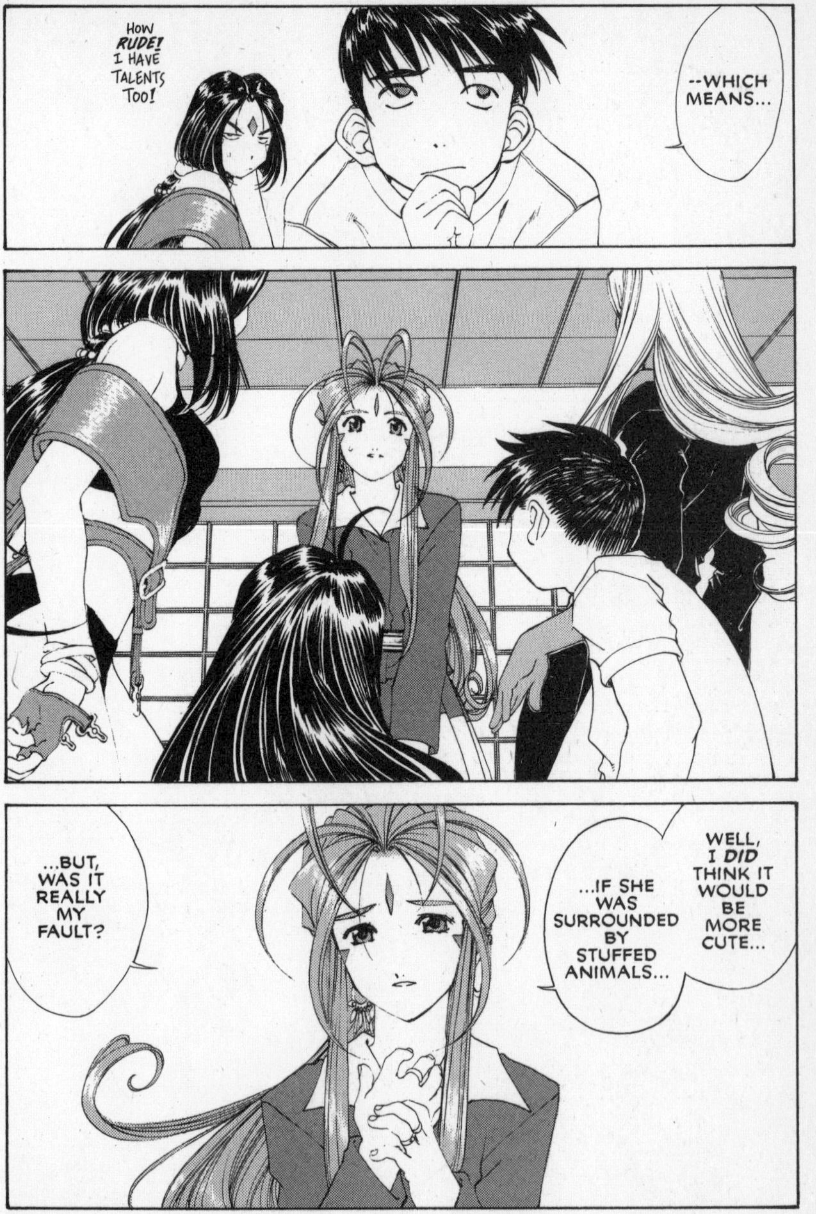

--WHICH MEANS...
HOW RUDE! I HAVE TALENTS TOO!
WELL, I DID THINK IT WOULD BE MORE CUTE...
...IF SHE WAS SURROUNDED BY STUFFED ANIMALS...
...BUT, WAS IT REALLY MY FAULT?

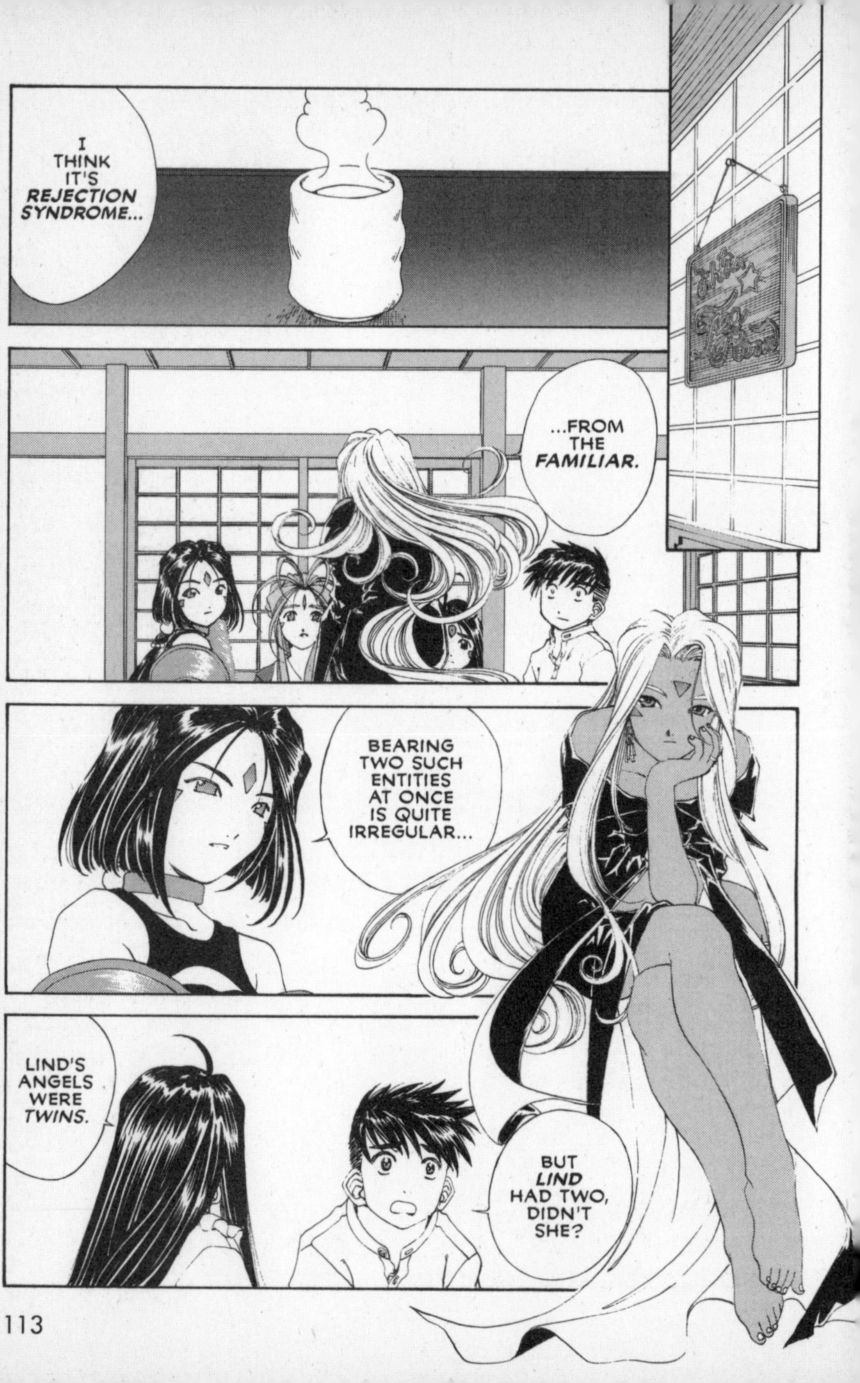
I THINK IT'S *REJECTION SYNDROME*...
...FROM THE *FAMILIAR*.
BEARING TWO SUCH ENTITIES AT ONCE IS QUITE IRREGULAR...
BUT *LIND* HAD TWO, DIDN'T SHE?
LIND'S ANGELS WERE *TWINS*.

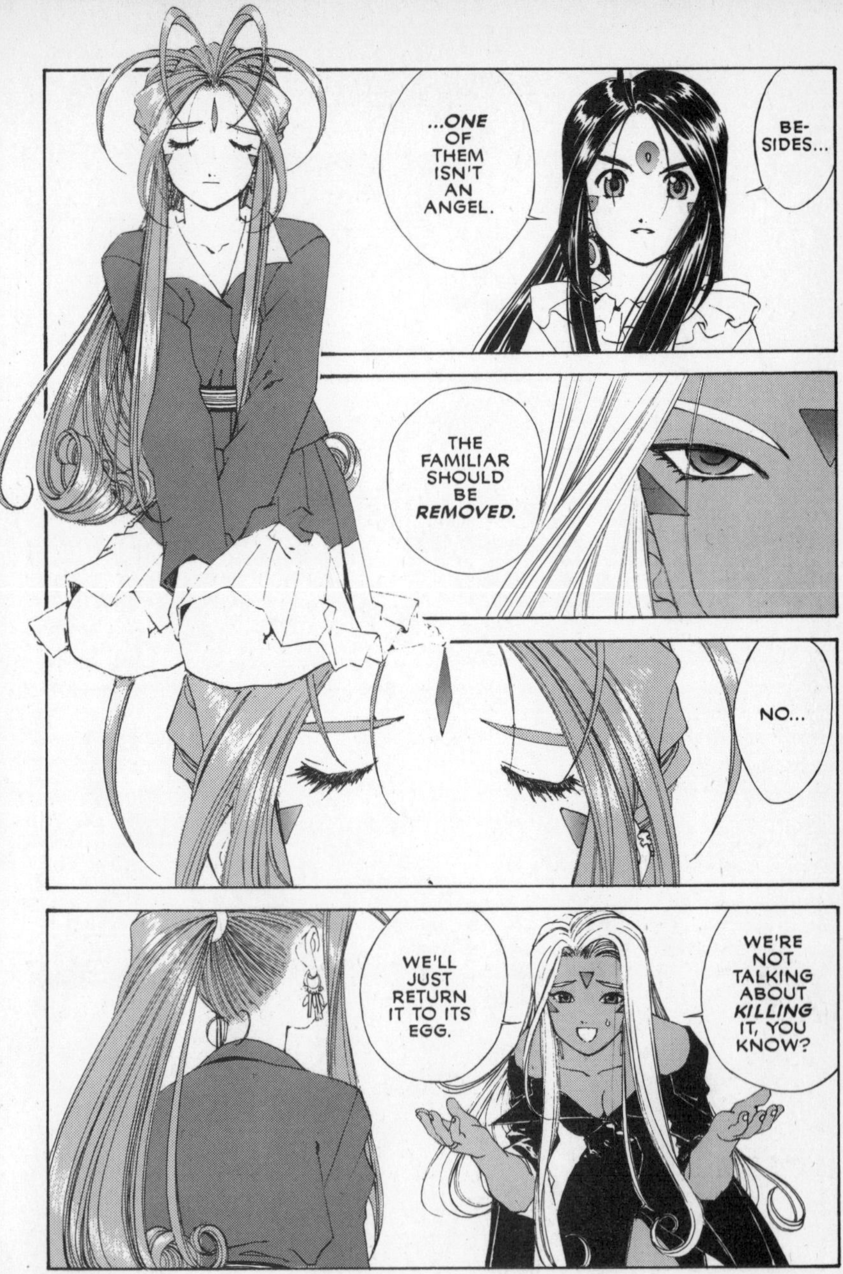
BE-SIDES...
...*ONE* OF THEM ISN'T AN ANGEL.
THE FAMILIAR SHOULD BE *REMOVED.*
NO...
WE'RE NOT TALKING ABOUT *KILLING* IT, YOU KNOW?
WE'LL JUST RETURN IT TO ITS EGG.

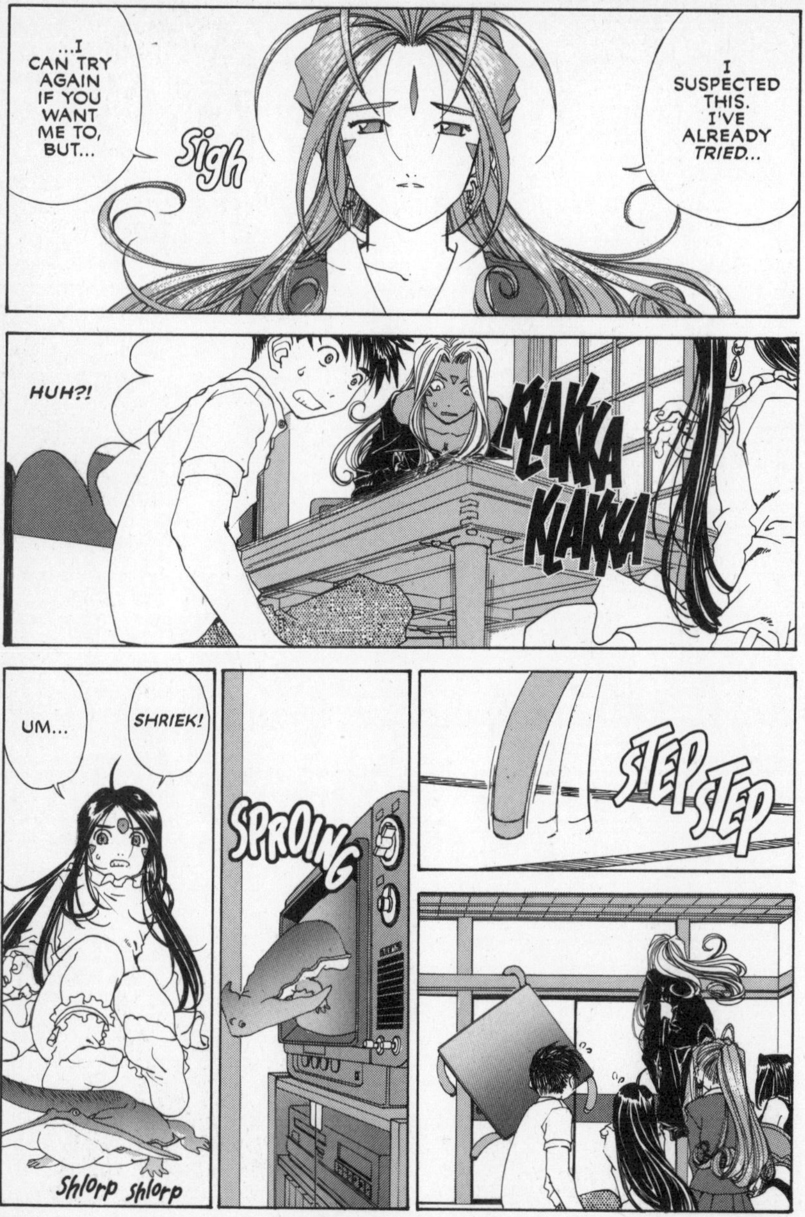
I SUSPECTED THIS. I'VE ALREADY *TRIED*...
...I CAN TRY AGAIN IF YOU WANT ME TO, BUT...
Sigh
KLAKKA KLAKKA
HUH?!
STEP STEP
SPROING
SHRIEK!
UM...
Shlorp shlorp

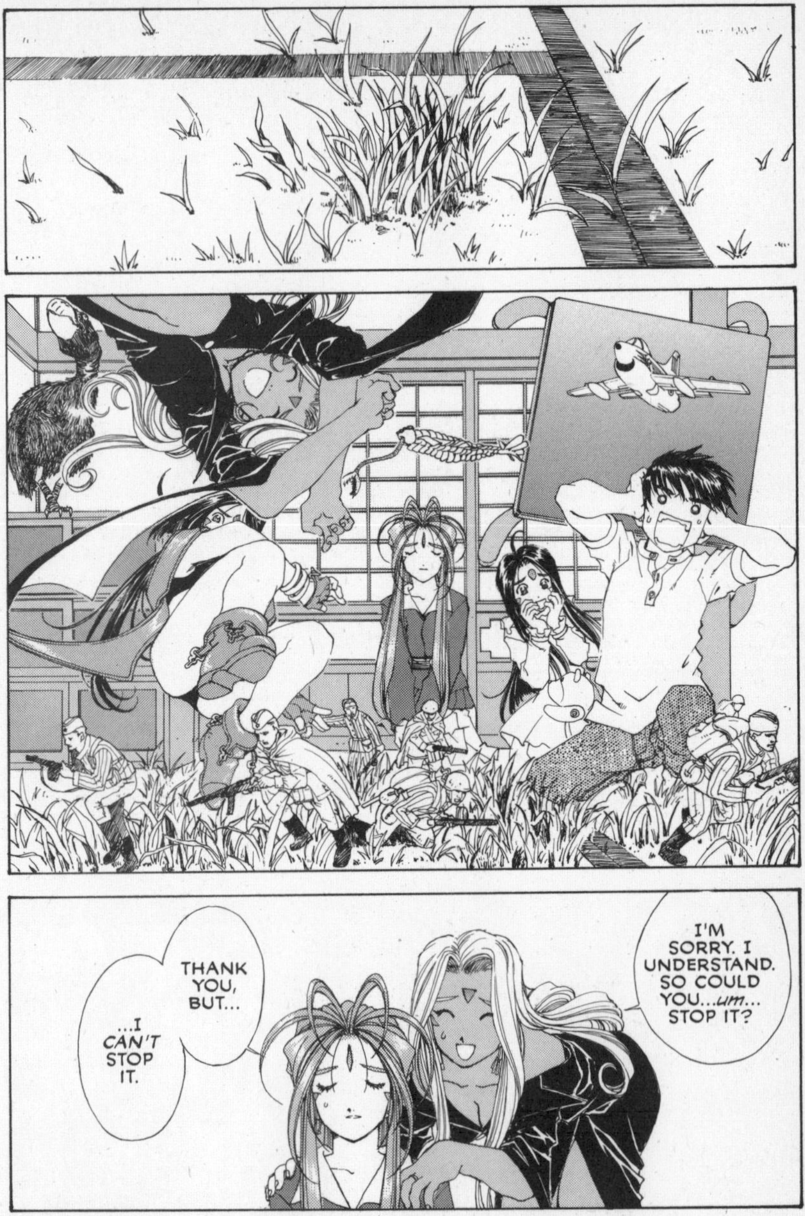
I'M SORRY. I UNDERSTAND. SO COULD YOU...*um*... STOP IT?
THANK YOU, BUT...
...I *CAN'T* STOP IT.

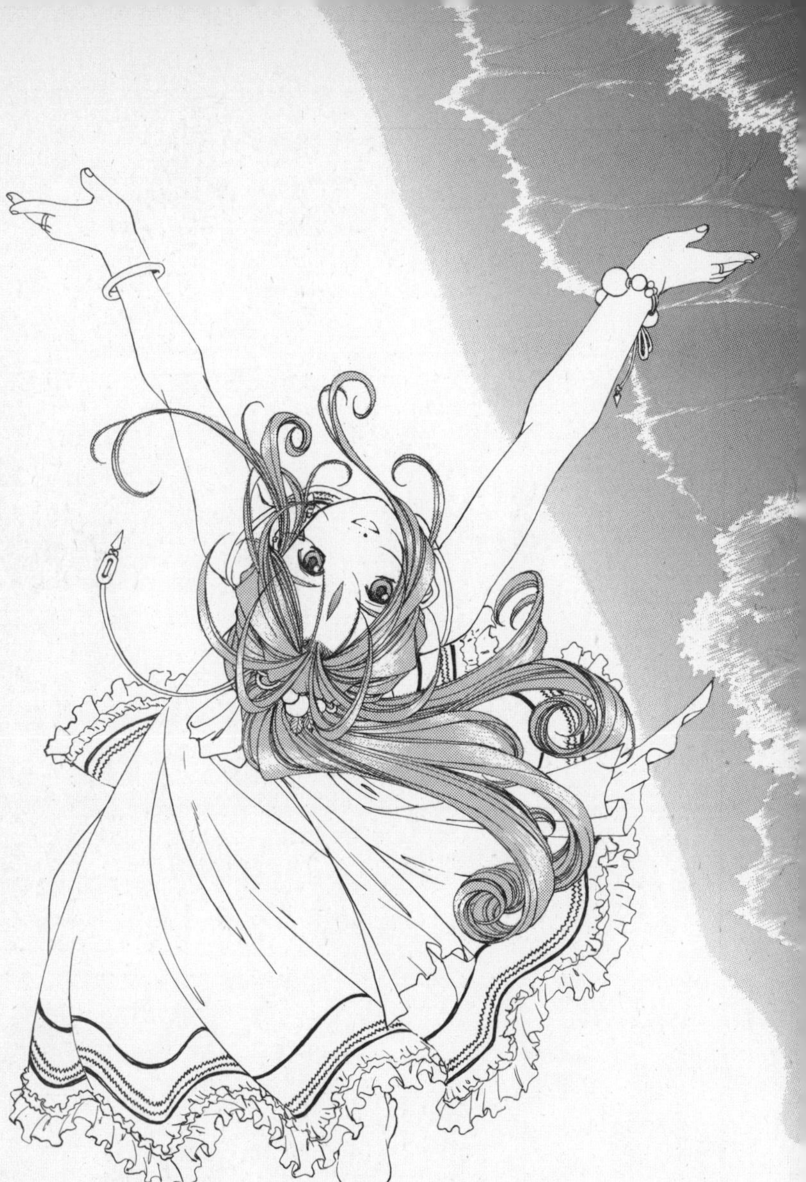

CHAPTER 168

Landscape with Angels

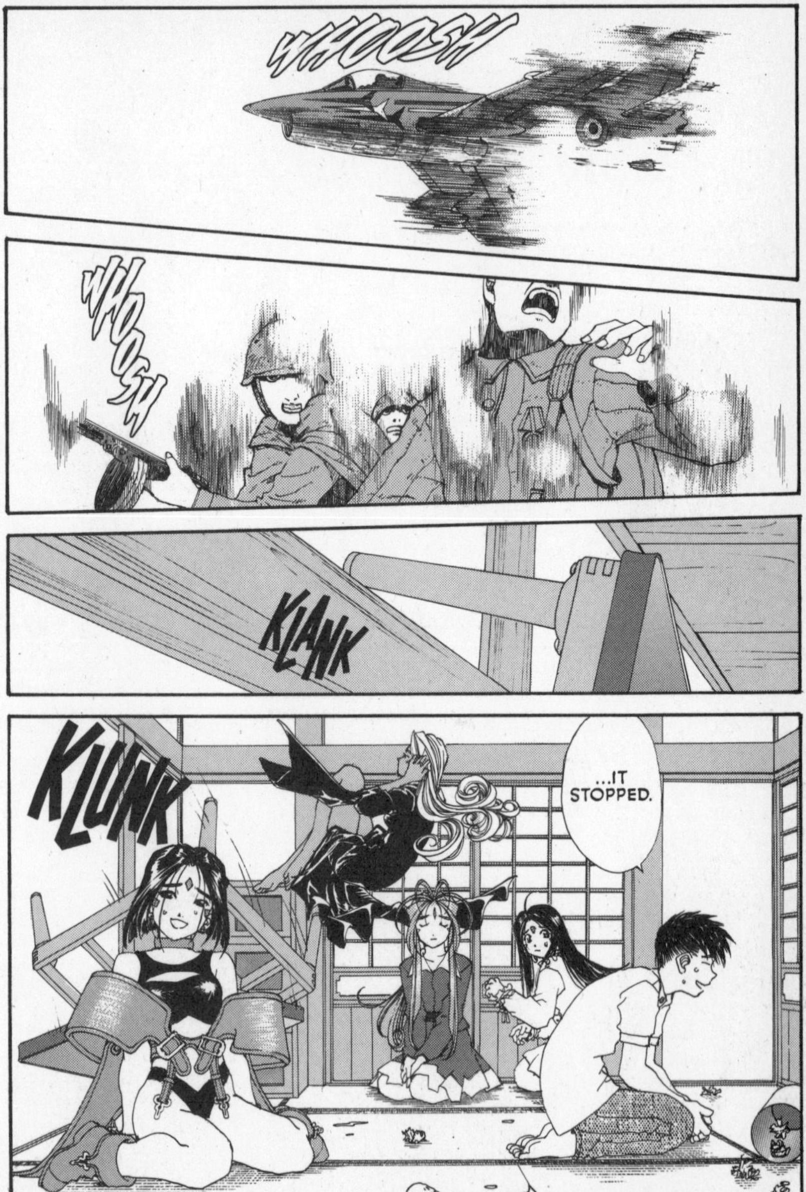
WHOOSH
WHOOSH
KLANK
...IT STOPPED.
KLUNK

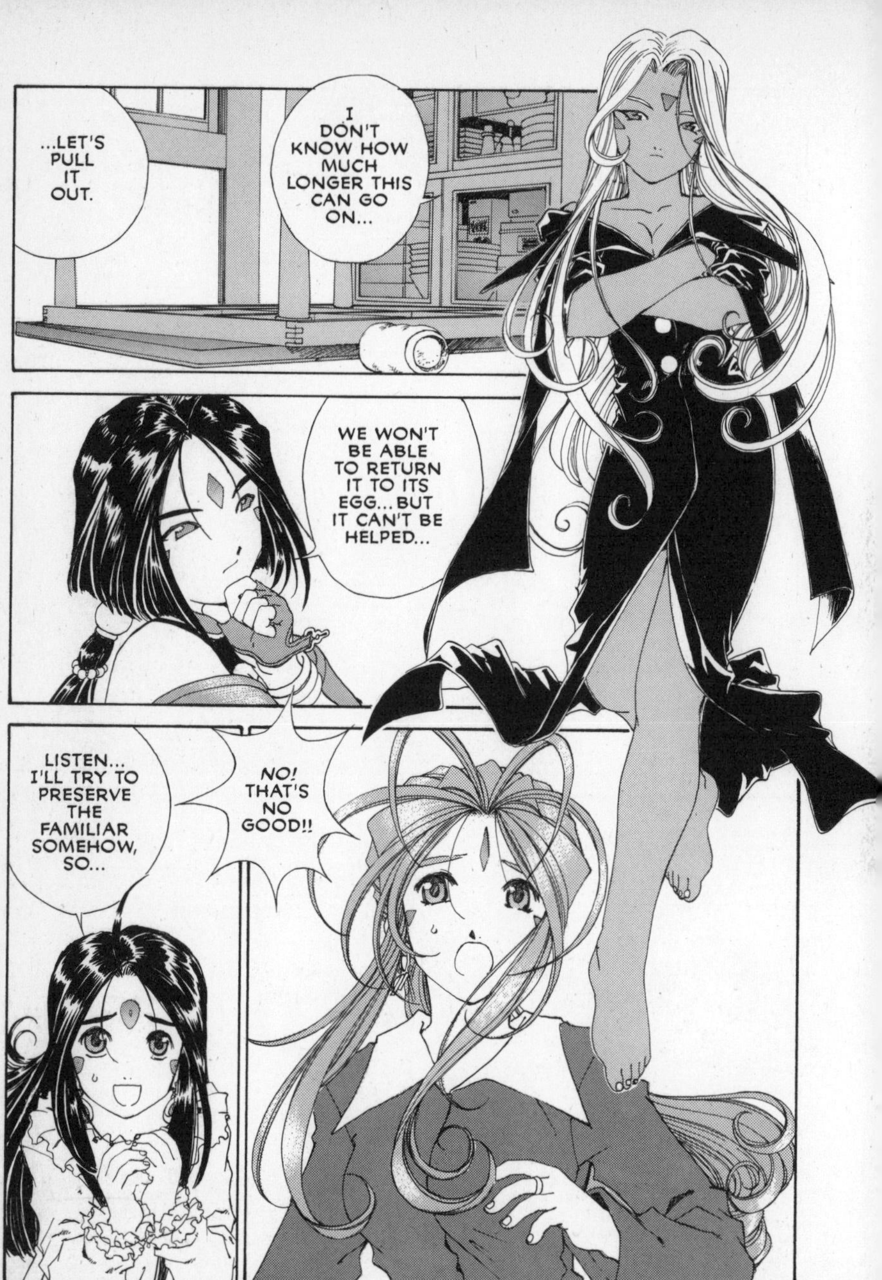
I DON'T KNOW HOW MUCH LONGER THIS CAN GO ON...
...LET'S PULL IT OUT.
WE WON'T BE ABLE TO RETURN IT TO ITS EGG... BUT IT CAN'T BE HELPED...
NO! THAT'S NO GOOD!!
LISTEN... I'LL TRY TO PRESERVE THE FAMILIAR SOMEHOW, SO...

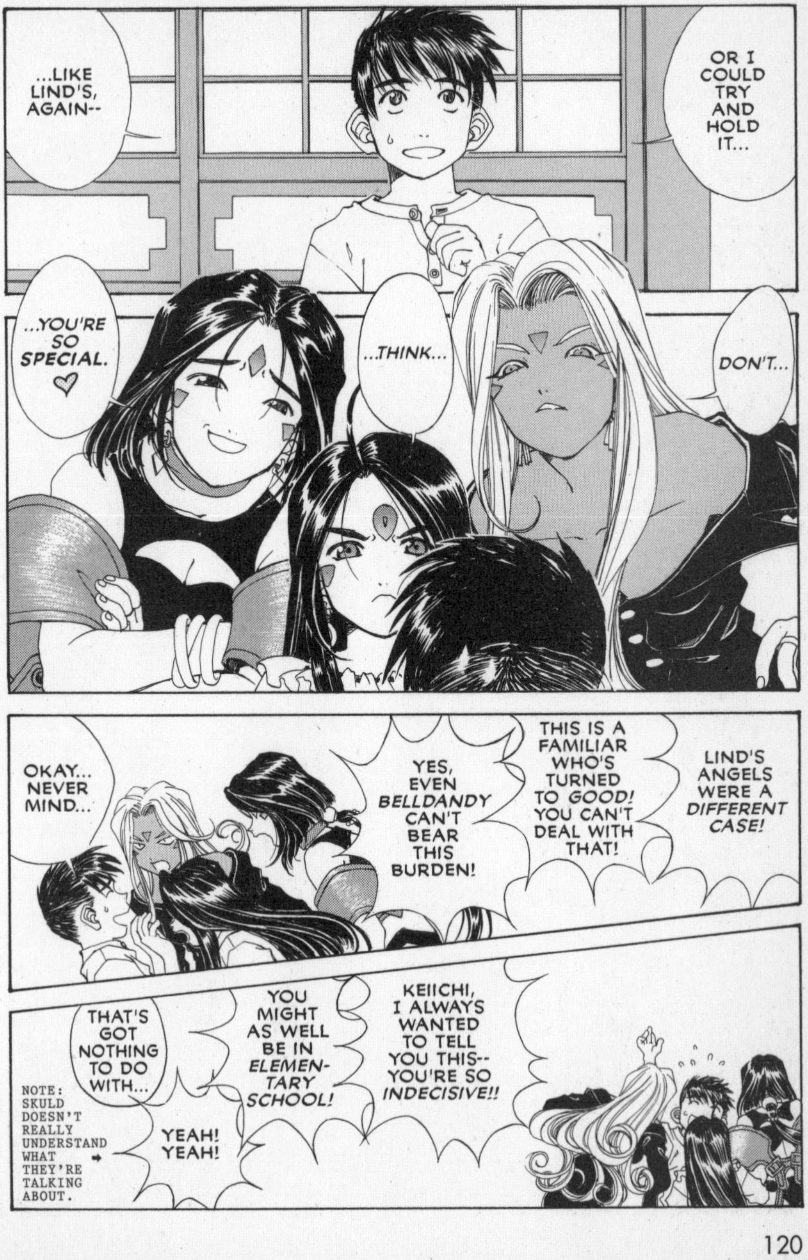
OR I COULD TRY AND HOLD IT...
...LIKE LIND'S, AGAIN--
DON'T...
...THINK...
...YOU'RE SO SPECIAL. ♡
LIND'S ANGELS WERE A DIFFERENT CASE!
THIS IS A FAMILIAR WHO'S TURNED TO GOOD! YOU CAN'T DEAL WITH THAT!
YES, EVEN BELLDANDY CAN'T BEAR THIS BURDEN!
OKAY... NEVER MIND...
KEIICHI, I ALWAYS WANTED TO TELL YOU THIS-- YOU'RE SO INDECISIVE!!
YOU MIGHT AS WELL BE IN ELEMEN-TARY SCHOOL!
THAT'S GOT NOTHING TO DO WITH...
YEAH! YEAH!
NOTE: SKULD DOESN'T REALLY UNDERSTAND WHAT THEY'RE TALKING ABOUT. ➡

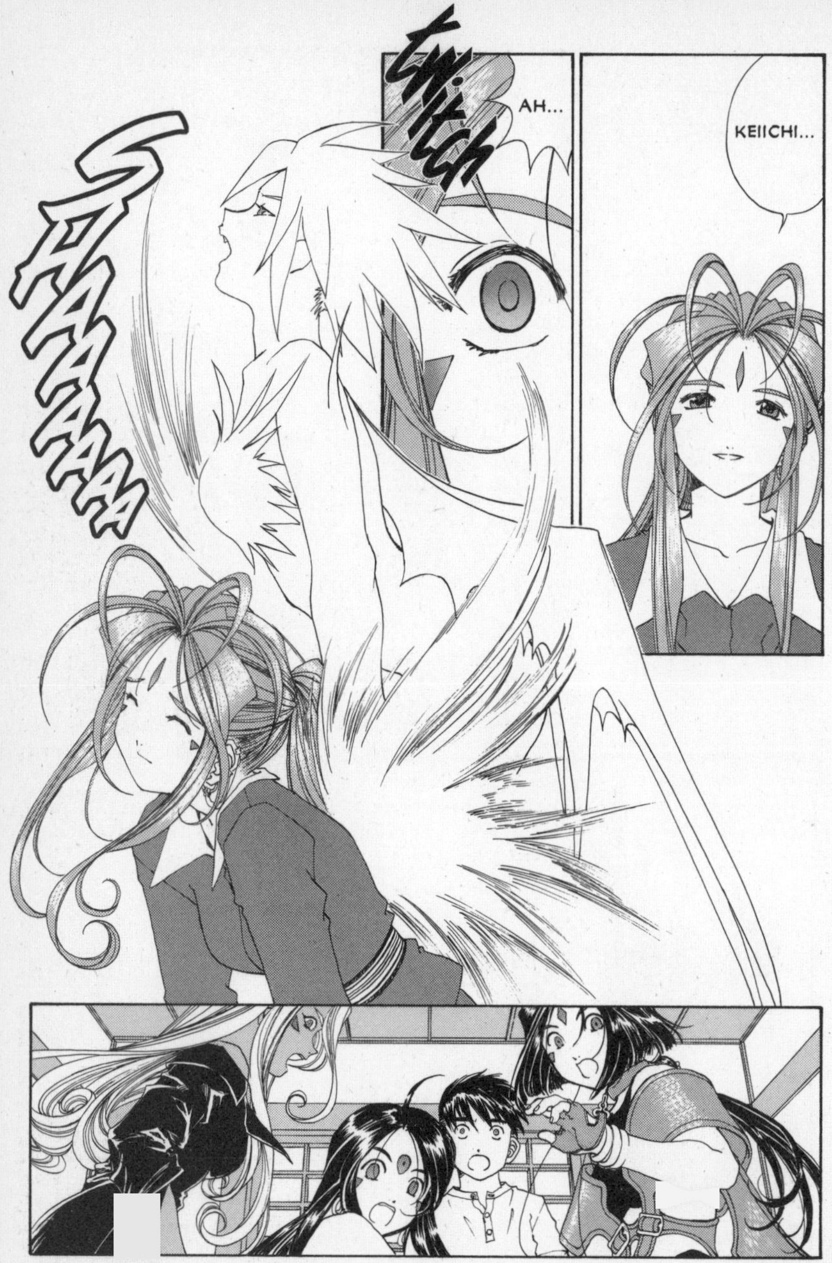
KEIICHI...
AH...
twitch
SHAAAAAA

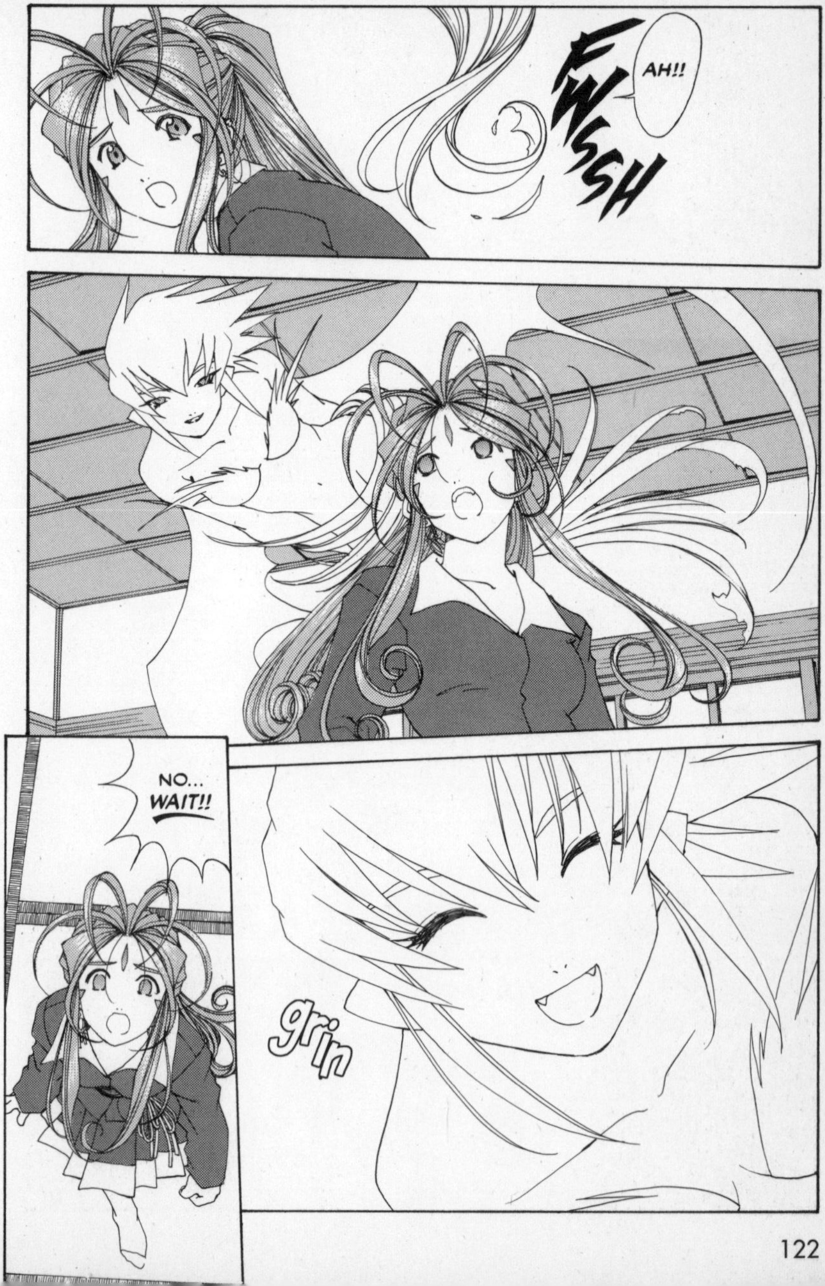
AH!!
FWSSH
grin
NO... WAIT!!

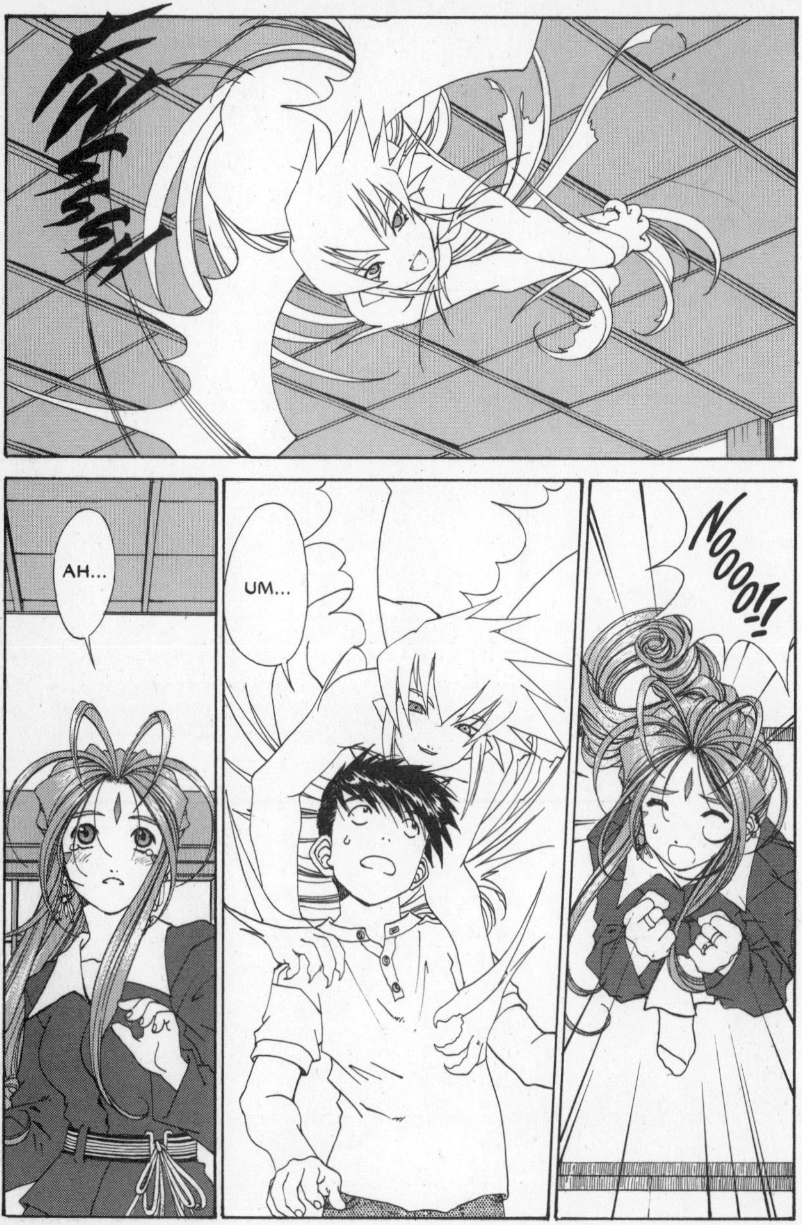
FWASSH
NOOOO!!
UM...
AH...

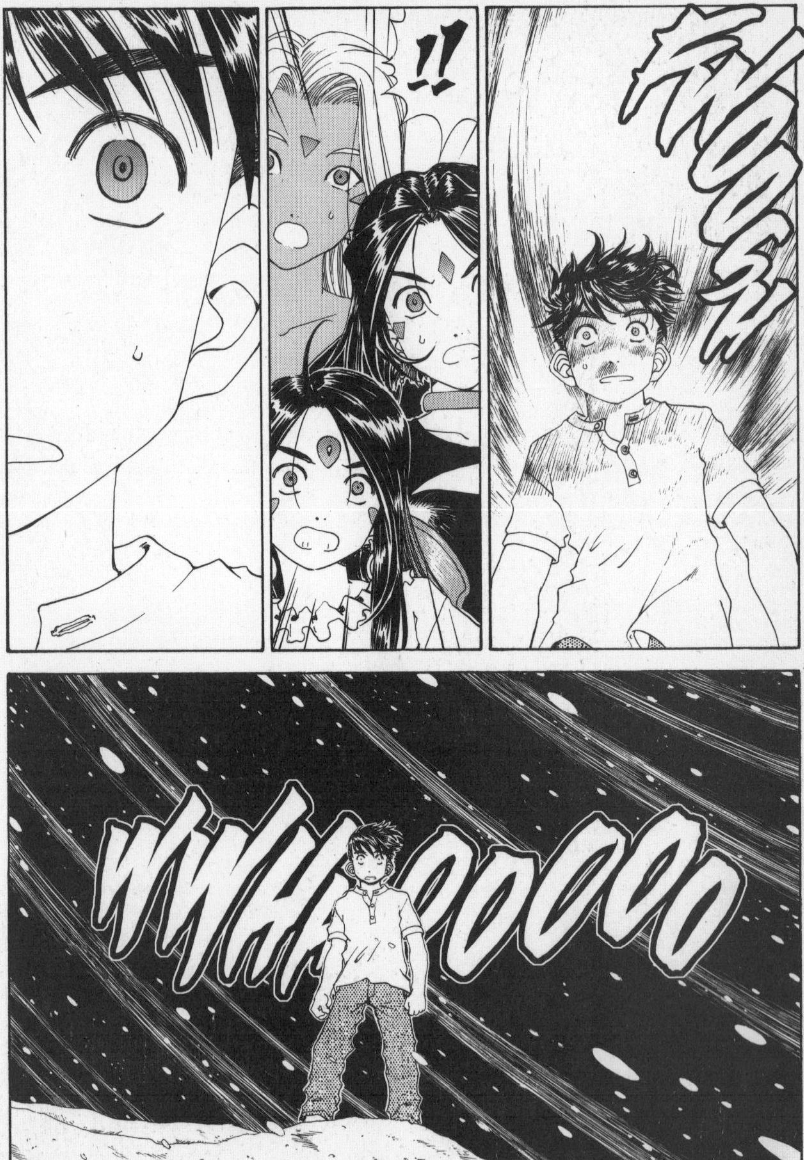
FWOOSH!
!!
WWHOOOOOO

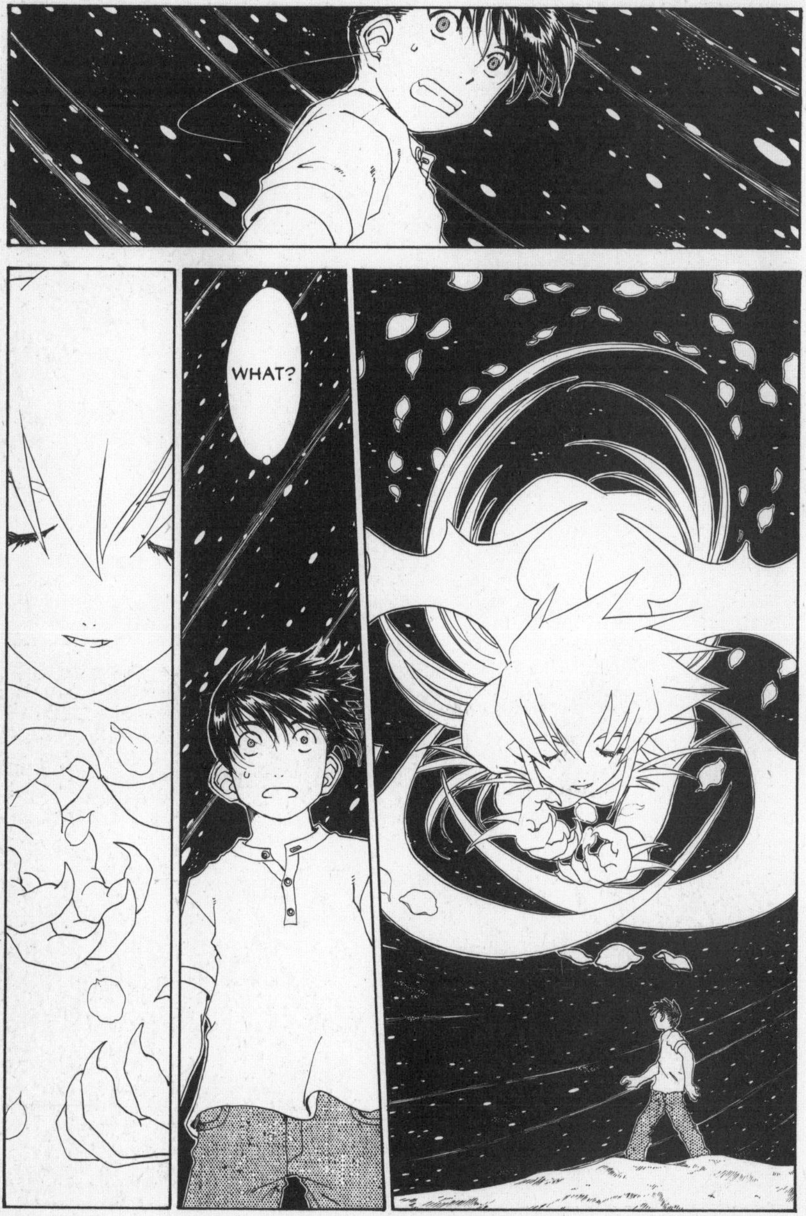
WHAT?

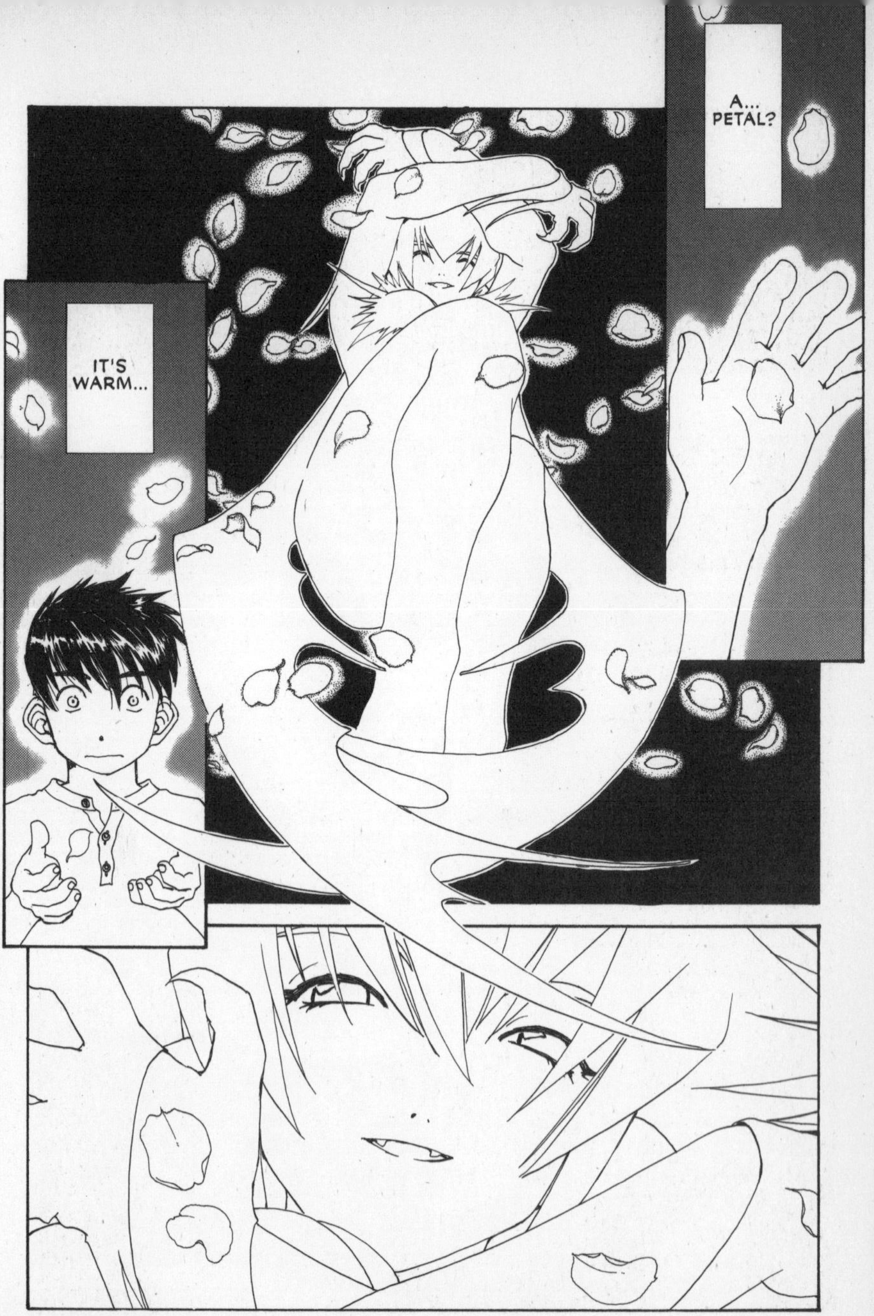
A... PETAL?
IT'S WARM...

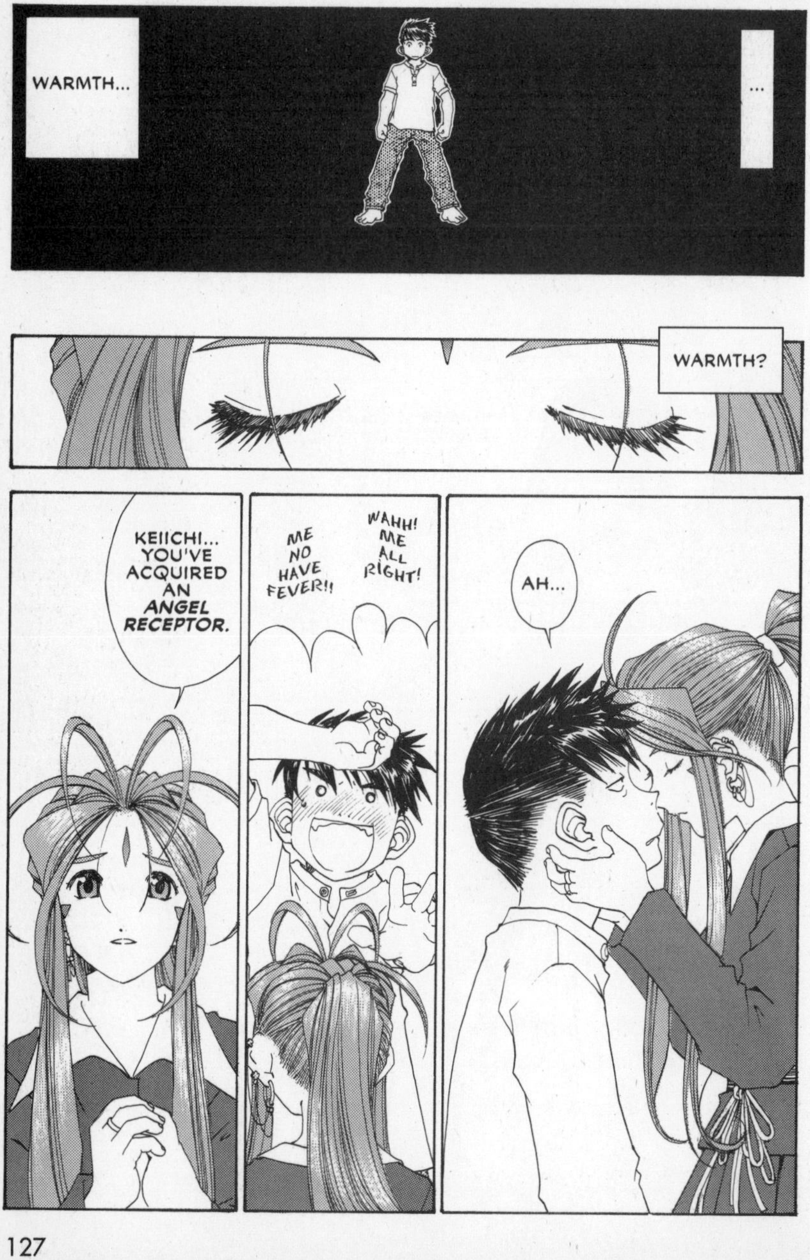
...
WARMTH...
WARMTH?
AH...
WAHH! ME ALL RIGHT!
ME NO HAVE FEVER!!
KEIICHI... YOU'VE ACQUIRED AN ANGEL RECEPTOR.

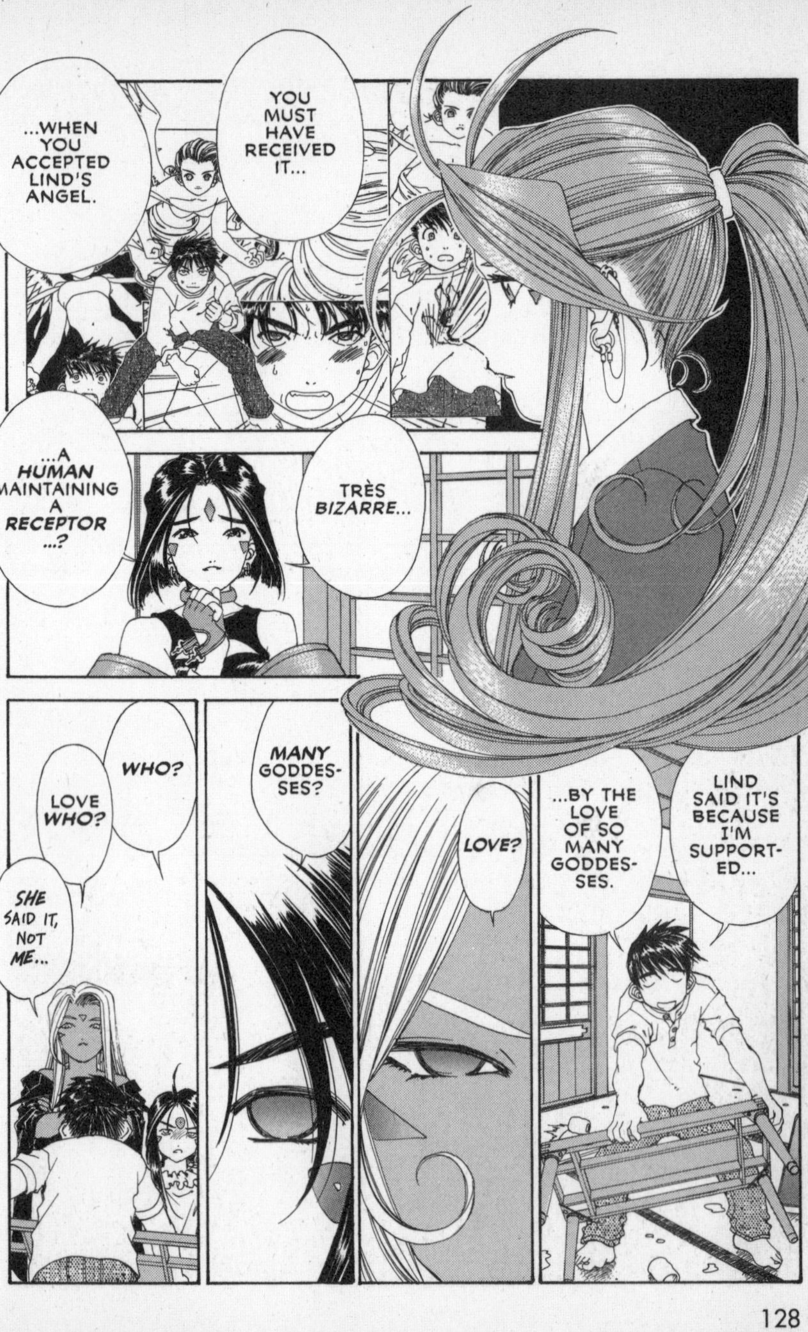
YOU MUST HAVE RECEIVED IT...
...WHEN YOU ACCEPTED LIND'S ANGEL.
TRÈS *BIZARRE*...
...A *HUMAN* MAINTAINING A *RECEPTOR* ...?
LIND SAID IT'S BECAUSE I'M SUPPORT-ED...
...BY THE LOVE OF SO MANY GODDES-SES.
LOVE?
MANY GODDES-SES?
WHO?
LOVE *WHO?*
SHE SAID IT, NOT *ME*...

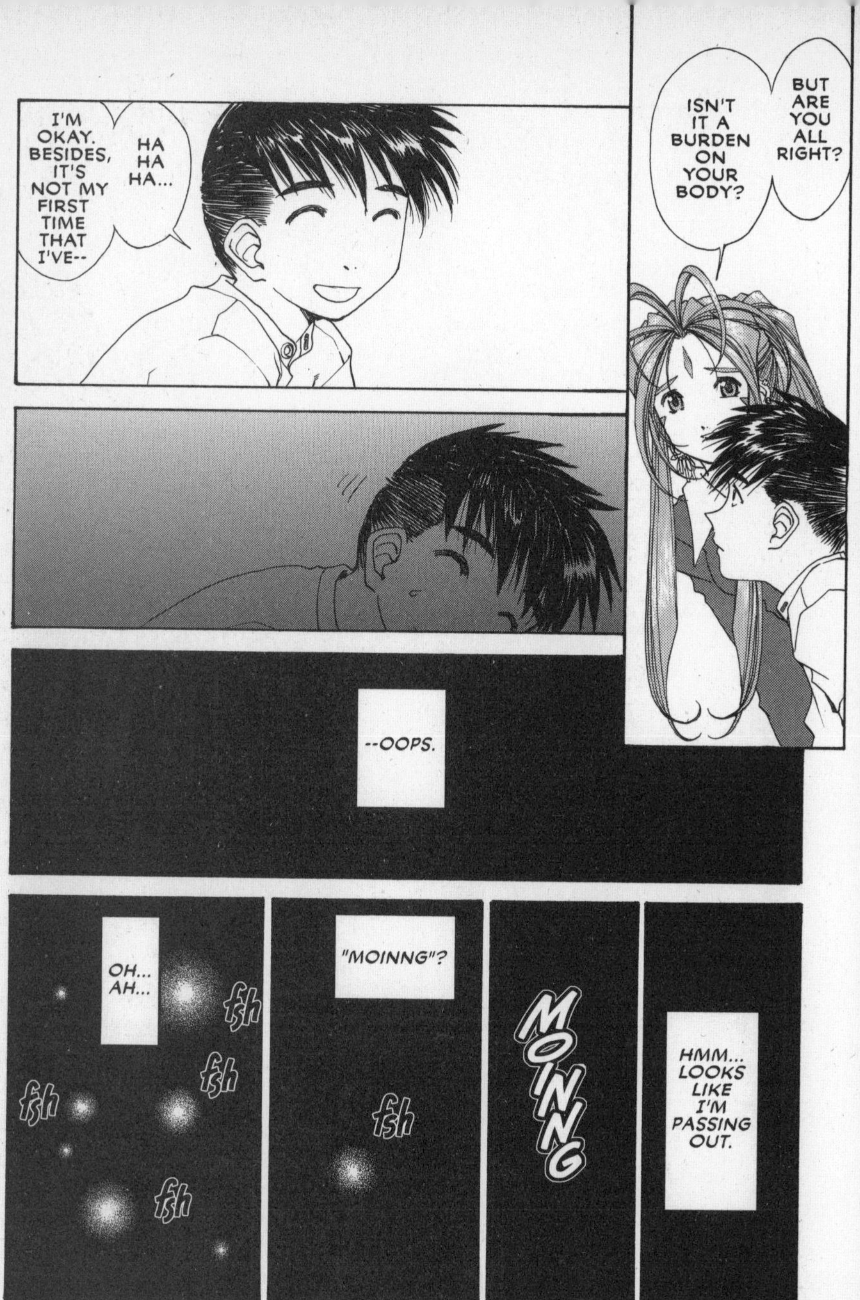
BUT ARE YOU ALL RIGHT?
ISN'T IT A BURDEN ON YOUR BODY?
HA HA HA...
I'M OKAY. BESIDES, IT'S NOT MY FIRST TIME THAT I'VE--
--OOPS.
HMM... LOOKS LIKE I'M PASSING OUT.
MOINNG
"MOINNG"?
fsh
OH... AH...
fsh
fsh
fsh
fsh

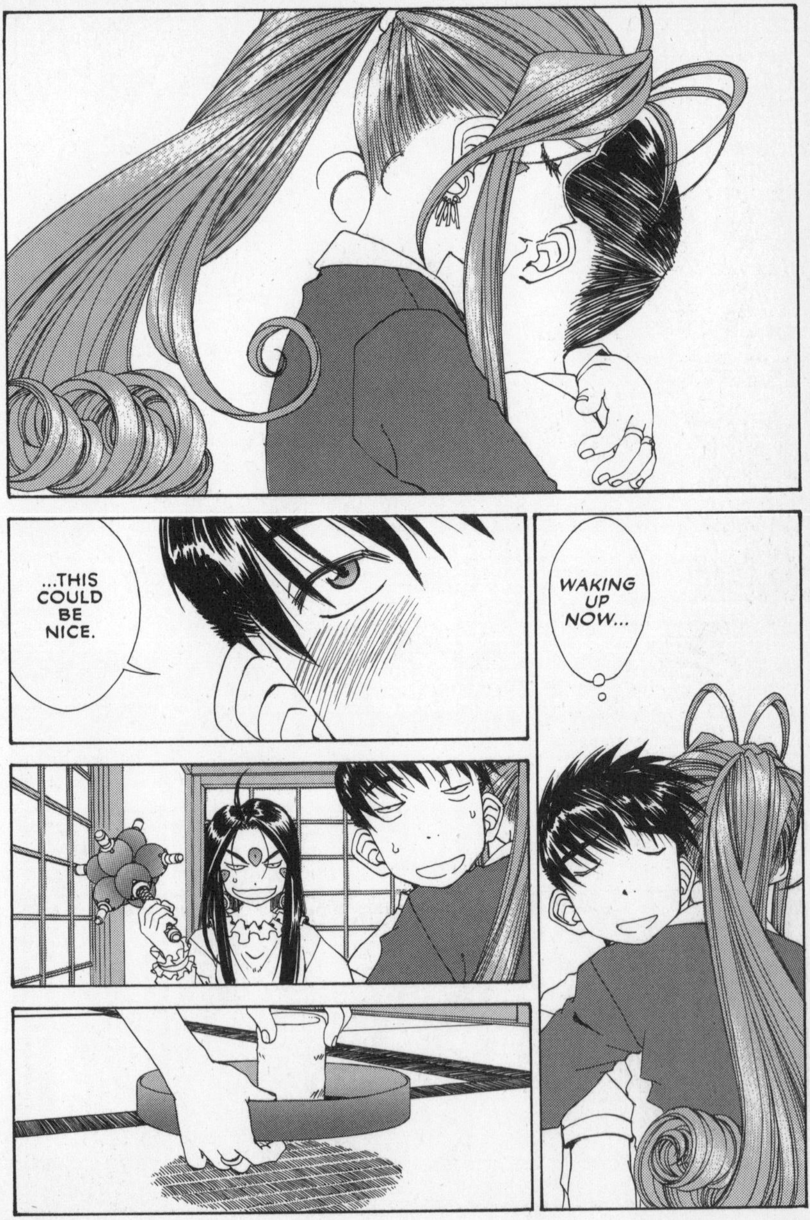
WAKING UP NOW...
...THIS COULD BE NICE.

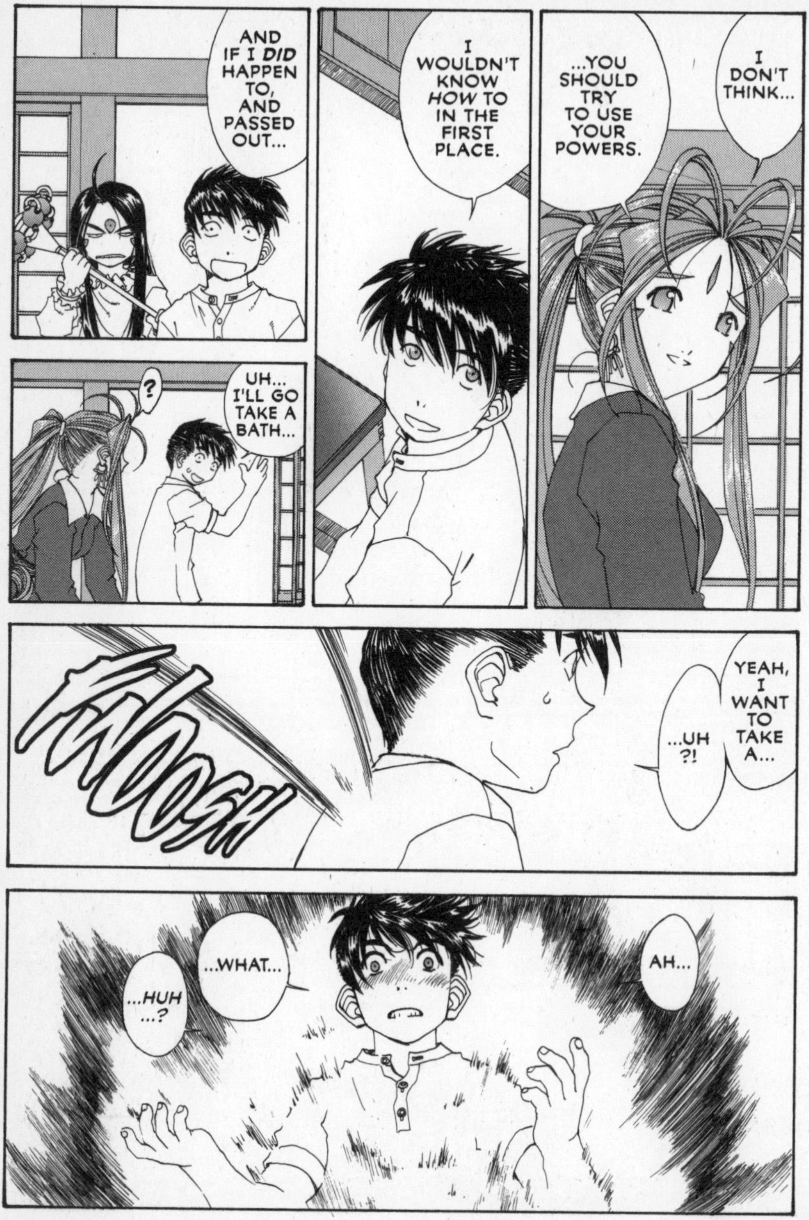

I DON'T THINK...
...YOU SHOULD TRY TO USE YOUR POWERS.
I WOULDN'T KNOW *HOW* TO IN THE FIRST PLACE.
AND IF I *DID* HAPPEN TO, AND PASSED OUT...
UH... I'LL GO TAKE A BATH...
?
YEAH, I WANT TO TAKE A...
...UH ?!
FWOOSH
AH...
...WHAT...
...HUH ...?

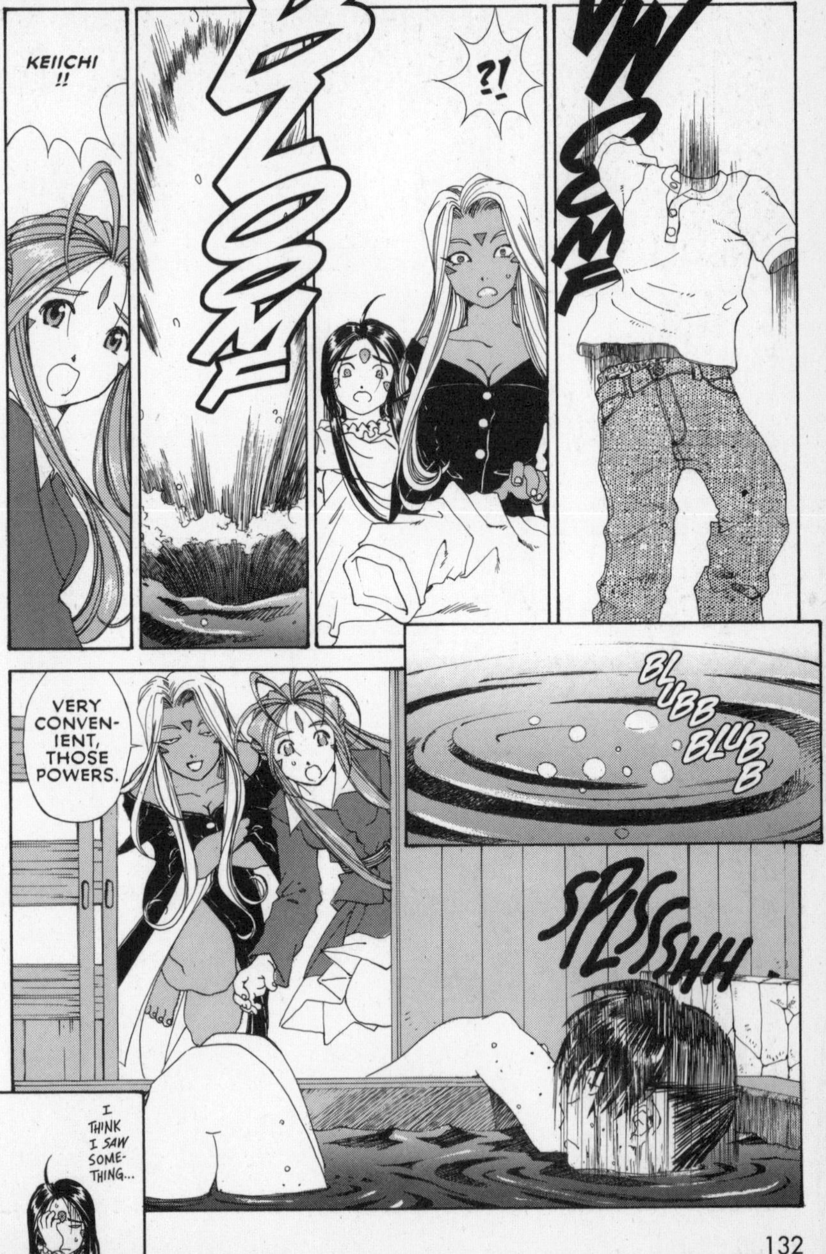
VWOOMF
?!
BLOOMF
KEIICHI !!
BLUBB BLUBB
VERY CONVENIENT, THOSE POWERS.
SPLSSSHH
I THINK I SAW SOMETHING...

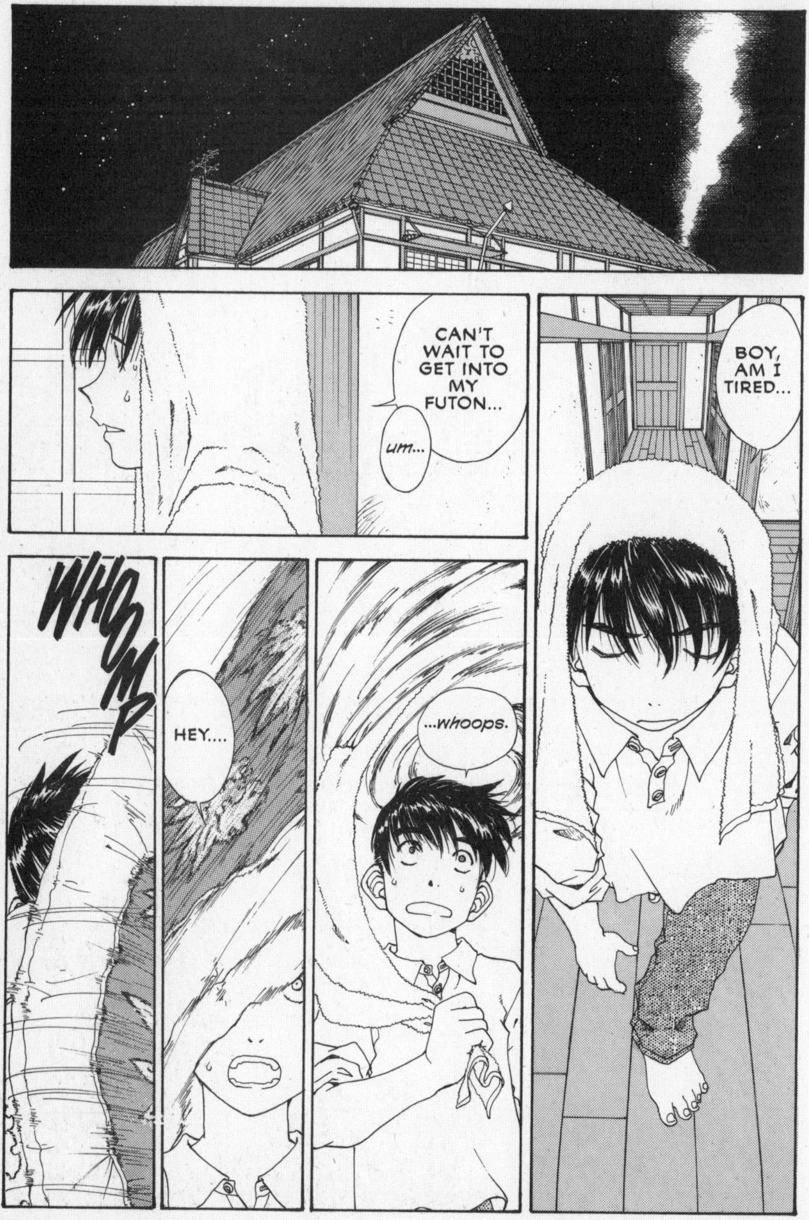
BOY, AM I TIRED...
CAN'T WAIT TO GET INTO MY FUTON...
um...
...whoops.
HEY....
WHOOMP

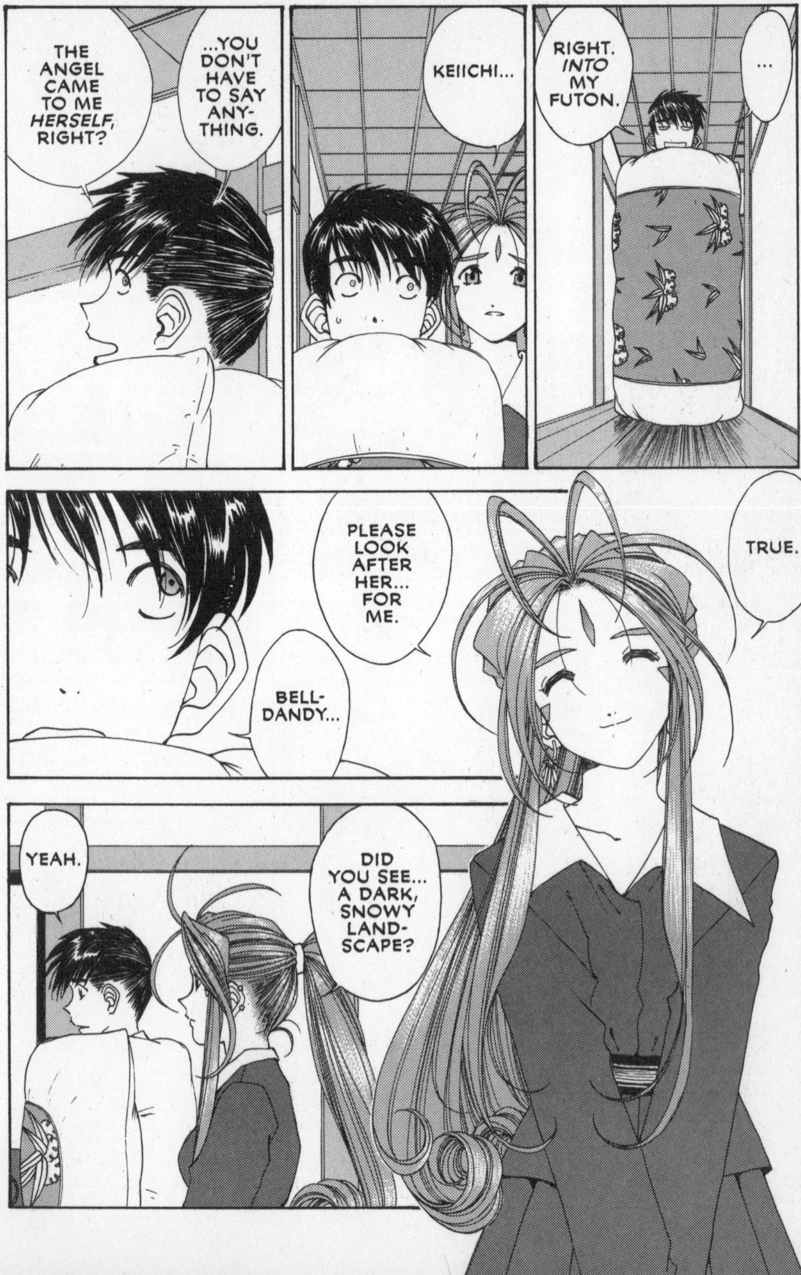
...
RIGHT. *INTO* MY FUTON.
KEIICHI...
...YOU DON'T HAVE TO SAY ANY-THING.
THE ANGEL CAME TO ME *HERSELF*, RIGHT?
TRUE.
PLEASE LOOK AFTER HER... FOR ME.
BELL-DANDY...
DID YOU SEE... A DARK, SNOWY LAND-SCAPE?
YEAH.

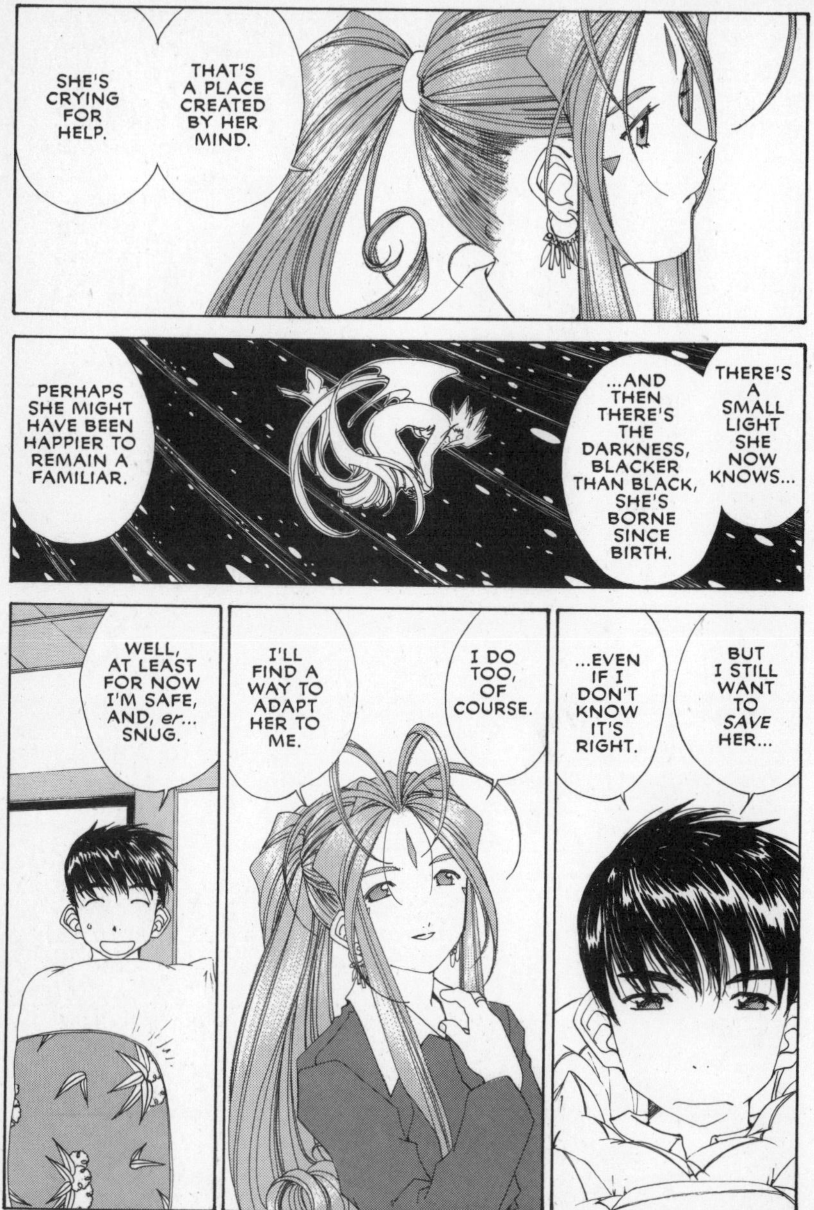
THAT'S A PLACE CREATED BY HER MIND.
SHE'S CRYING FOR HELP.
THERE'S A SMALL LIGHT SHE NOW KNOWS...
...AND THEN THERE'S THE DARKNESS, BLACKER THAN BLACK, SHE'S BORNE SINCE BIRTH.
PERHAPS SHE MIGHT HAVE BEEN HAPPIER TO REMAIN A FAMILIAR.
BUT I STILL WANT TO *SAVE* HER...
...EVEN IF I DON'T KNOW IT'S RIGHT.
I DO TOO, OF COURSE.
I'LL FIND A WAY TO ADAPT HER TO ME.
WELL, AT LEAST FOR NOW I'M SAFE, AND, *er*... SNUG.

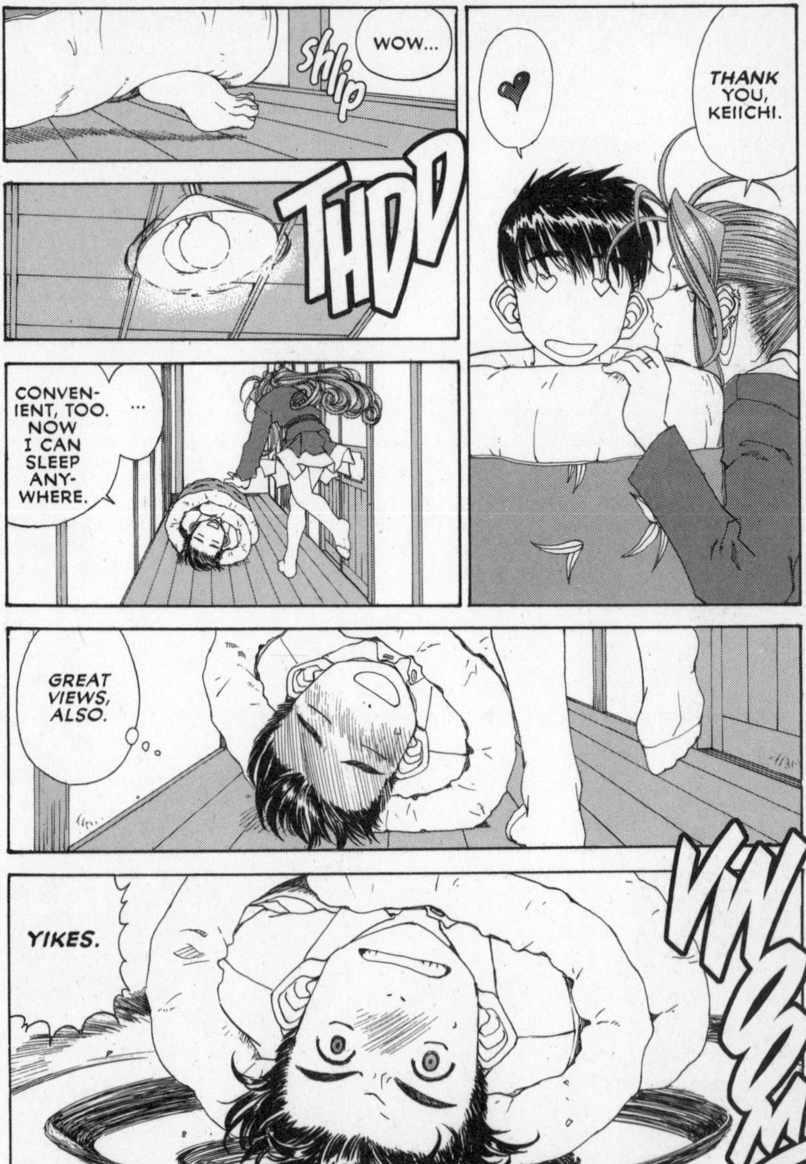
THANK YOU, KEIICHI.
♥
WOW...
shlip
THDD
CONVEN-IENT, TOO. NOW I CAN SLEEP ANY-WHERE.
...
GREAT VIEWS, ALSO.
YIKES.

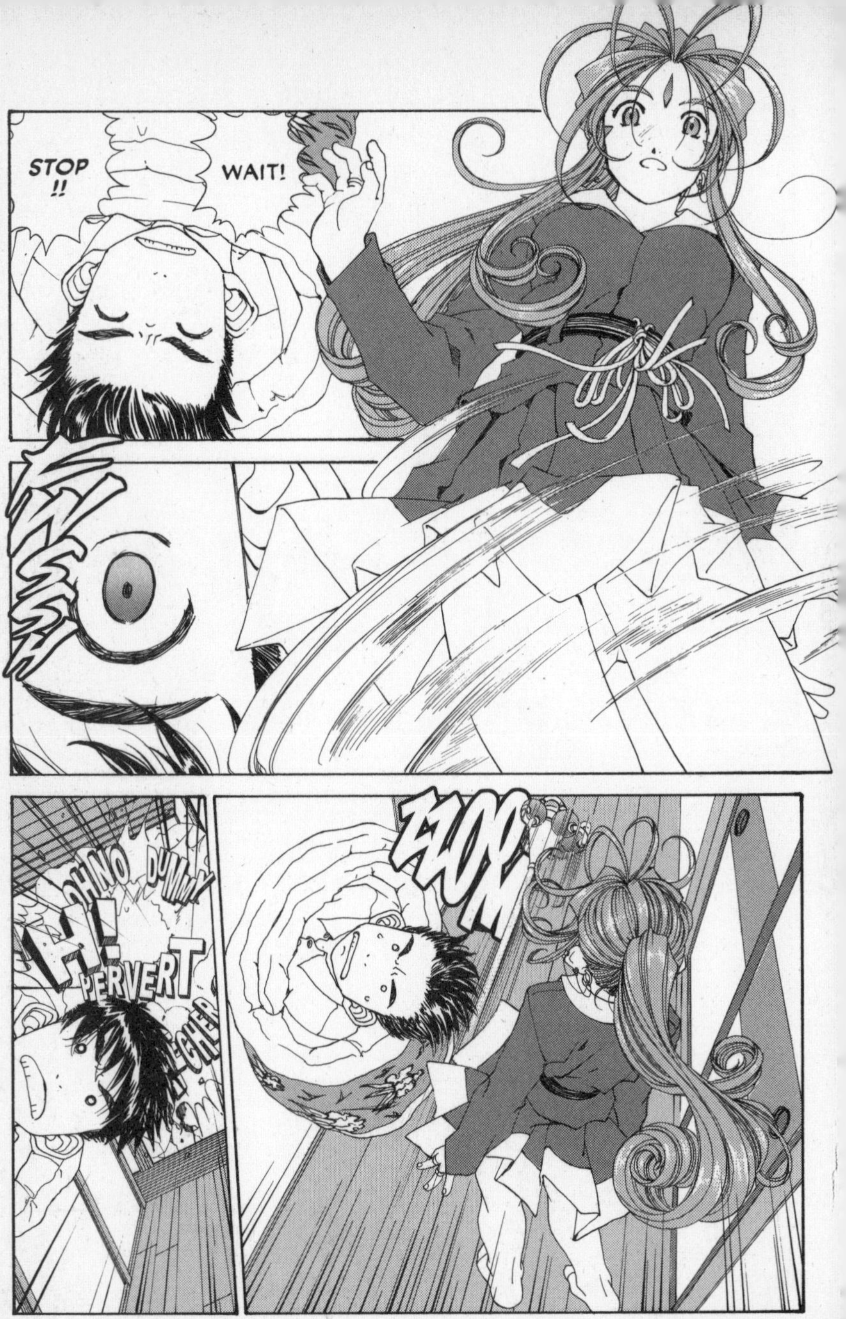
WAIT!
STOP !!
ZZOOM
OHNO DUMMY
H!
PERVERT
LECHER

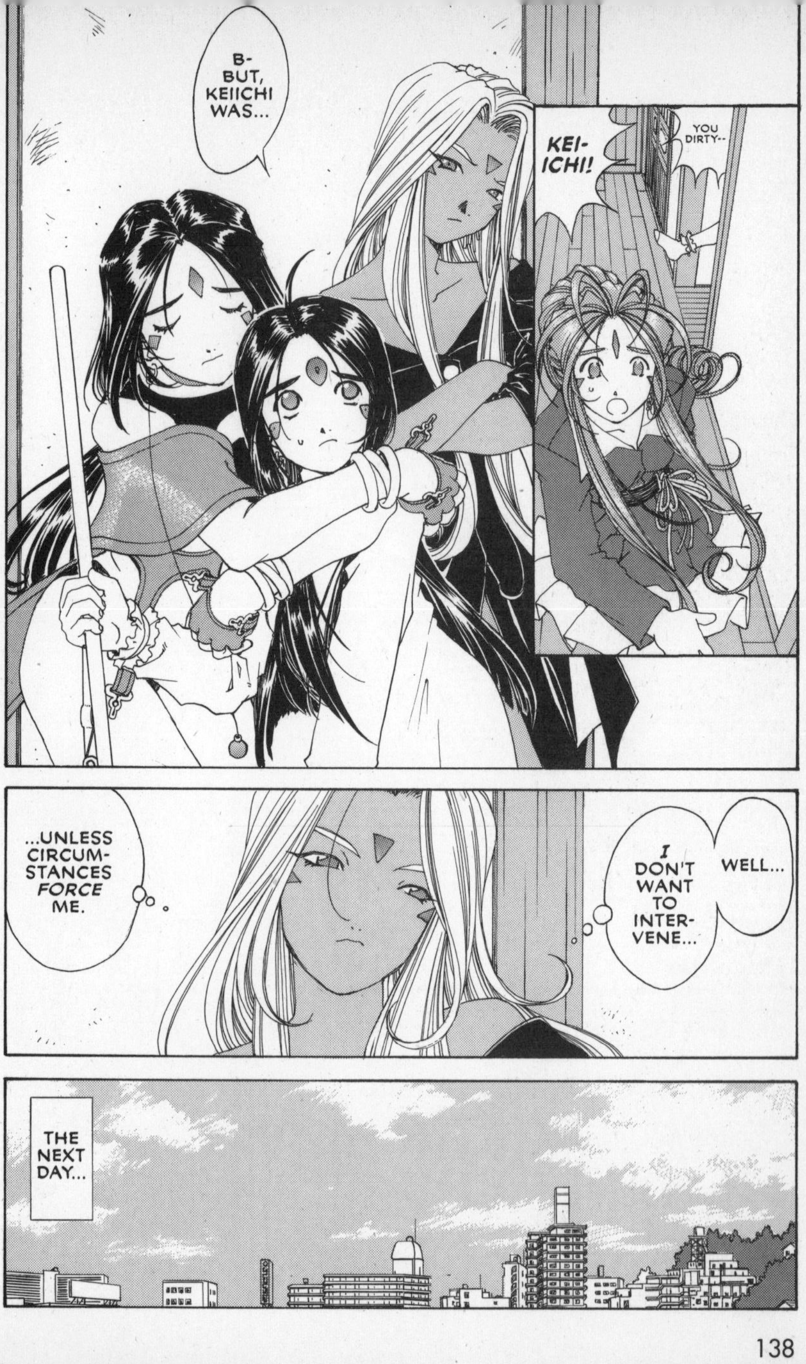
YOU DIRTY--
KEI-ICHI!
B-BUT, KEIICHI WAS...
WELL...
I DON'T WANT TO INTERVENE...
...UNLESS CIRCUMSTANCES *FORCE* ME.
THE NEXT DAY...

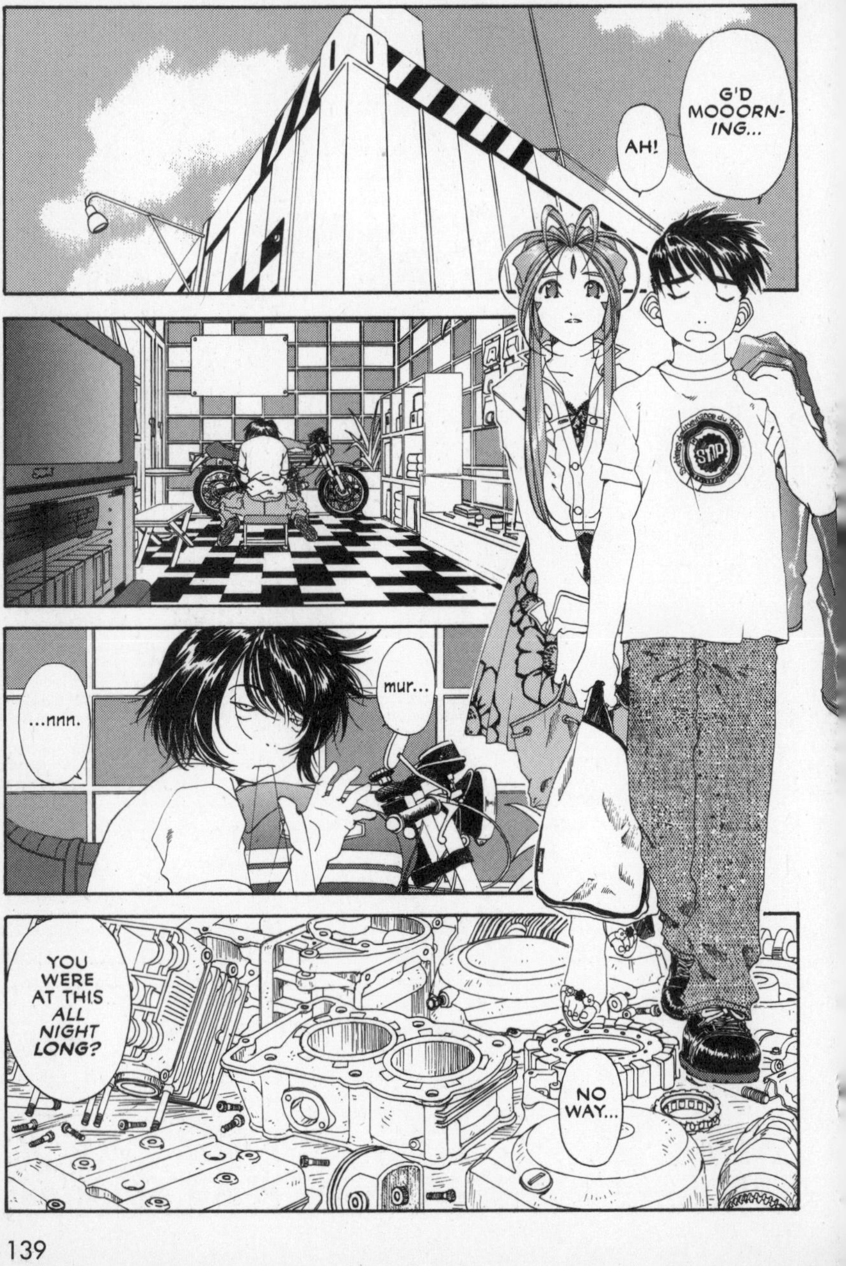
G'D MOOORN-ING...
AH!
mur...
...nnn.
YOU WERE AT THIS ALL NIGHT LONG?
NO WAY...

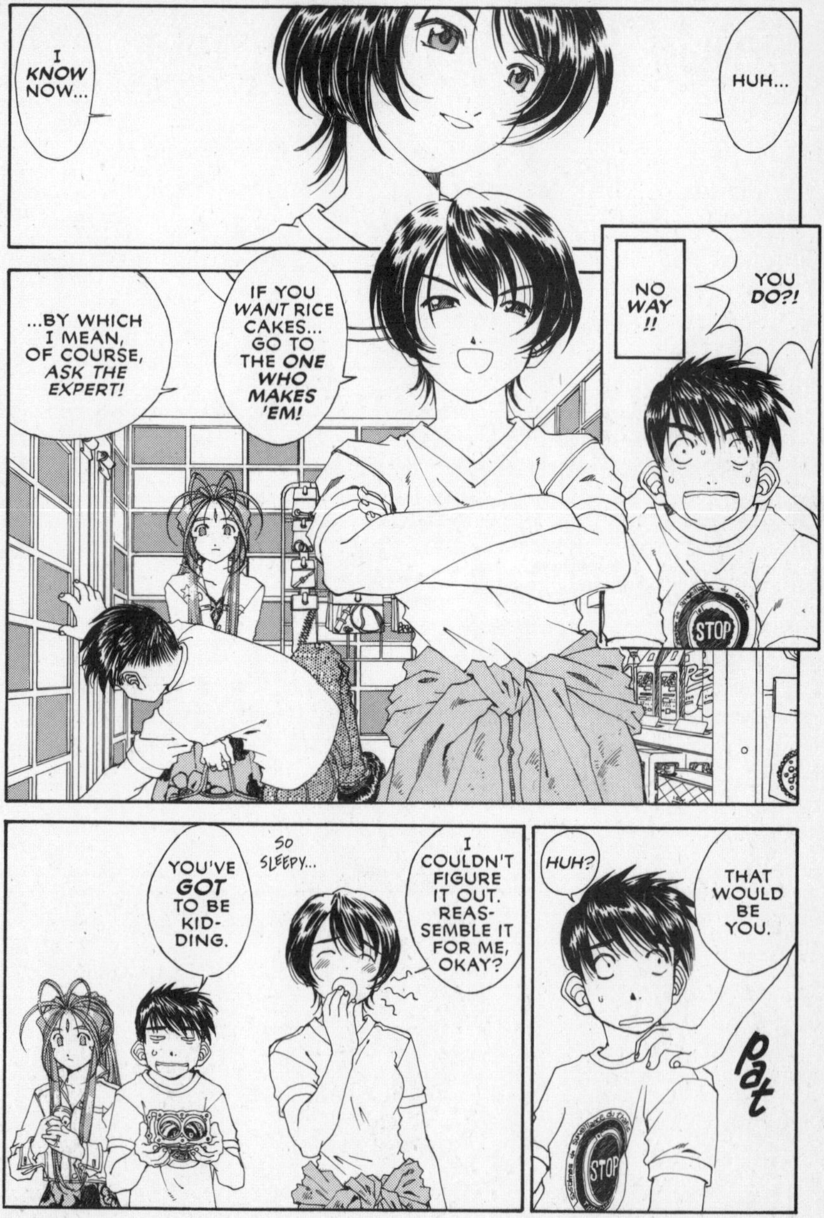
HUH...
I KNOW NOW...
YOU DO?!
NO WAY!!
IF YOU WANT RICE CAKES... GO TO THE ONE WHO MAKES 'EM!
...BY WHICH I MEAN, OF COURSE, ASK THE EXPERT!
THAT WOULD BE YOU.
HUH?
pat
I COULDN'T FIGURE IT OUT. REAS-SEMBLE IT FOR ME, OKAY?
SO SLEEPY...
YOU'VE GOT TO BE KID-DING.
STOP

CHAPTER 169

What We Would Save

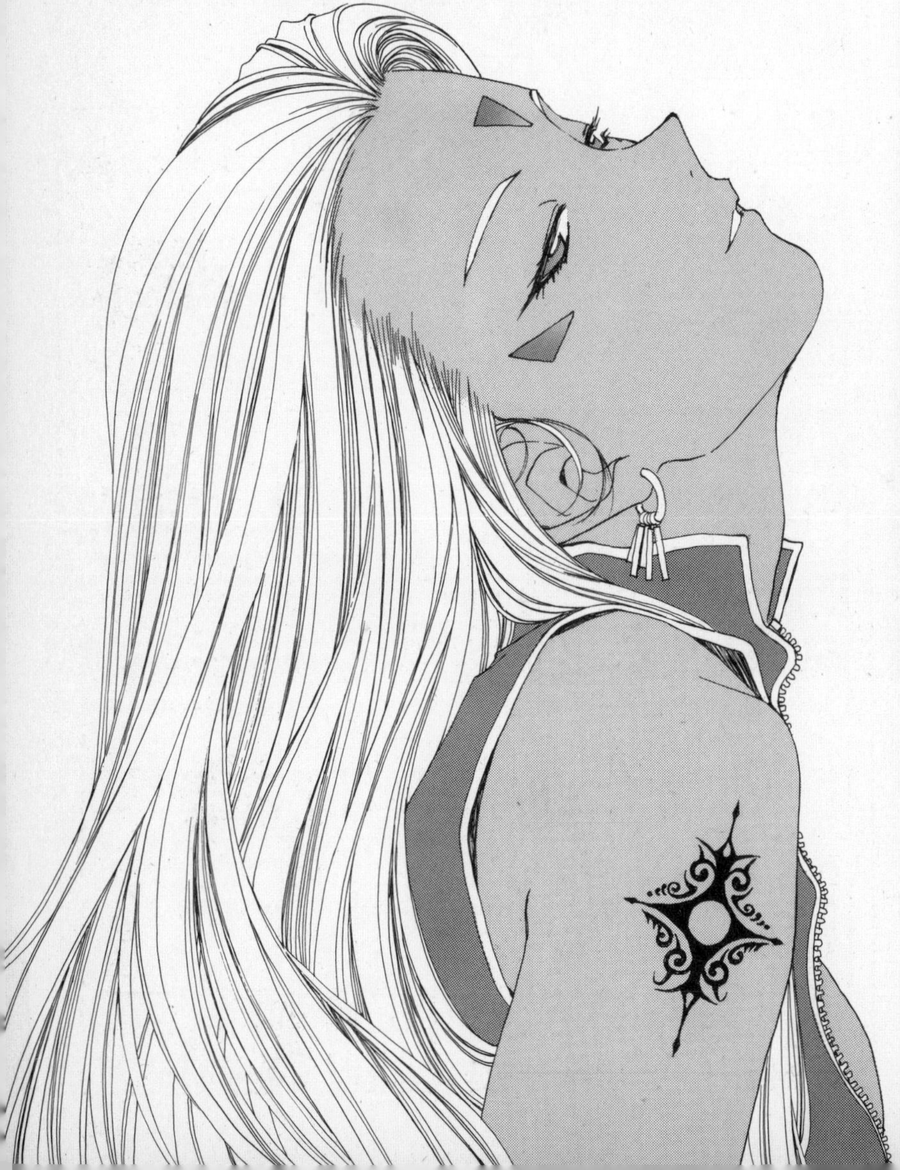

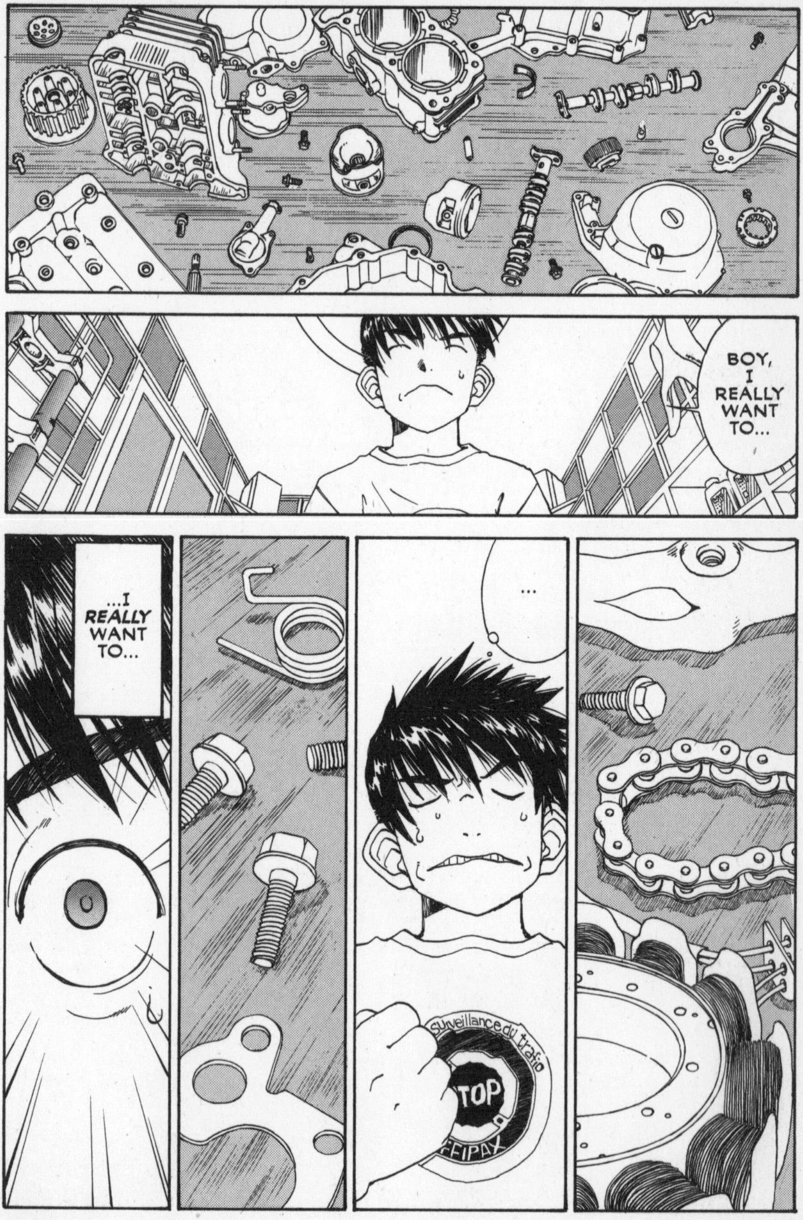
BOY, I REALLY WANT TO...
...
...I *REALLY* WANT TO...

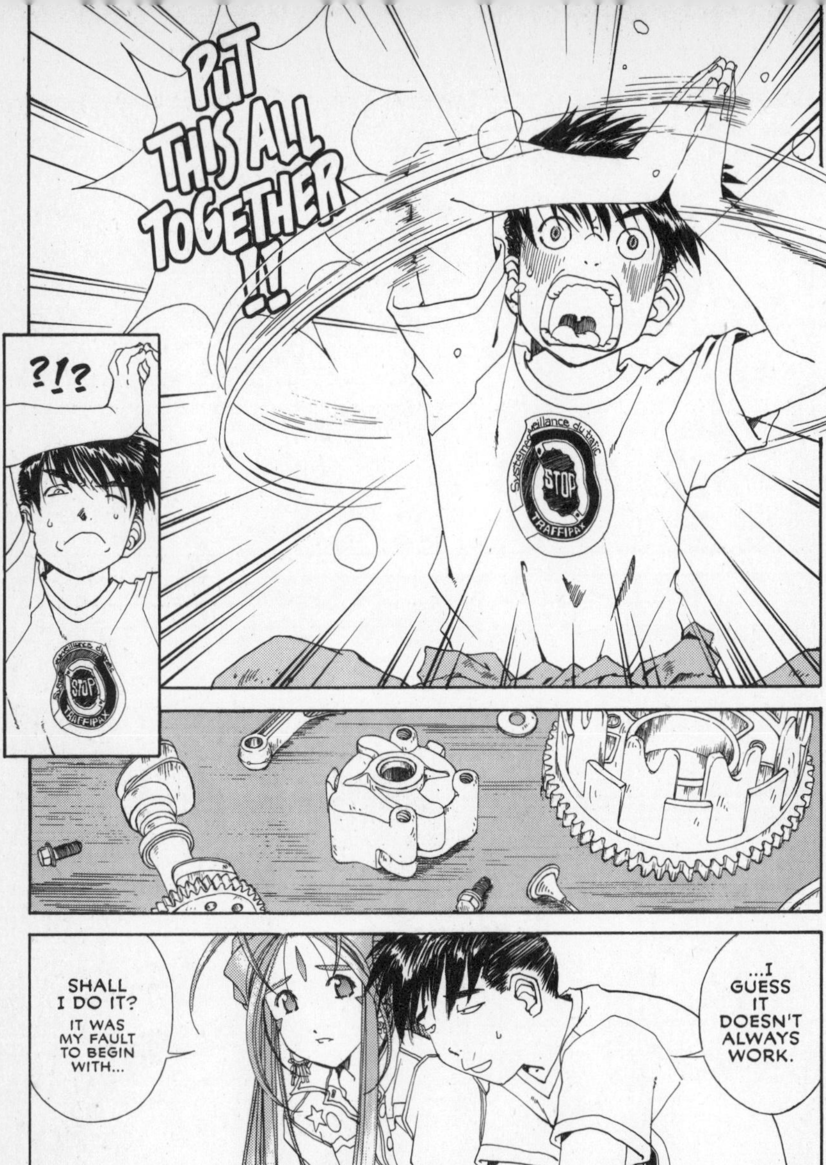
PUT THIS ALL TOGETHER!!
STOP
TRAFFIPAX
?!?
...I GUESS IT DOESN'T ALWAYS WORK.
SHALL I DO IT? IT WAS MY FAULT TO BEGIN WITH...

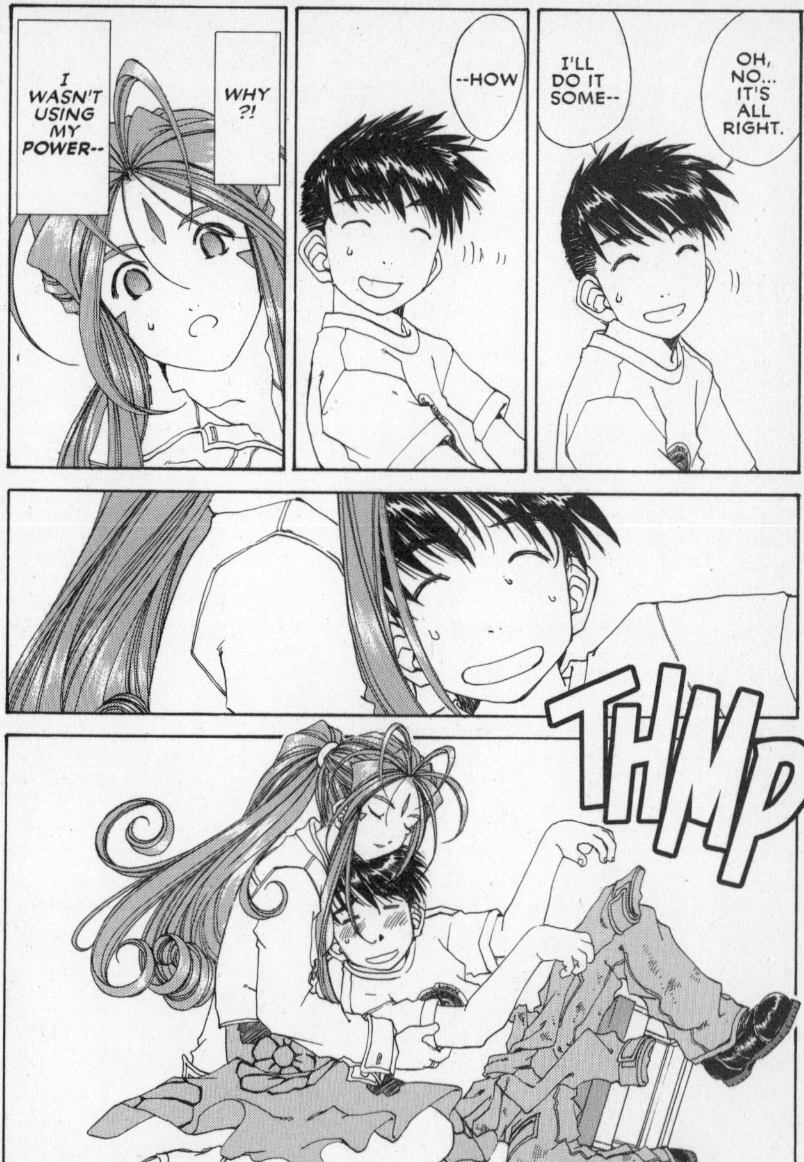
OH, NO... IT'S ALL RIGHT.
I'LL DO IT SOME--
--HOW
WHY ?!
I WASN'T USING MY POWER--
THMP

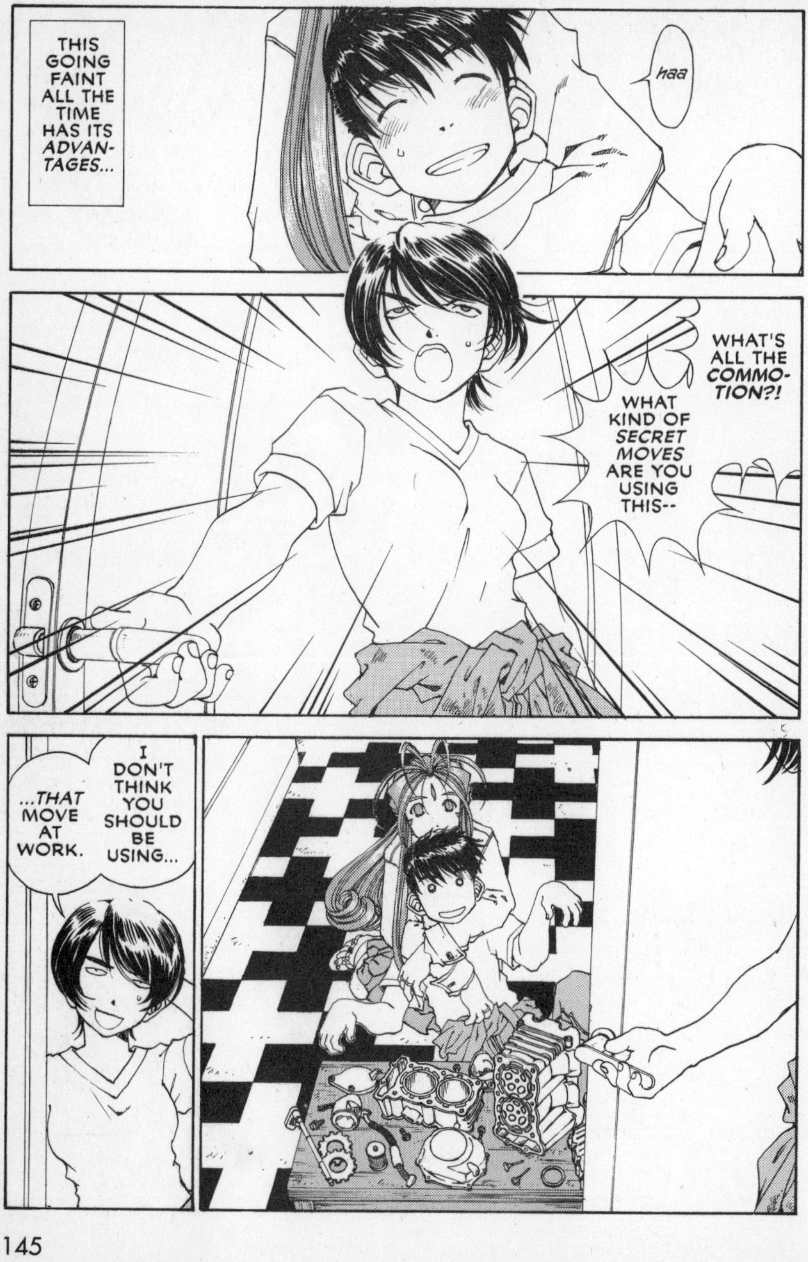
haa
THIS GOING FAINT ALL THE TIME HAS ITS *ADVANTAGES*...
WHAT'S ALL THE *COMMOTION?!*
WHAT KIND OF *SECRET MOVES* ARE YOU USING THIS--
I DON'T THINK YOU SHOULD BE USING...
...*THAT* MOVE AT WORK.

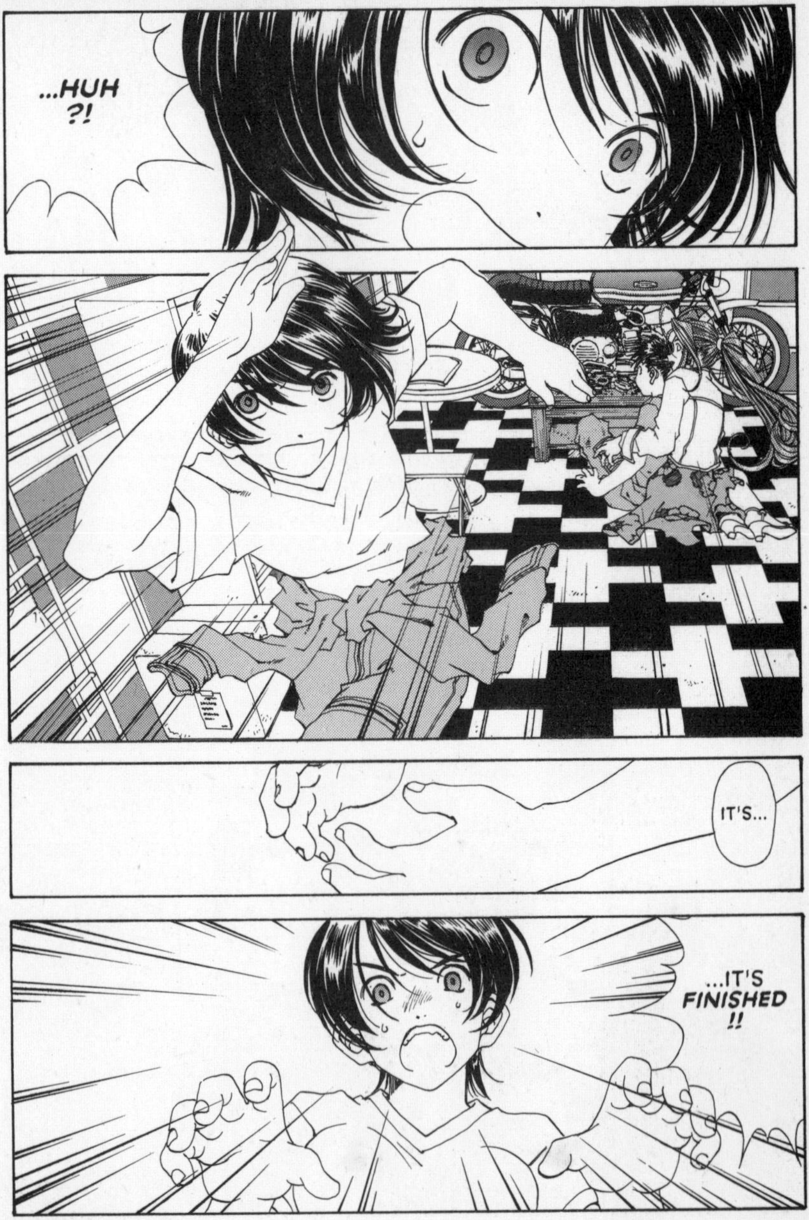
...HUH ?!
IT'S...
...IT'S FINISHED !!

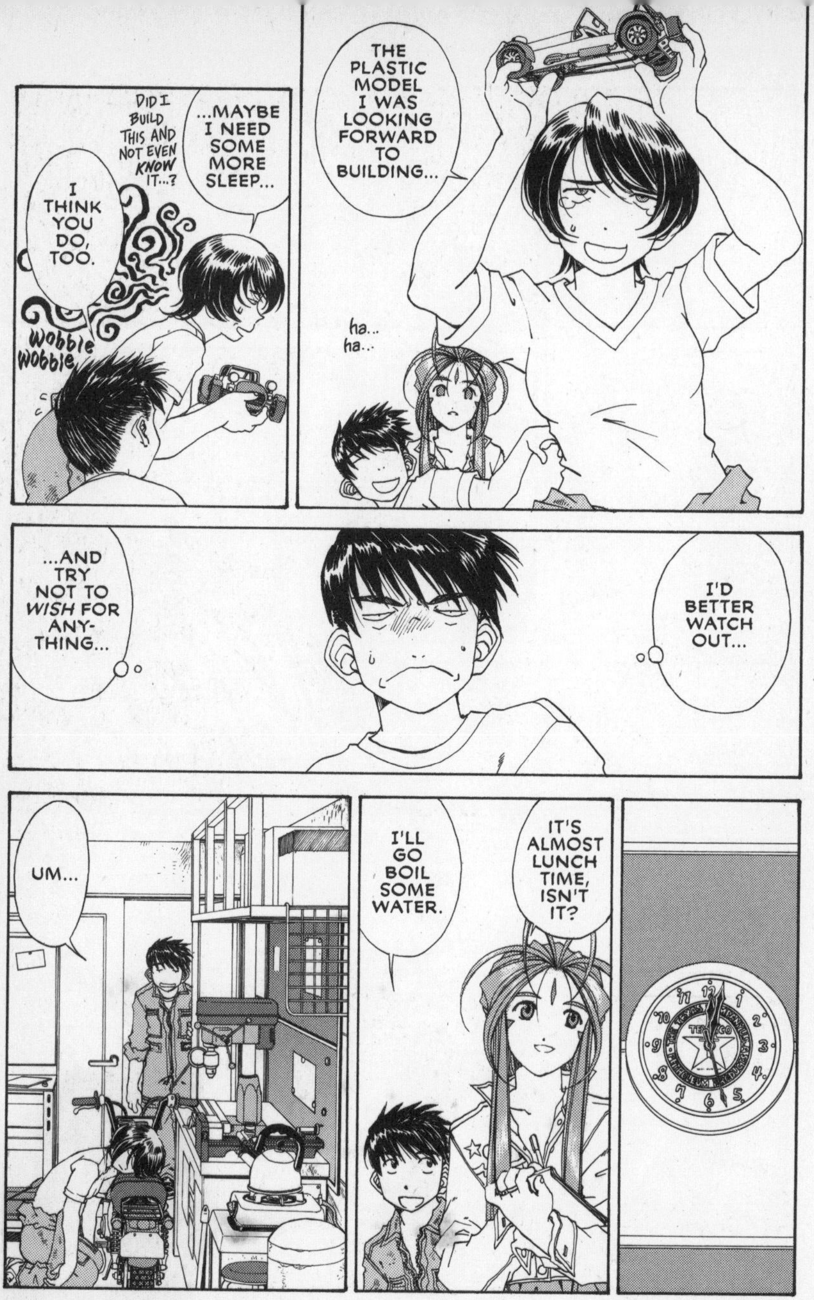
THE PLASTIC MODEL I WAS LOOKING FORWARD TO BUILDING...
ha... ha...
...MAYBE I NEED SOME MORE SLEEP...
DID I BUILD THIS AND NOT EVEN *KNOW* IT...?
I THINK YOU DO, TOO.
wobble wobble
I'D BETTER WATCH OUT...
...AND TRY NOT TO *WISH* FOR ANYTHING...
IT'S ALMOST LUNCH TIME, ISN'T IT?
I'LL GO BOIL SOME WATER.
UM...

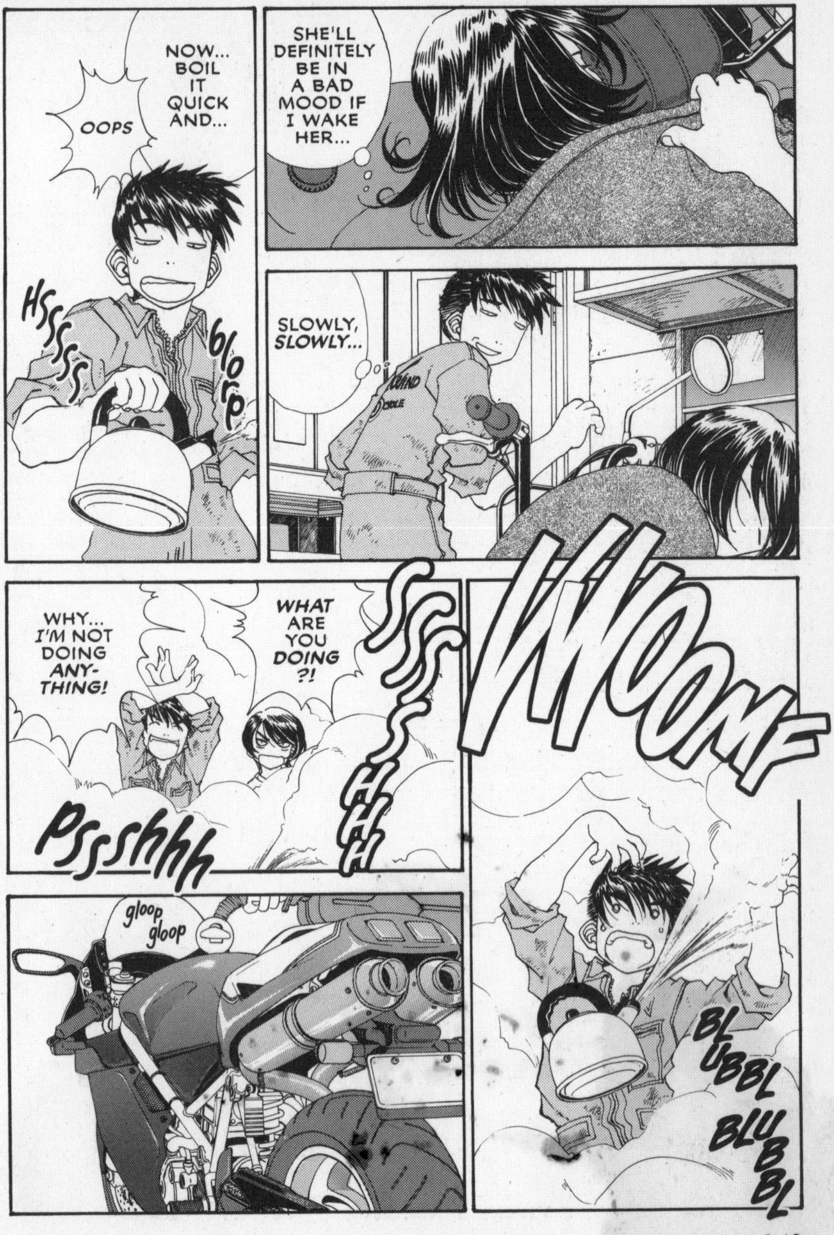

SHE'LL DEFINITELY BE IN A BAD MOOD IF I WAKE HER...
SLOWLY, *SLOWLY*...
NOW... BOIL IT QUICK AND...
OOPS
HSSSSSS
blorp
WOOMF
BLUBBL BLUBBL
WHAT ARE YOU *DOING* ?!
WHY... *I'M* NOT DOING *ANY-THING!*
SSS~HHH
Pssshhh
gloop gloop

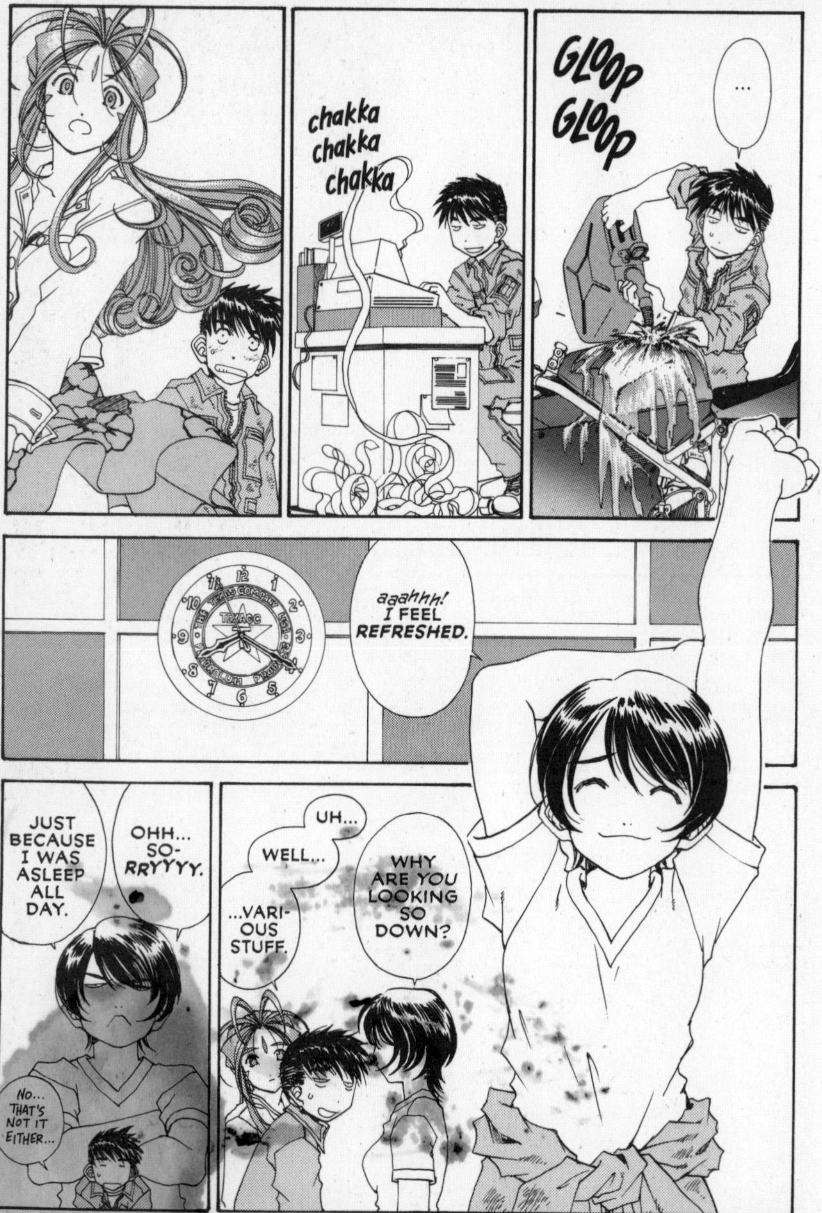
GLOOP GLOOP
...
chakka chakka chakka
aaahhh! I FEEL REFRESHED.
WHY ARE YOU LOOKING SO DOWN?
UH...
WELL...
...VARIOUS STUFF.
OHH... SO-RRYYYY.
JUST BECAUSE I WAS ASLEEP ALL DAY.
NO... THAT'S NOT IT EITHER...

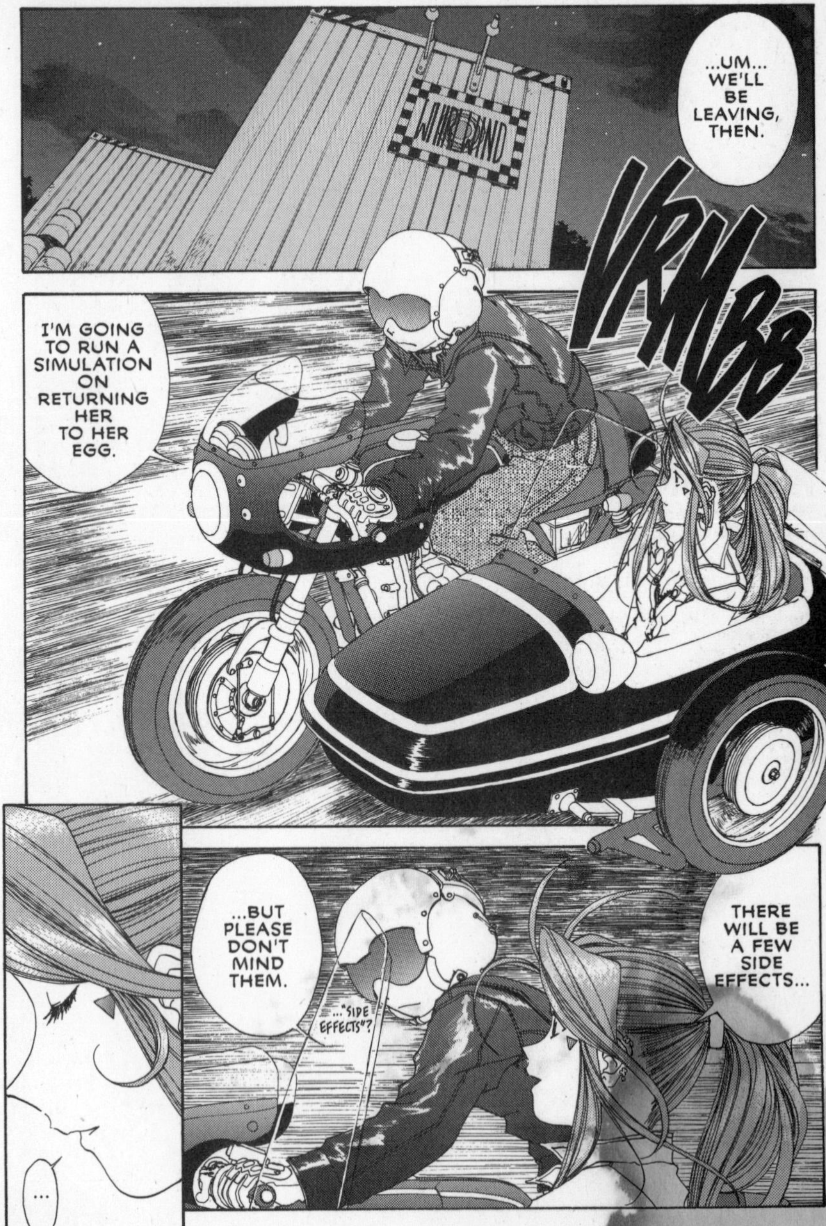
...UM... WE'LL BE LEAVING, THEN.
VRMBB
I'M GOING TO RUN A SIMULATION ON RETURNING HER TO HER EGG.
THERE WILL BE A FEW SIDE EFFECTS...
...BUT PLEASE DON'T MIND THEM.
..."SIDE EFFECTS"?
...

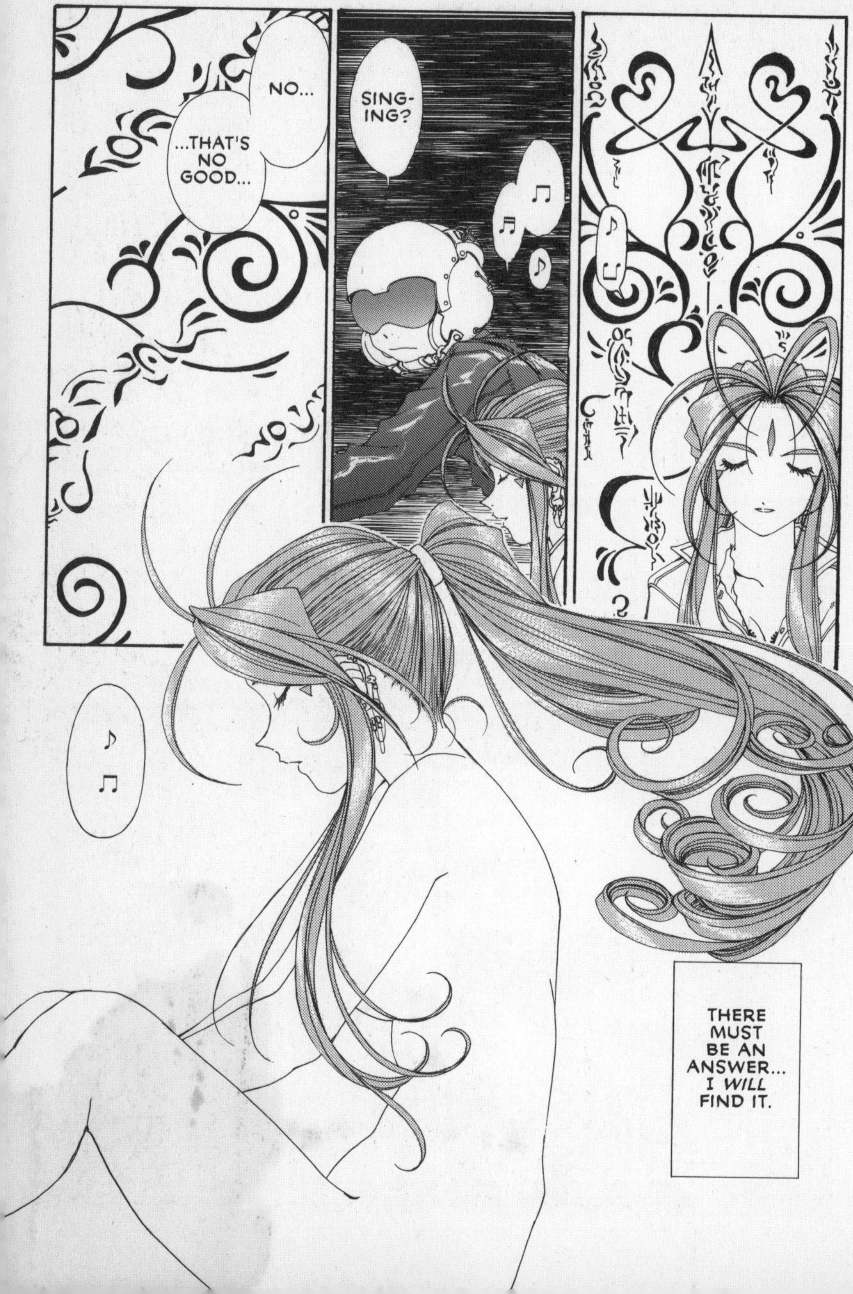
♪ ♫
SING-ING?
♫ ♫ ♪
NO...
...THAT'S NO GOOD...
♪ ♫
THERE MUST BE AN ANSWER... I *WILL* FIND IT.

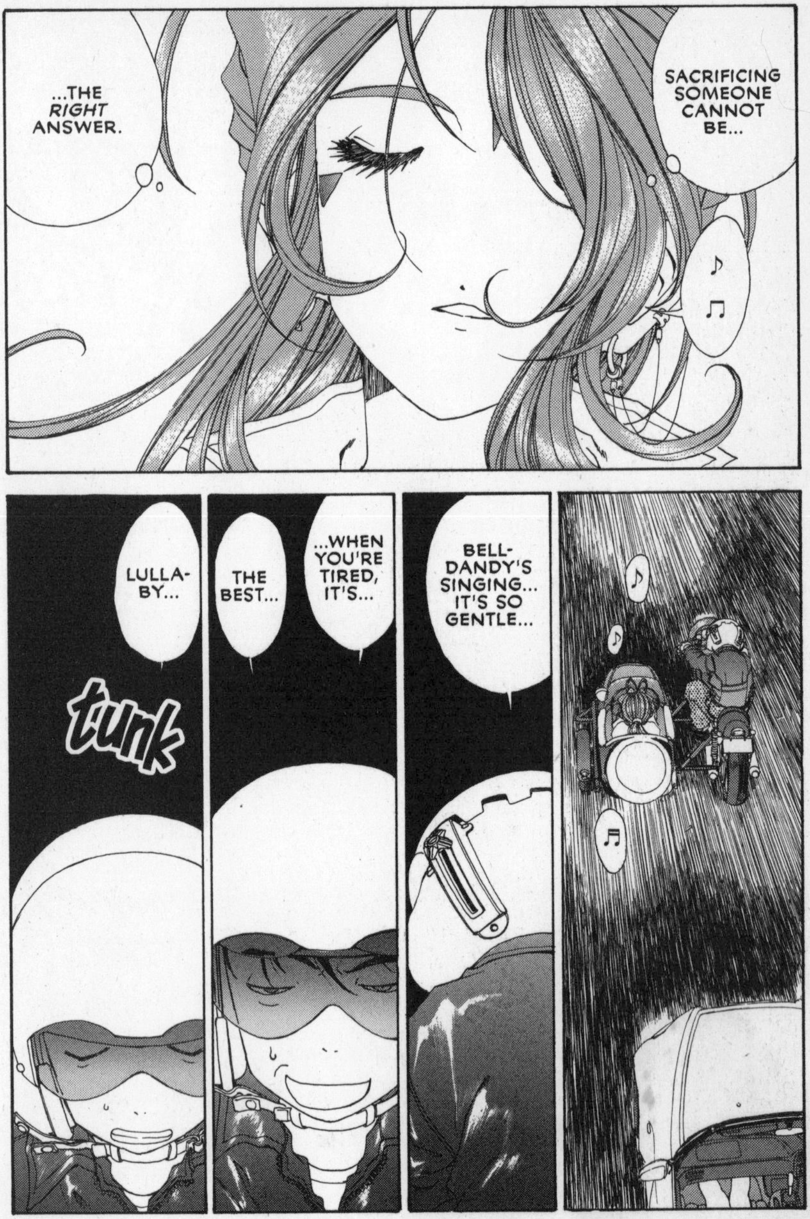
SACRIFICING SOMEONE CANNOT BE...
...THE *RIGHT* ANSWER.
♪ ♫
♪ ♪ ♫
BELL-DANDY'S SINGING... IT'S SO GENTLE...
...WHEN YOU'RE TIRED, IT'S...
THE BEST...
LULLA-BY...
tunk

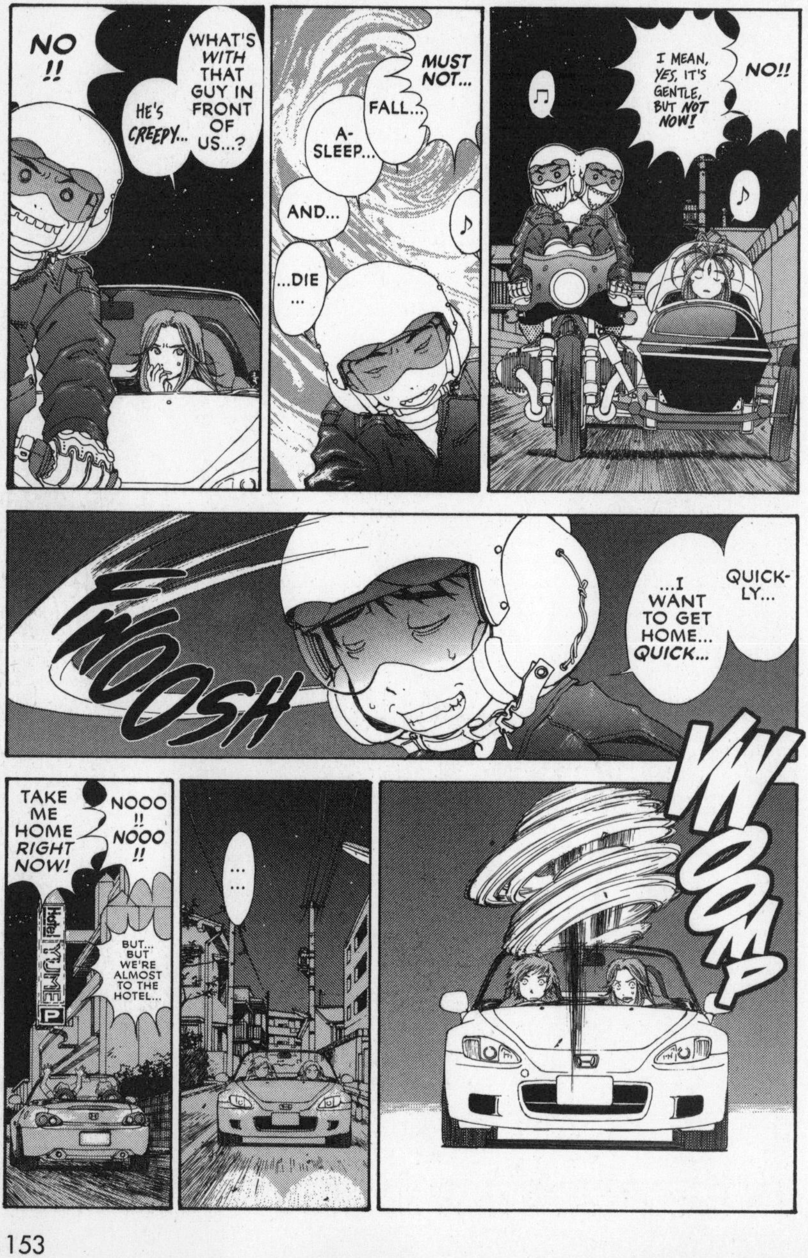
NO!!
I MEAN, YES, IT'S GENTLE, BUT NOT NOW!
♪
♪
MUST NOT...
FALL...
A-SLEEP...
AND...
...DIE...
♪
WHAT'S WITH THAT GUY IN FRONT OF US...?
HE'S CREEPY...
NO!!
QUICKLY...
...I WANT TO GET HOME... QUICK...
FWOOSH
VWOOMP
......
NOOO!! NOOO!!
TAKE ME HOME RIGHT NOW!
Hotel YUME P
BUT... BUT WE'RE ALMOST TO THE HOTEL...

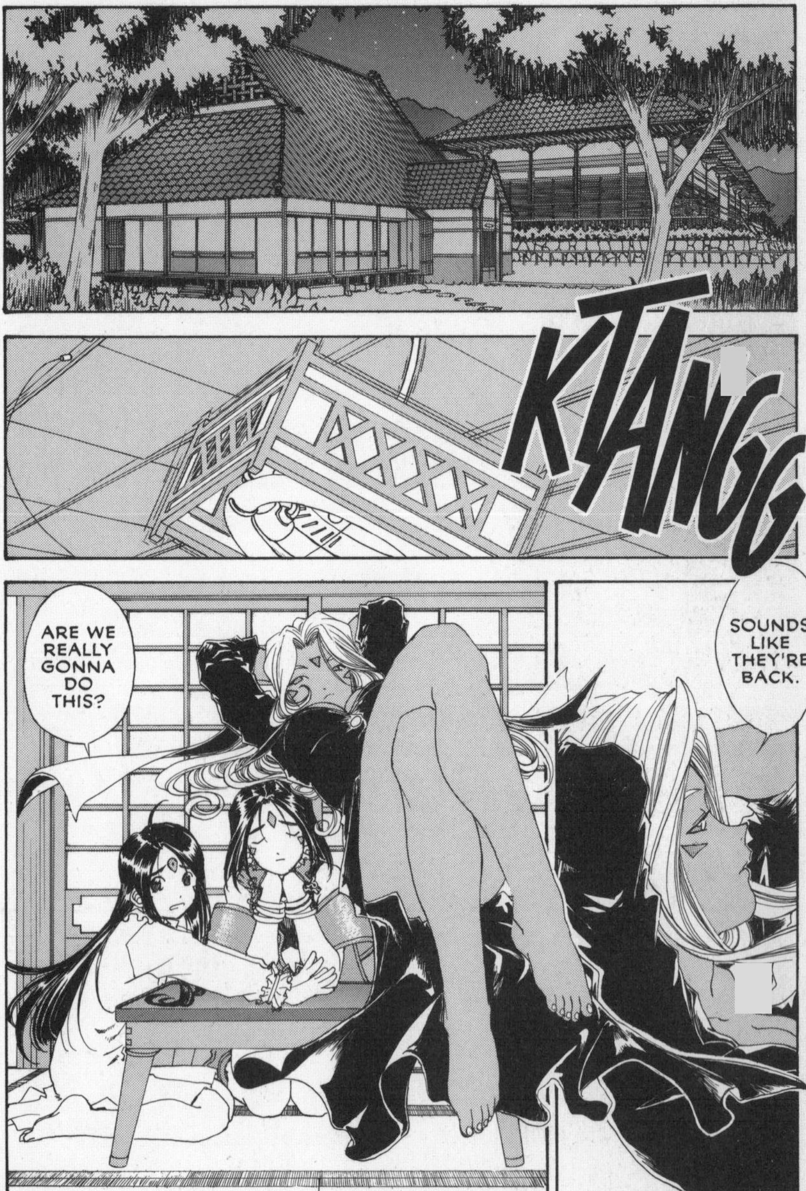
KTANGG
SOUNDS LIKE THEY'RE BACK.
ARE WE REALLY GONNA DO THIS?

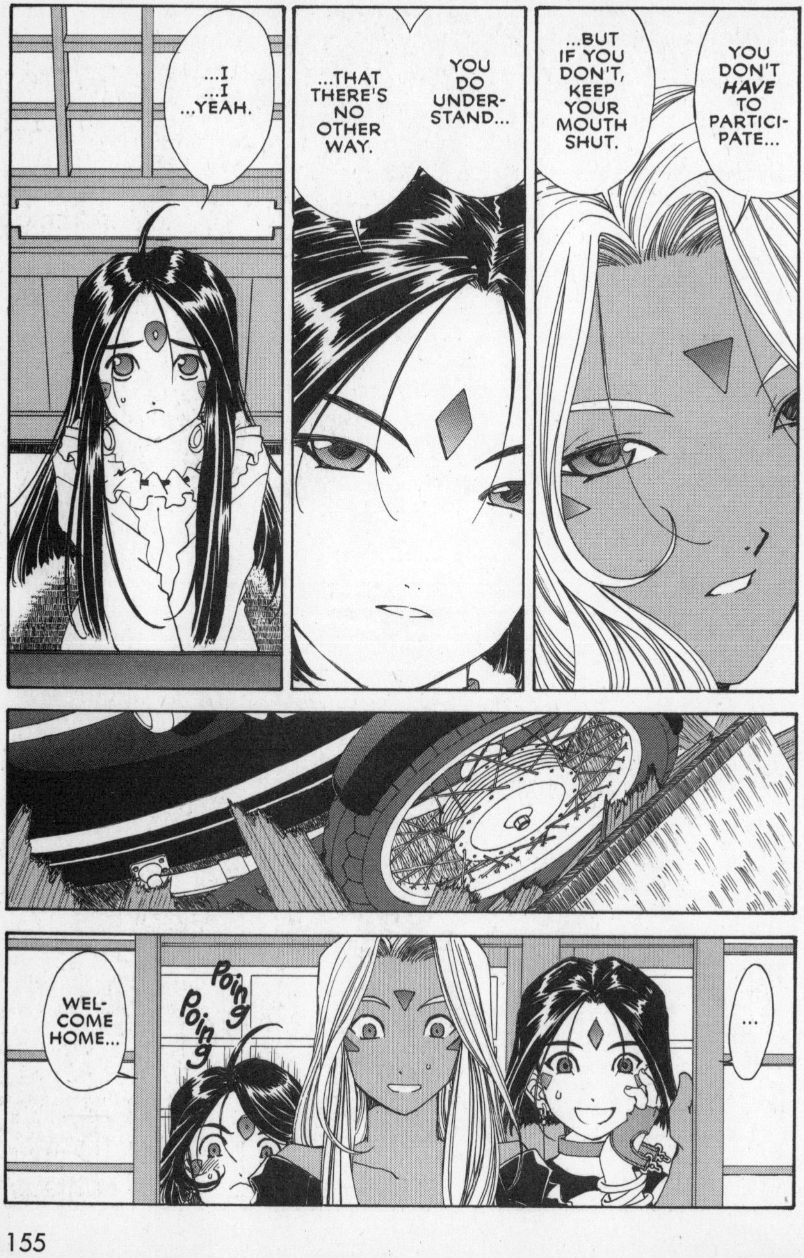
YOU DON'T *HAVE* TO PARTICI-PATE...
...BUT IF YOU DON'T, KEEP YOUR MOUTH SHUT.
YOU DO UNDER-STAND...
...THAT THERE'S NO OTHER WAY.
...I ...I ...YEAH.
...
Poing Poing
WEL-COME HOME...

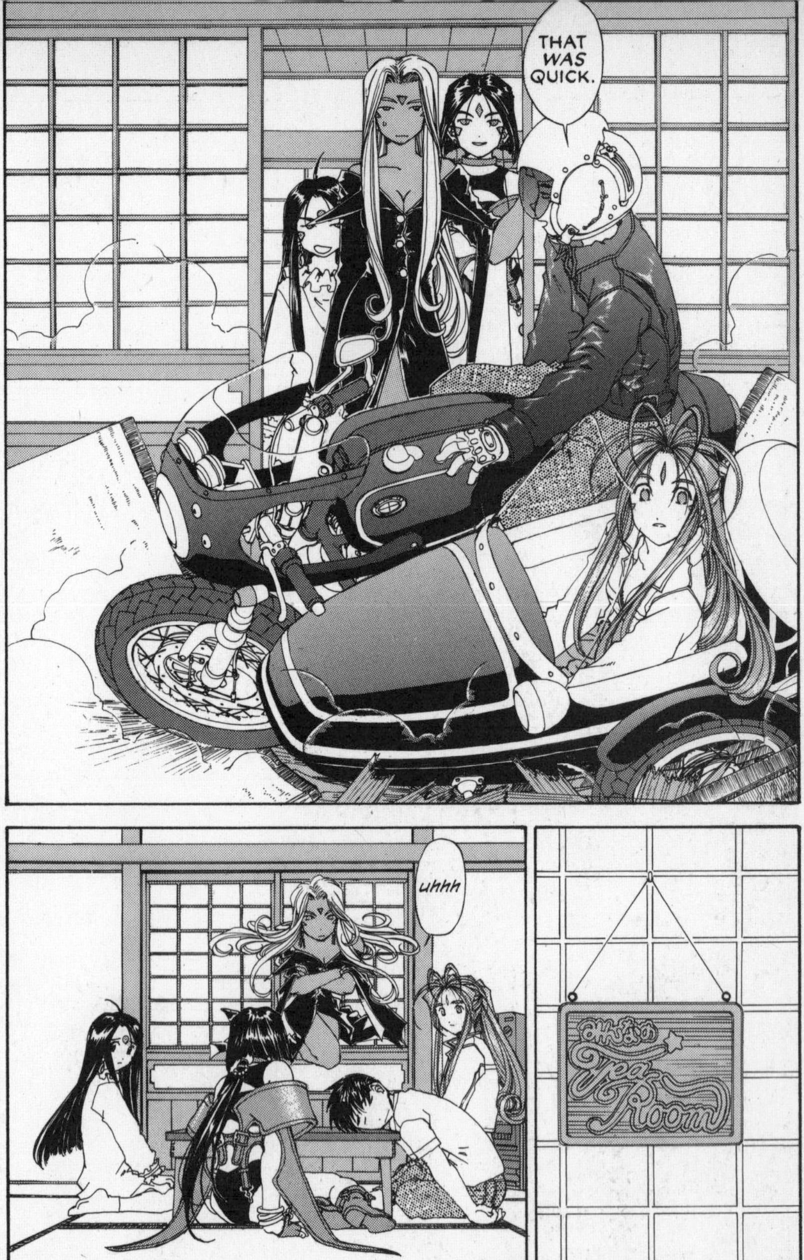
THAT WAS QUICK.
uhhh
Tea Room

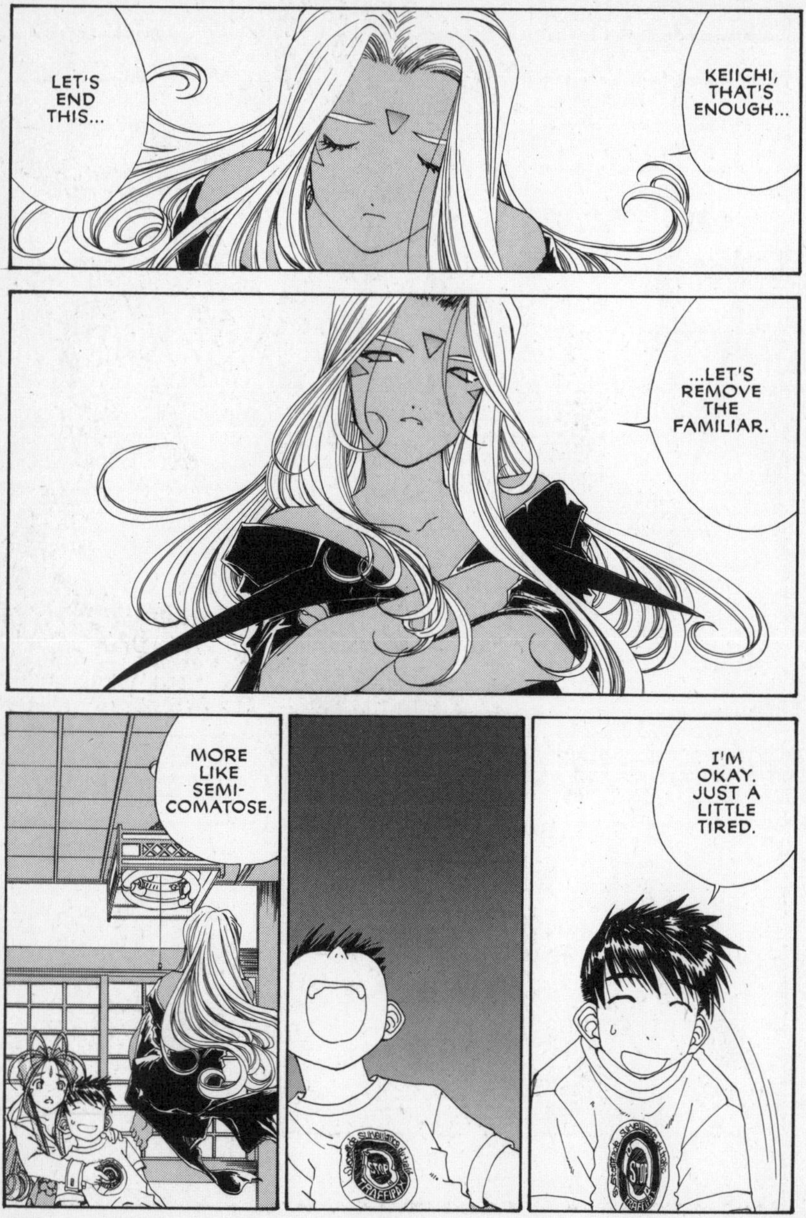
KEIICHI, THAT'S ENOUGH...
LET'S END THIS...
...LET'S REMOVE THE FAMILIAR.
I'M OKAY. JUST A LITTLE TIRED.
MORE LIKE SEMI-COMATOSE.

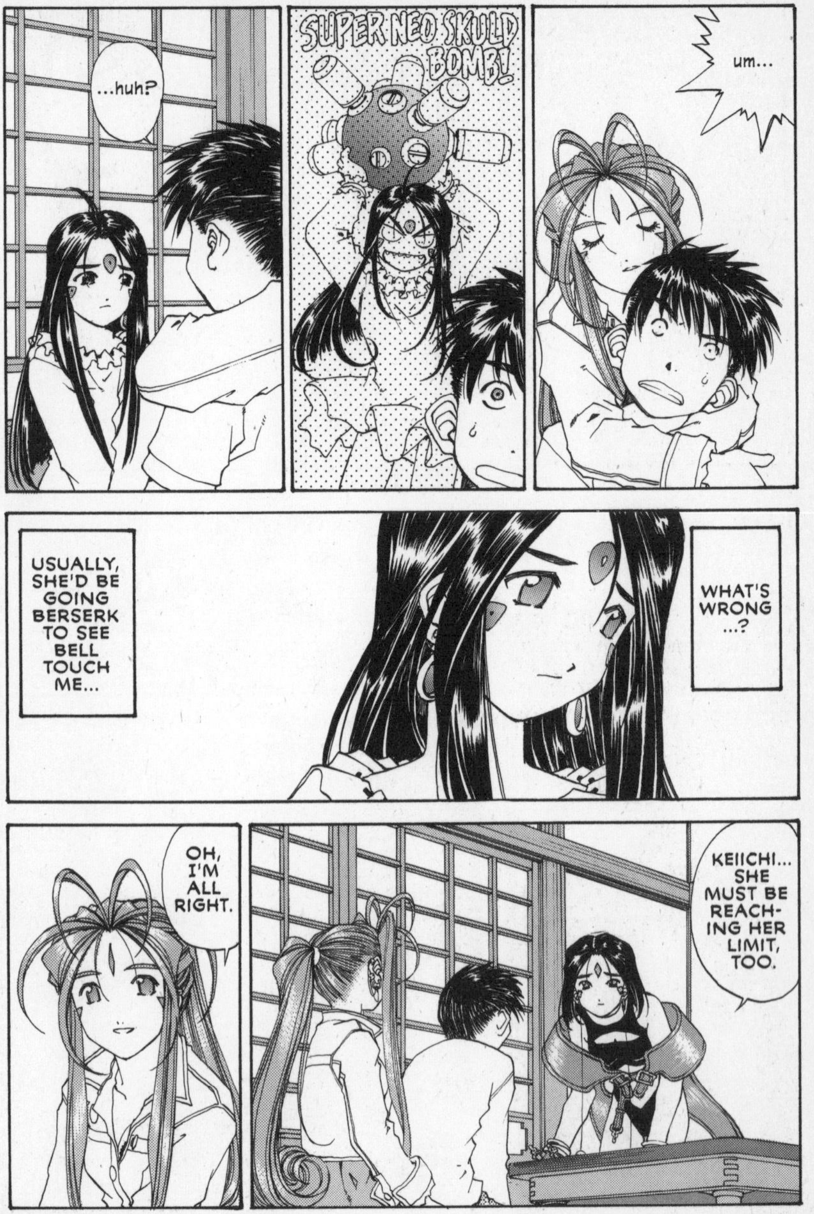
um...
SUPER NEO SKULD BOMB!
...huh?
WHAT'S WRONG ...?
USUALLY, SHE'D BE GOING BERSERK TO SEE BELL TOUCH ME...
KEIICHI... SHE MUST BE REACHING HER LIMIT, TOO.
OH, I'M ALL RIGHT.

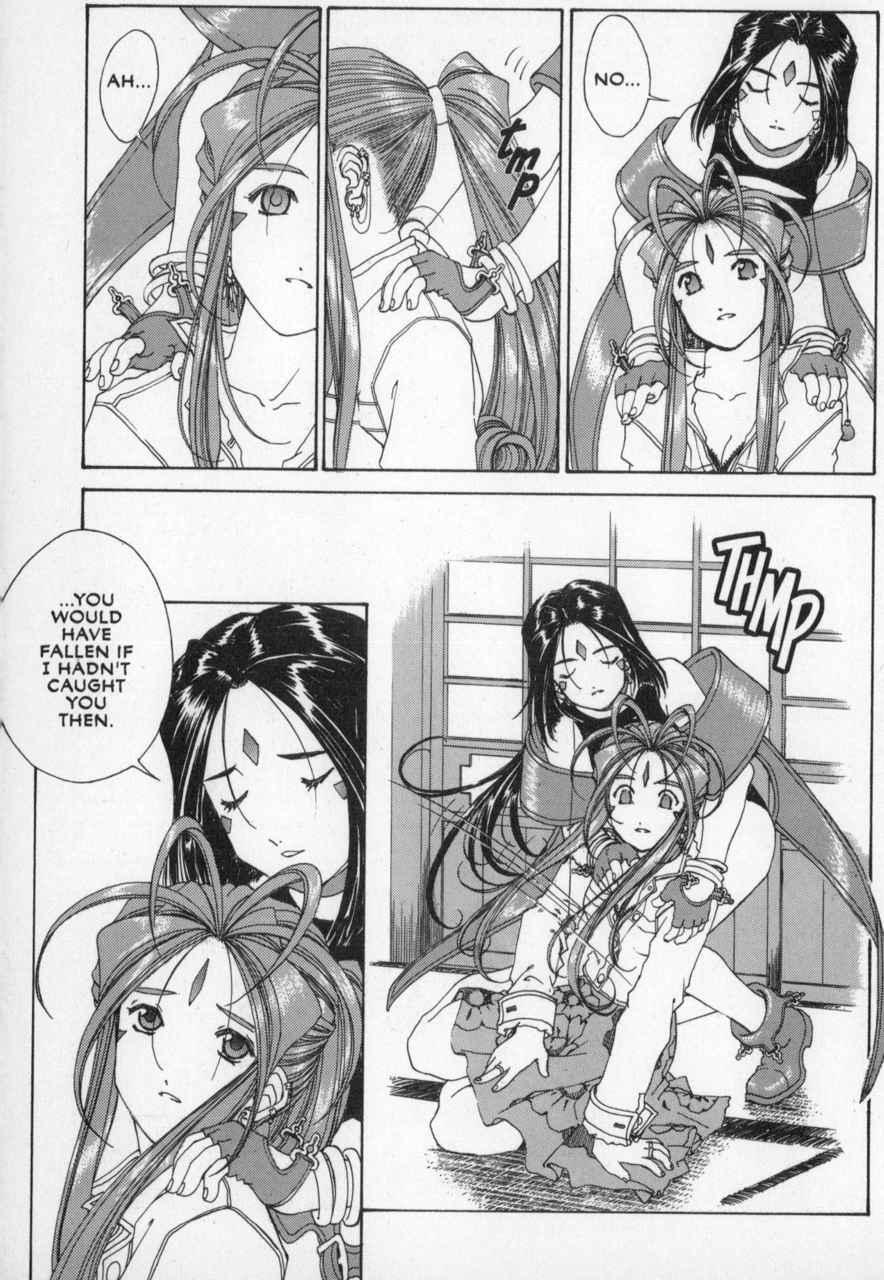
NO...
tmp
AH...
THMP
...YOU WOULD HAVE FALLEN IF I HADN'T CAUGHT YOU THEN.

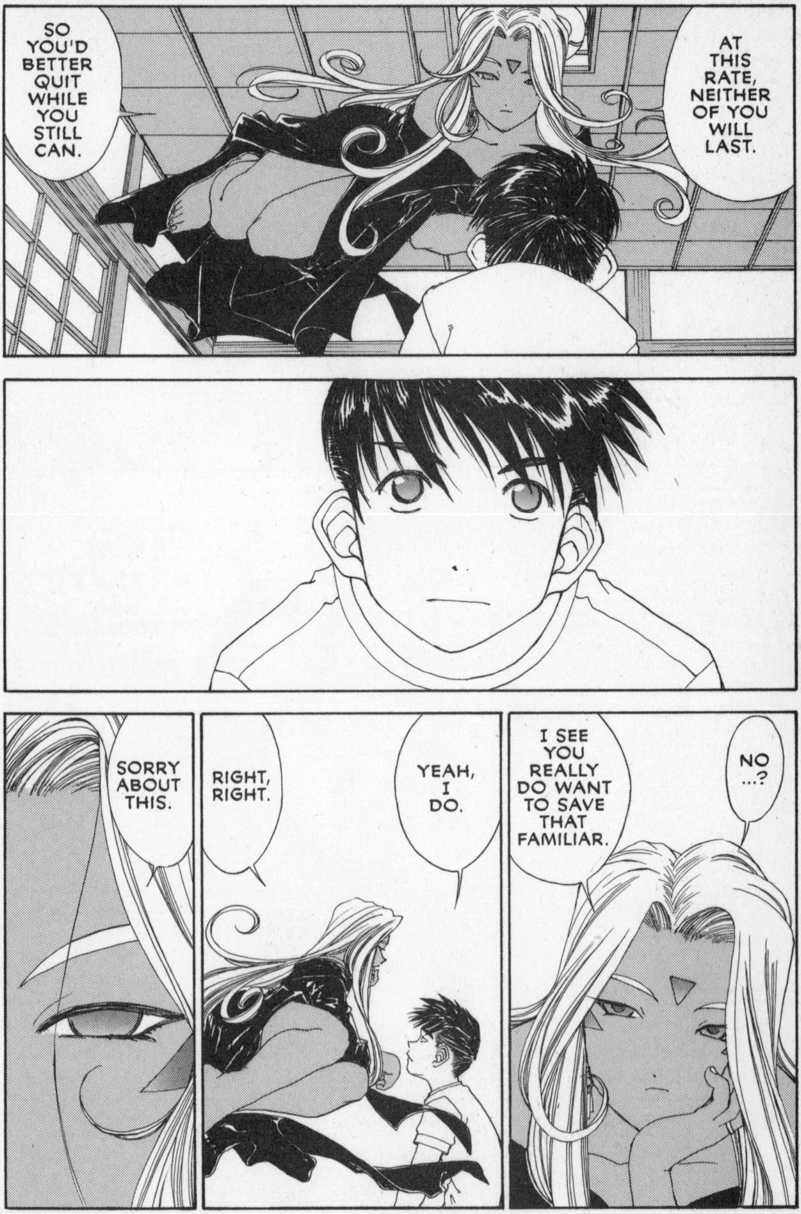
AT THIS RATE, NEITHER OF YOU WILL LAST.
SO YOU'D BETTER QUIT WHILE YOU STILL CAN.
NO ...?
I SEE YOU REALLY DO WANT TO SAVE THAT FAMILIAR.
YEAH, I DO.
RIGHT, RIGHT.
SORRY ABOUT THIS.

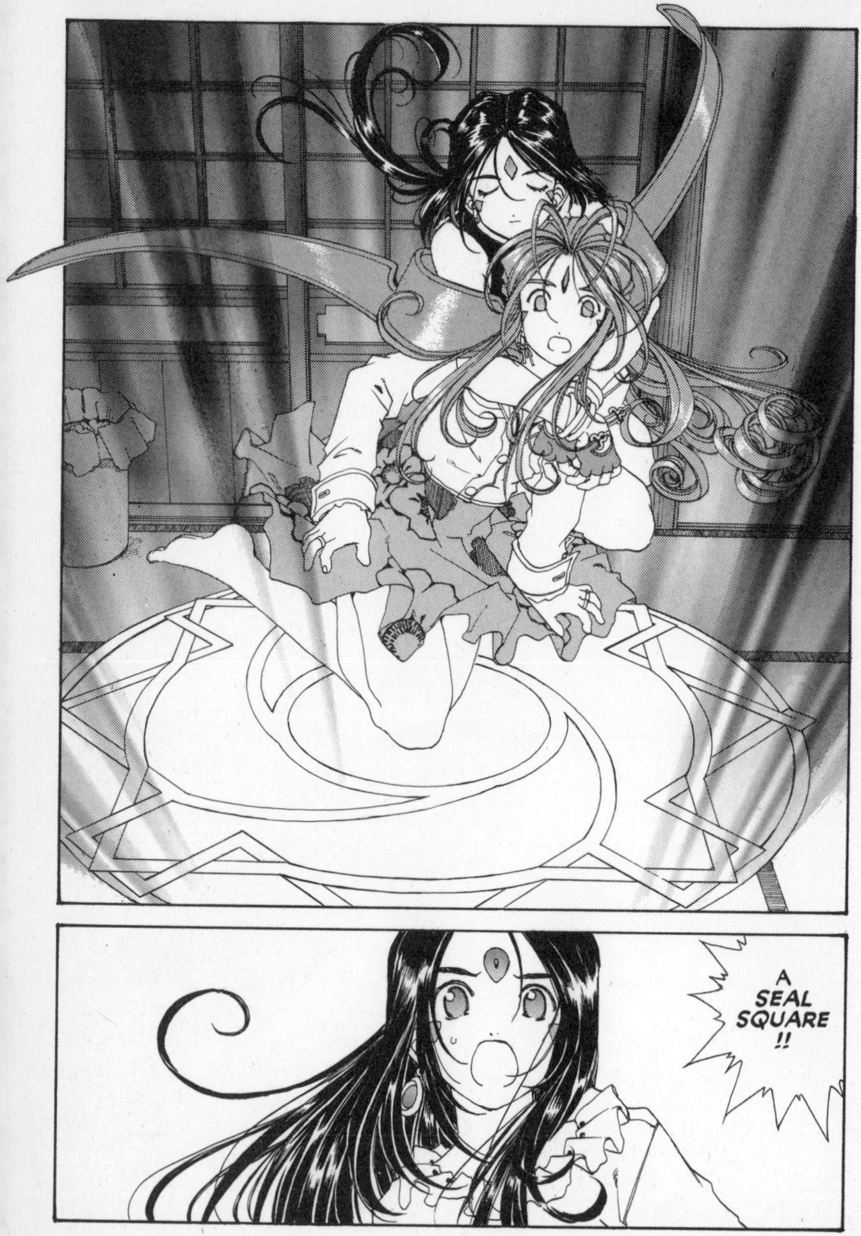
A SEAL SQUARE !!

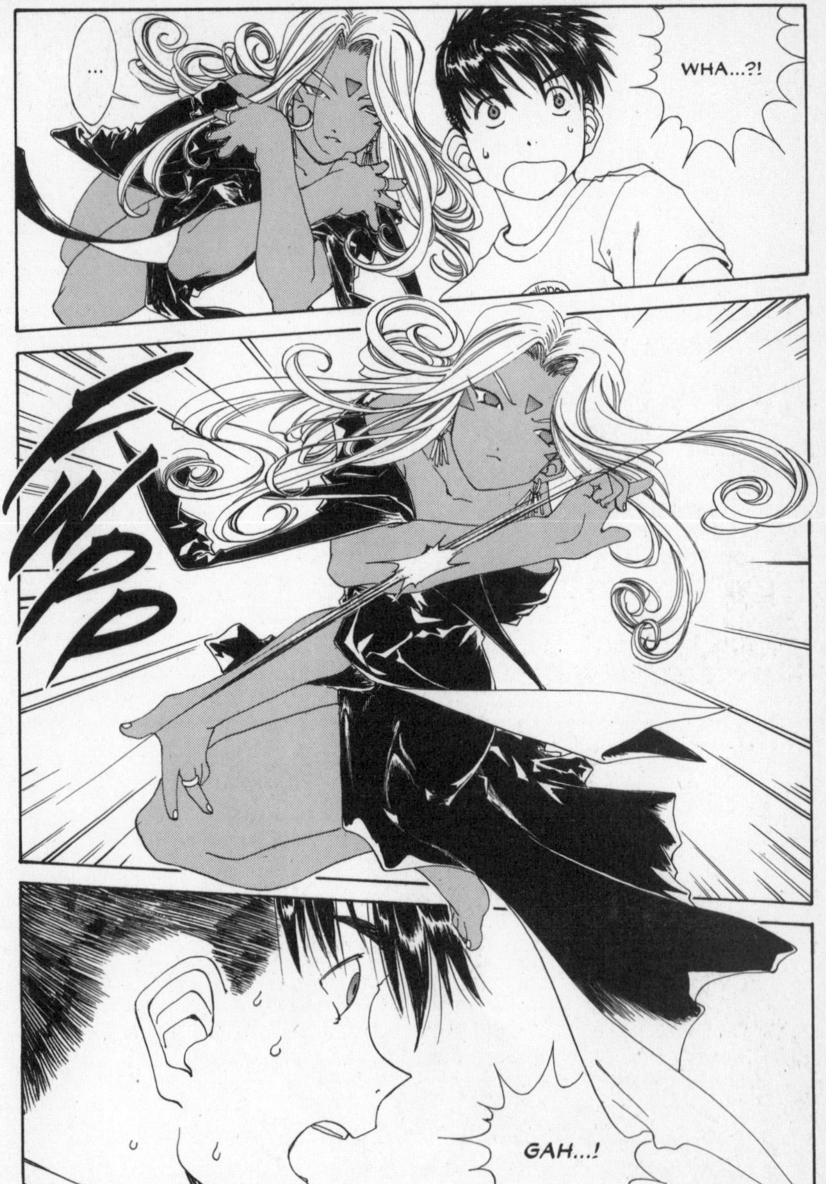
WHA...?!
...
GAH...!

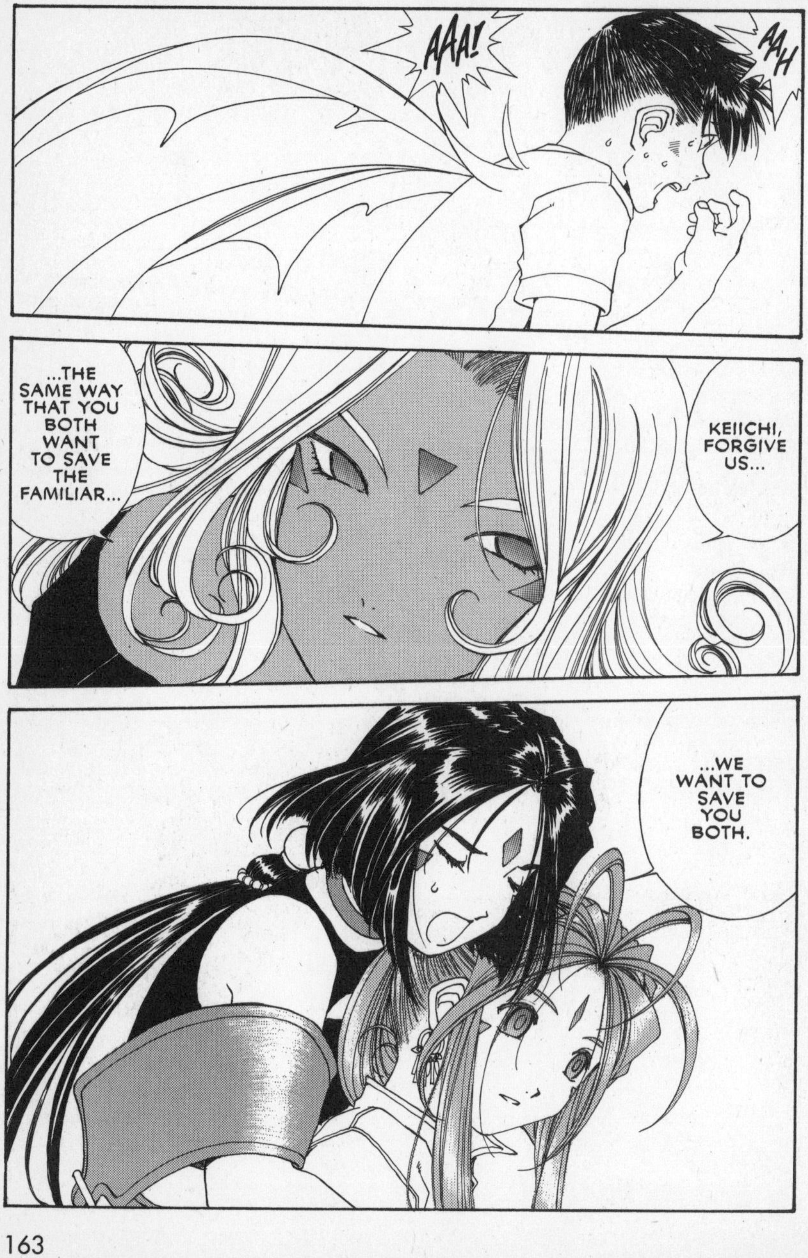
AAH
AAA!
KEIICHI, FORGIVE US...
...THE SAME WAY THAT YOU BOTH WANT TO SAVE THE FAMILIAR...
...WE WANT TO SAVE YOU BOTH.

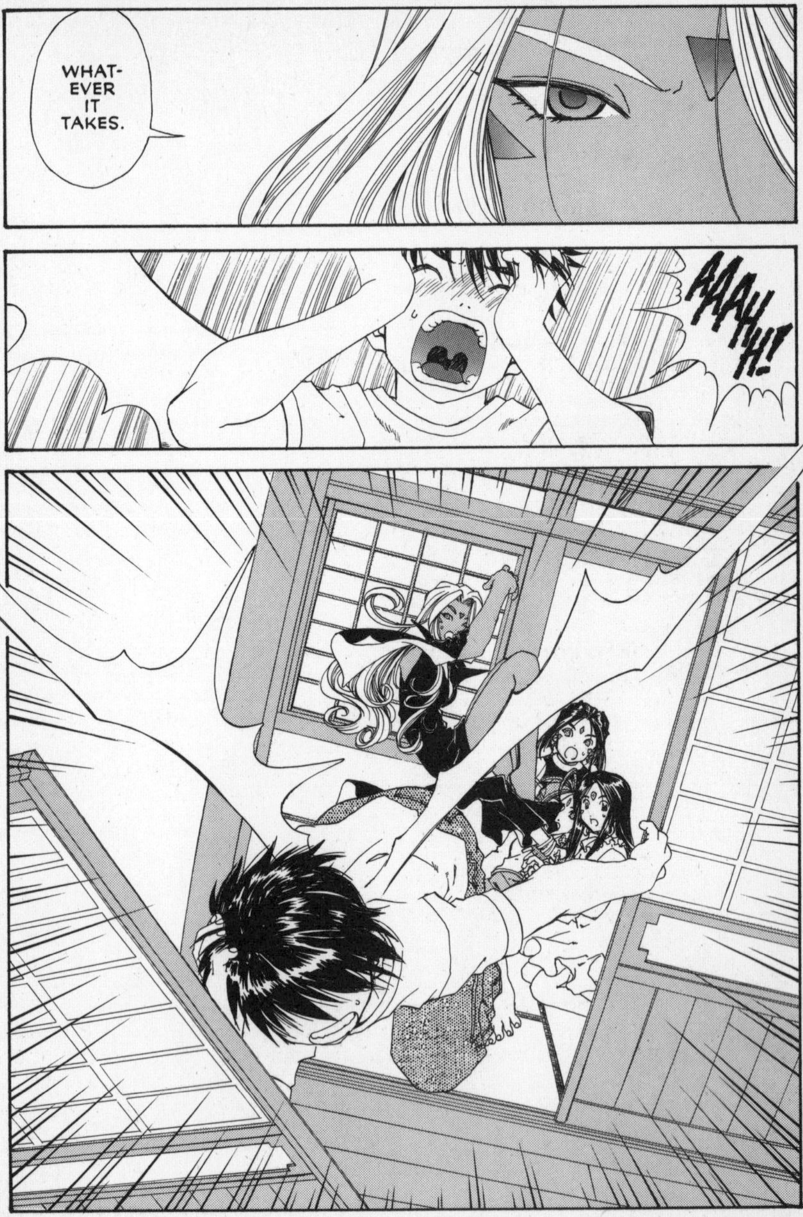
WHAT-EVER IT TAKES.
AAAHH!

EDITOR
Carl Gustav Horn

DESIGNER
Scott Cook

ART DIRECTOR
Lia Ribacchi

PUBLISHER
Mike Richardson

English-language version
produced by Dark Horse Comics

OH MY GODDESS! Vol. 26
©2007 Kosuke Fujishima. All rights reserved. First published in
Japan in 2003 by Kodansha, Ltd., Tokyo. Publication rights for this
English edition arranged through Kodansha Ltd. All other material
©2007 by Dark Horse Comics, Inc. All rights reserved. No portion of this
publication may be reproduced or transmitted, in any form or by any
means, without the express written permission of the copyright holders.
Names, characters, places, and incidents featured in this publication are
either the product of the author's imagination or are used fictitiously. Any
resemblance to actual persons (living or dead), events, institutions, or
locales, without satiric intent, is coincidental. Dark Horse Manga™ is a
trademark of Dark Horse Comics, Inc. All rights reserved.

Published by Dark Horse Manga
A division of Dark Horse Comics, Inc.
10956 SE Main Street
Milwaukie, OR 97222
www.darkhorse.com

To find a comics shop in your area,
call the Comic Shop Locator Service
toll-free at 1-888-266-4226

First edition: April 2007
ISBN-10: 1-59307-715-7
ISBN-13: 978-1-59307-715-0

1 3 5 7 9 10 8 6 4 2

Printed in Canada

letters to the
ENCHANTRESS

10956 SE Main Street, Milwaukie, Oregon 97222
omg@darkhorse.com • www.darkhorse.com

NOTE: Full addresses and e-mail addresses will not be printed, unless you ask! All fan art-work, letters, and e-mails submitted become the property of Dark Horse Comics.

Since everyone else is talking about the new format, I will put in my two cents' worth as well. While I will admit that the unflipped format does take some getting used to, in the end it makes manga (Japanese comics) easier to read, especially in the case of very complex works such as those by manga-ka (artists) such as Shirow Masamune (*Ghost in the Shell, Orion, Appleseed . . .*). It is also closer to what the manga-ka intended.

There is another factor that seldom gets mentioned. Flipping a manga takes time. Time is money. Compare the price of the old flipped format to the new unflipped format (not the only factor, to be sure, but . . .). This means more people can afford to buy a manga, or perhaps they can buy more of them.

One way the new format is *not* the same as the original is the lack of a slipcover. While the cover is the same, there are two illustrations on the inside of the slipcovers' flaps. The Japanese Volume 24 of *OMG!* (ISBN4-06-321136-3) has an illustration of Peorth wearing even less than she usually does (sorry guys, still PG).

I think Dana Lewis has done a great job in the translation, and the transition to using the Japanese honorifics was done very well. I almost missed it. However, there is a problem with the series that has nothing to do with the translation. In the Norse myths,

Urd, Belldandy (Verdandi), and Skuld all are born at the beginning of time. Their appearances are different only because, as fates, they each govern a different aspect of time. Yet in the *OMG!* series, Urd is said to be the older, and Skuld, the younger, sisters of Belldandy. Skuld has to practice and discover her power because of her young age. Fair enough. But in Volume 21, page 77, Peorth says to Keiichi "We're voyagers across time. Always have been. Always will be." Both cannot be true, and it begs the question, were there other goddesses serving as fates before the current ones?

By the way, some people are confused about what is going on with the video crew on pages 15 through 33 in Volume 24. The person being interviewed is the Drag Racing Queen that Megumi raced in (flopped) Volume 15, *Hand in Hand*, and the "IT" they are talking about is the ghost of Chihiro's old motorcycle featured in a volume I don't recall **[Vol. 18—CGH]**.

Living in Los Angeles, I get to see a lot of what goes on in manga and anime before it hits the rest of the United States. I fell in love with the character of Hild from a plastic model kit I saw, and there is more of Peorth and Hild in upcoming issues, as well as a new outfit for Belldandy. Yet, sadly some of the characters are lost forever. Otaki's bride-to-be, Satoko Yamano (*OMG!* Vol. 1 *Wrong Number ISBN 1-56971-669-2*) never reap-pears, and Sora Hasegawa's crush on Sayoko's slimy cousin, Toshiyuki Aoshima, is never resolved. And Keiichi's *kawaii* sister Megumi never gets a boyfriend. Come on, Fujishima-san, let's give some others a little *aio* (romantic love interest).

As a side note, the Japanese love a play on words, and this shows up in the Nekomi Tech's MCC attire. Neko = a cat, so their logo is a cat's head. Ichi = the number one, so Keiichi's jacket reads K (ke) 1 (ichi). Hasegawa and Tamiya are the names of model kit manufacturers.

Yours,
Andrew F. Gillis
Torrance, CA

Torrance has what is probably the most important Japanese-American community in Southern California, and was moreover for three glorious years between 1999 and 2002 blessed with having the U.S. branch of the world's greatest otaku boutique, Mandarake. Many fans, including myself, still mourn the loss of this store, which was located in Mitsuwa Marketplace. And any fan going to Tokyo, of course, should never mind Akiba—head for Mandarake's home store (actually, a complex of *nineteen* stores on three stories!) in Nakano. They have English, Spanish, and French-speaking staff, and you will truly recall Tanaka's line from *Otaku no Video*, "Welcome, comrade. This is our homeland."

As you point out, the slipcover format of the original Japanese books provides extra space for illustrations, although sometimes we do try to feature them in the English editions as well—for example, the picture of Lind on page one of this book is from the inside front cover flap of the original Japanese volume. In the case of *Oh My Goddess!*, the new, unflopped editions actually take almost as much work to produce as the old, flopped ones, for the simple reason the sound FX are still retouched (as Dark Horse's longest-running manga title—actually, its longest-running title, period—I was reluctant as editor to make too many stylistic changes besides the obvious one of unflopping the manga itself).

The flopped-to-unflopped transition has meant therefore going from the equivalent of producing one chapter of *Oh My Goddess!* a month (as for many years it was a monthly comic book series) to three to four chapters a month (that is, one graphic novel's worth every two months)—a 350-400% increase in output without the production itself becoming any simpler. Moreover, several of the unflopped volumes contain bonus material not featured in the original flopped editions. With Volume 26, I believe, we have finally completed that transition, which is owed to the very hard work (which is, of course, continuing even as I type this) of the adaptation staff.

Because of such things as its emotional sensitivity and penchant for elegant, flowing costumes, *Oh My Goddess!* isn't usually thought of as a fan service–oriented title, although perhaps that reputation is in truth unwarranted ^_^ Sometimes things will suddenly pop out at you, as on the title page for Vol. 4's Chapter 26—but what about Belldandy, of all people, leaving us behind in Vol. 25, p. 41, or the pose with which Hild ended that volume and began this one—which, as translator Dana Lewis points out, is straight out of Shirow Masamune?

And, just as Shirow in *Appleseed* uses Greek mythology with considerable artistic license, so, I think, does Fujishima do the same in *Oh My Goddess!* with Norse mythology, mixing it with scientific concepts, traditional Western and Japanese magic, and other elements. I believe he leaves in enough ambiguity that we can't be sure of such contradictions (likewise, we don't know for sure about whether "loose ends" of the plot will ever be resolved). Of course, some fans also go to great lengths to "resolve" possible contradictions on Mr. Fujishima's behalf, theorizing how things might fit together—actually, this is a classic fan activity, and I tried it myself ten years ago on *Neon Genesis Evangelion*, and ten years before that, on *Robotech* ^_^

The titles "Wrong Number" and "Hand in Hand" that Mr. Gillis refers to, are, of course, the older, flopped versions of *Oh My Goddess!* As mentioned before, between 1996 and 2005, Dark Horse published the equivalent of the first 20 Japanese volumes of *Oh My Goddess!* in 19 books (the reason there were 19, not 20 of these flopped books wasn't because chapters were left out, but because the flopped books were organized by story arc instead of ending in the middle of a story as the Japanese editions often do). Some of these flopped books had volume numbers on them, and some didn't, but one way you can always tell the difference without seeing them is that the flopped books all had volume titles such as "Wrong Number" and "Hand in Hand," whereas the current unflopped editions only have volume numbers, never volume titles. For more information on the flopped editions, please see the ad in the back of this volume.

As you can see from the next few pages, the fan art is still coming in strong, and if you're considering sending in some of your own, then stop considering, and start sending! The following four illustrations are courtesy of Maggie Mei Lewis, AKA Xiu Xiu. Thank you very much, and see you all again in the next volume!

—CGH

By Maggie Mei Lewis

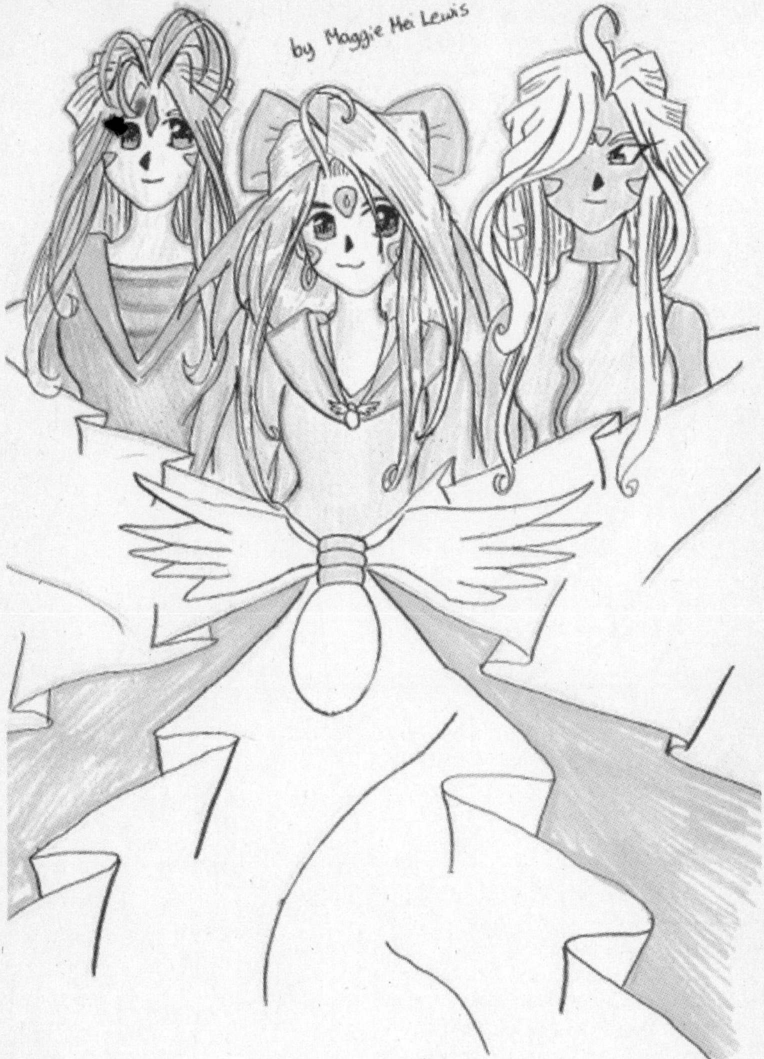
by Maggie Mei Lewis

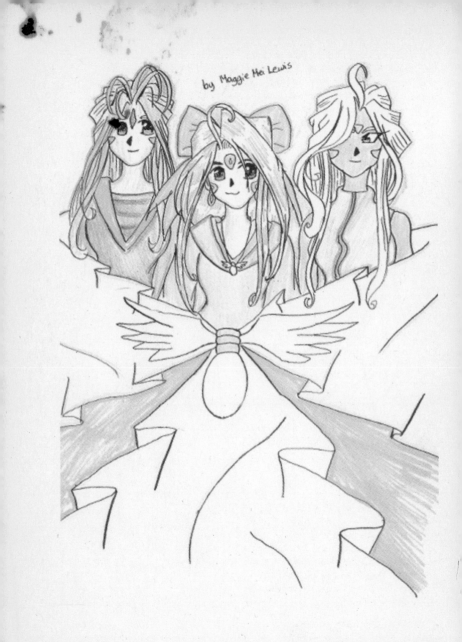

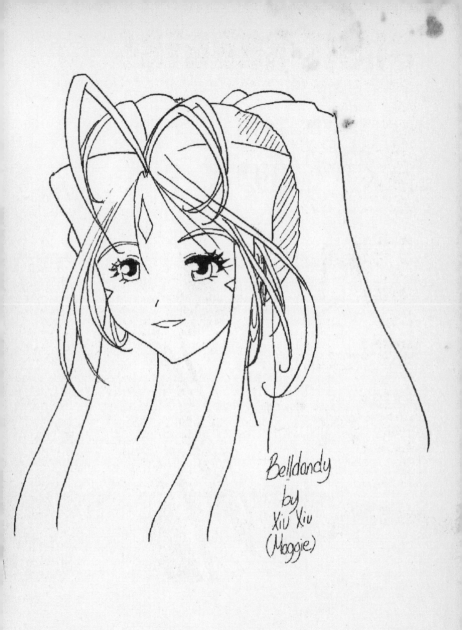

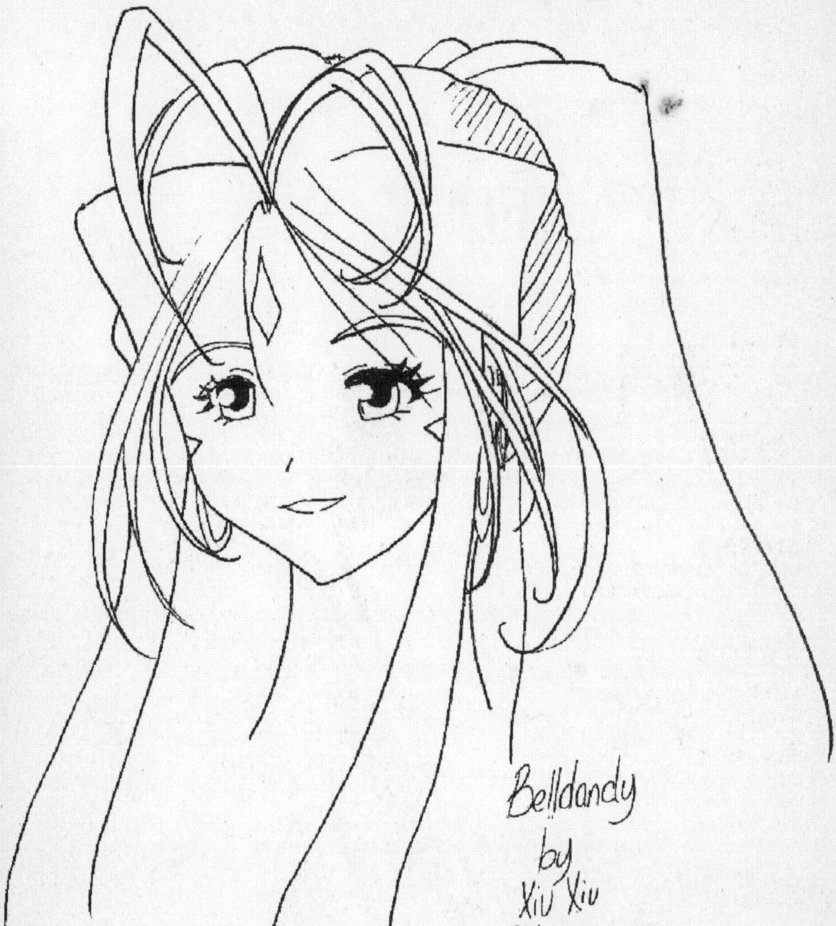
Belldandy
by
Xiu Xiu
(Maggie)

GIANT ROBOTS!

ALIEN INVASION! FUTURISTIC TECHNOLOGY! SEXY ANDROIDS! TEEN ANGST!

Kenichi Sonoda's

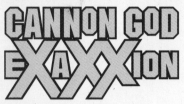

CANNON GOD EXAXXION

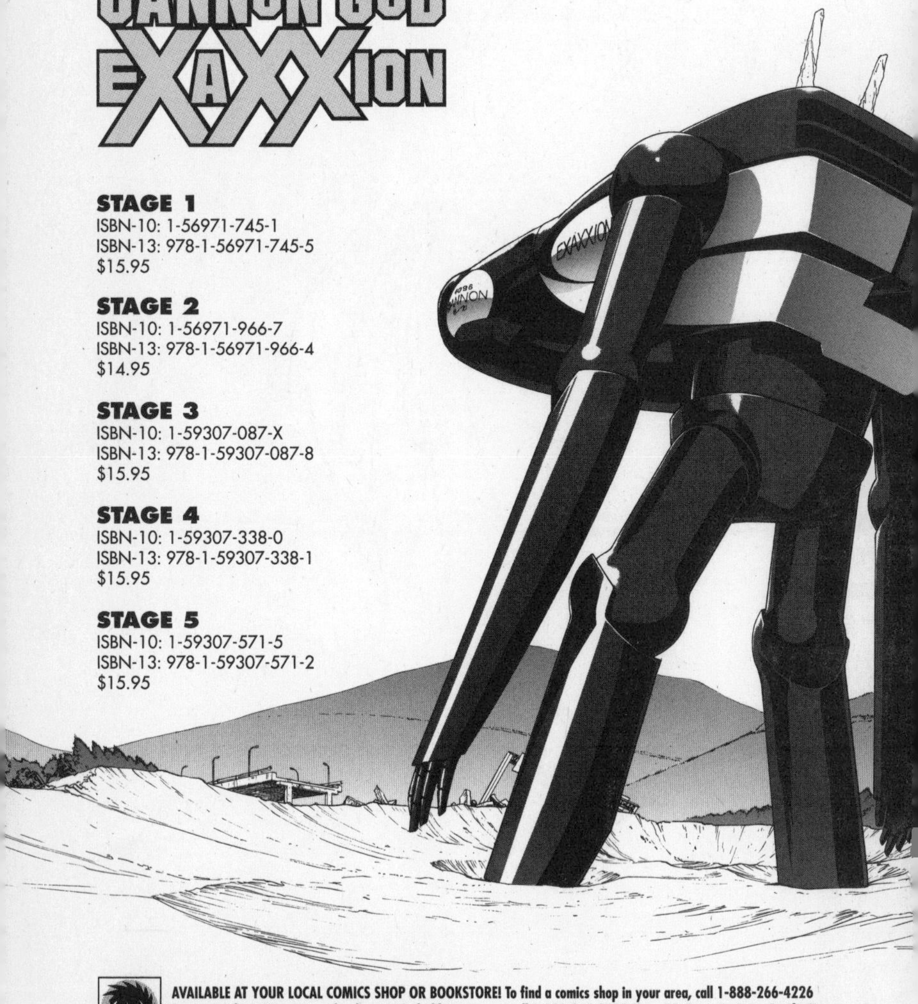
EXAXXION

STAGE 1
ISBN-10: 1-56971-745-1
ISBN-13: 978-1-56971-745-5
$15.95

STAGE 2
ISBN-10: 1-56971-966-7
ISBN-13: 978-1-56971-966-4
$14.95

STAGE 3
ISBN-10: 1-59307-087-X
ISBN-13: 978-1-59307-087-8
$15.95

STAGE 4
ISBN-10: 1-59307-338-0
ISBN-13: 978-1-59307-338-1
$15.95

STAGE 5
ISBN-10: 1-59307-571-5
ISBN-13: 978-1-59307-571-2
$15.95

DARK HORSE MANGA

AVAILABLE AT YOUR LOCAL COMICS SHOP OR BOOKSTORE! To find a comics shop in your area, call 1-888-266-4226
For more information or to order direct visit darkhorse.com or call 1-800-862-0052 Mon.-Fri. 9 A.M. to 5 P.M. Pacific Time.
***Prices and availability subject to change without notice.**

B U R S T

Don't miss the latest adventures of the most fun-loving, well-armed bounty hunters in Chicago! Rally Vincent and Minnie-May Hopkins return with *Gunsmith Cats: Burst*, back in action and back in trouble!

Presented in the authentic right-to-left reading format, and packed full of bounty-hunting, gun-slinging, property-damaging action, *Gunsmith Cats: Burst* aims to please.

VOLUME 1
ISBN-10: 1-59307-750-5
ISBN-13: 978-59307-750-1

VOLUME 2
ISBN-10: 1-59307-767-X
ISBN-13: 978-1-59307-767-9
Coming in July 2007!

$10.95 EACH!

DARK
HORSE
MANGA

AVAILABLE AT YOUR LOCAL COMICS SHOP OR BOOKSTORE!

To find a comics shop in your area, call 1-888-266-4226. For more information or to order direct visit darkhorse.com or call 1-800-862-0052 Mon.-Fri. 9 A.M. to 5 P.M. Pacific Time. *Prices and availability subject to change without notice.

(vertical left margin) GUNSMITH CATS

Kosuke Fujishima's

Oh My Goddess!

Can't wait on the Goddesses? Change directions!

Just gotten into the new unflopped editions of *Oh My Goddess!*, and found you can't wait to see what happens next? Have no fear! The first ***20 volumes*** of *Oh My Goddess!* are available ***right now*** in Western-style editions! Released between 1994 and 2005, our *OMG!* Western-style volumes feature premium paper, and pages 40% larger than those of the unflopped editions! If you've already got some of the unflopped volumes and want to know which Western-style ones to get to catch up, check out darkhorse.com's "Manga Zone" for a complete breakdown of how the editions compare!

Vol. 1: Wrong Number
ISBN: 1-56971-669-2 / $13.95

Vol. 2: Leader of the Pack
ISBN: 1-56971-764-8 / $13.95

Vol. 3: Final Exam
ISBN: 1-56971-765-6 / $13.95

Vol. 4: Love Potion No. 9
ISBN: 1-56971-252-2 / $14.95

Vol. 5: Sympathy for the Devil
ISBN: 1-56971-329-4 / $13.95

Vol. 6: Terrible Master Urd
ISBN: 1-56971-369-3 / $14.95

Vol. 7: The Queen of Vengeance
ISBN: 1-56971-431-2 / $13.95

Vol. 8: Mara Strikes Back!
ISBN: 1-56971-449-5 / $14.95

Vol. 9: Ninja Master
ISBN: 1-56971-474-6 / $13.95

Vol. 10: Miss Keiichi
ISBN: 1-56971-522-X / $16.95

Vol. 11: The Devil in Miss Urd
ISBN: 1-56971-540-8 / $14.95

Vol. 12: The Fourth Goddess
ISBN: 1-56971-551-3 / $18.95

Vol. 13: Childhood's End
ISBN: 1-56971-685-4/ $15.95

Vol. 14: Queen Sayoko
ISBN: 1-56971-766-4 / $16.95

Vol. 15: Hand in Hand
ISBN: 1-56971-921-7 / $17.95

Vol. 16: Mystery Child
ISBN: 1-56971-950-0 / $18.95

Vol. 17: Traveler
ISBN: 1-56971-986-1 / $17.95

Vol. 18: The Phantom Racer
ISBN: 1-59307-217-1 / $17.95

Vol. 19/20: Sora Unchained
ISBN: 1-59307-316-X / $18.95

Adventures of the Mini-Goddesses
ISBN: 1-56971-421-5 / $9.95

AVAILABLE AT YOUR LOCAL COMICS SHOP OR BOOKSTORE
*To find a comics shop in your area, call 1-888-266-4226

For more information or to order direct:
- On the web: darkhorse.com
- E-mail: mailorder@darkhorse.com
- Phone: 1-800-862-0052 Mon.-Fri. 9 A.M. to 5 P.M. Pacific Time.

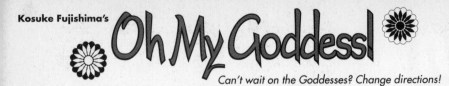

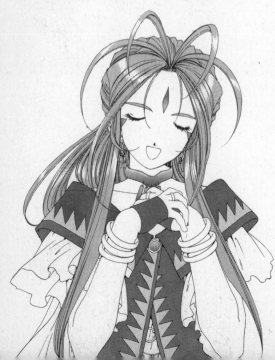

OMNIBUS EDITIONS!

Kenichi Sonoda's Gunsmith Cats is back!

Rally Vincent and Minnie-May Hopkins are experts in their respective fields of marksmanship and explosives, but they're so cute you'd never know! Neither would the perps unlucky enough to be hunted by these two bounty-hunting girls on the dangerous streets of Chicago.

Presented for the first time in their authentic Japanese format, these giant-sized volumes are action-packed, unretouched, unflopped, and sure to please.

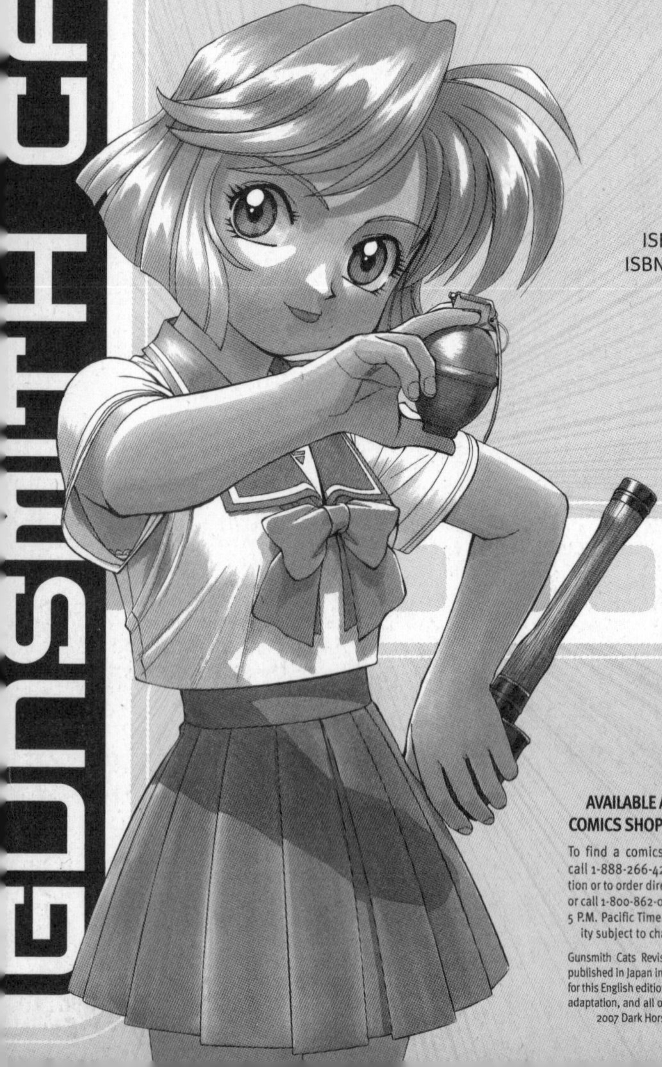
GUNSMITH CATS

VOLUME 1
ISBN-10: 1-56971-215-8
ISBN-13: 978-1-56971-215-3
$13.95

AVAILABLE AT YOUR LOCAL COMICS SHOP OR BOOKSTORE!

To find a comics shop in your area, call 1-888-266-4226. For more information or to order direct visit darkhorse.com or call 1-800-862-0052 Mon.-Fri. 9 A.M. to 5 P.M. Pacific Time. *Prices and availability subject to change without notice.

DARK HORSE MANGA

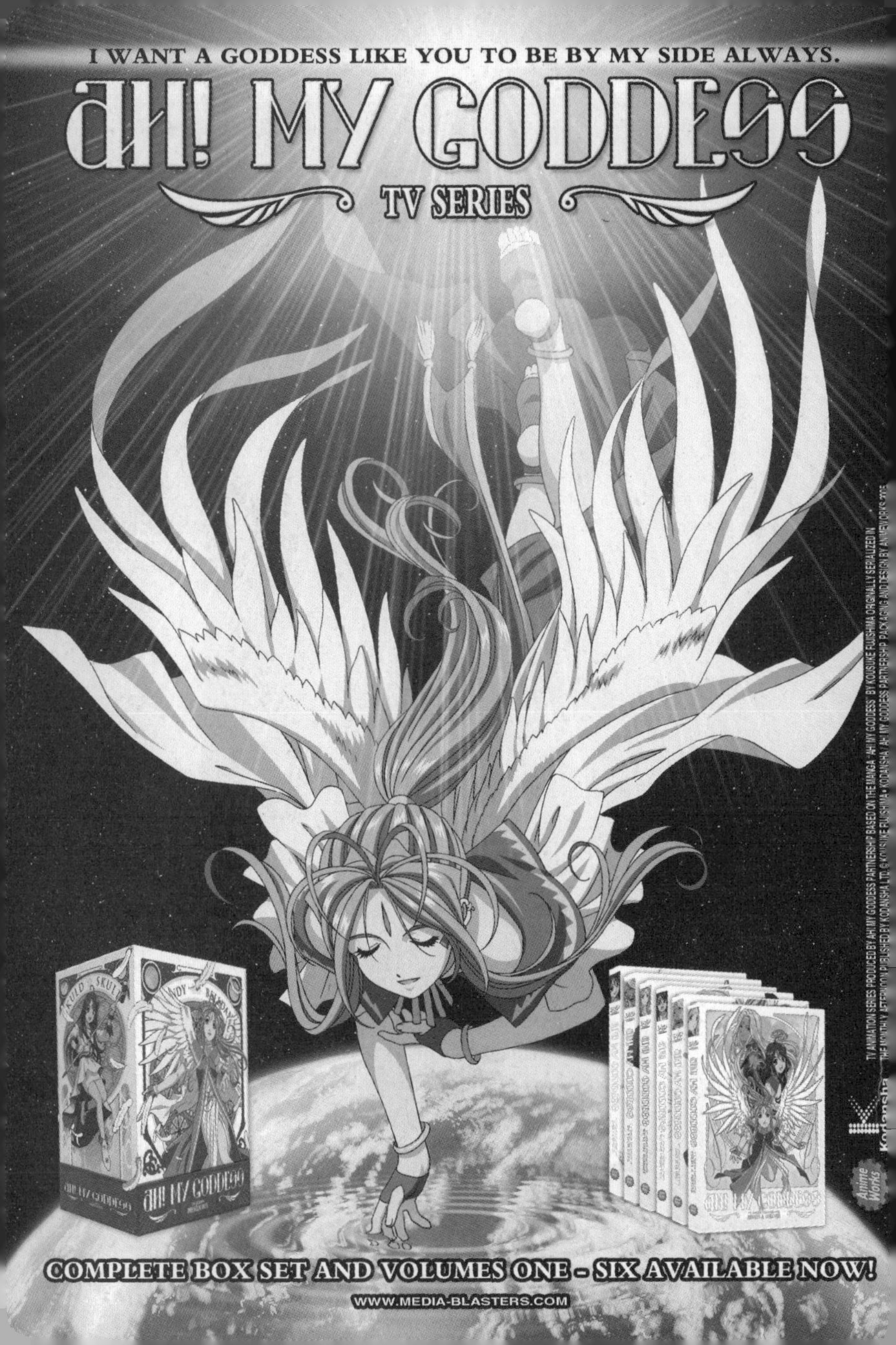
I WANT A GODDESS LIKE YOU TO BE BY MY SIDE ALWAYS.
AH! MY GODDESS
TV SERIES
COMPLETE BOX SET AND VOLUMES ONE - SIX AVAILABLE NOW!
WWW.MEDIA-BLASTERS.COM
TV ANIMATION SERIES PRODUCED BY AH! MY GODDESS PARTNERSHIP BASED ON THE MANGA "AH! MY GODDESS" BY KOUSUKE FUJISHIMA ORIGINALLY SERIALIZED IN THE MONTHLY AFTERNOON PUBLISHED BY KODANSHA LTD. © KOUSUKE FUJISHIMA • KODANSHA / AH! MY GODDESS PARTNERSHIP. PACKAGING AND DESIGN BY ANIMEWORKS 2005
Kodansha
Anime Works

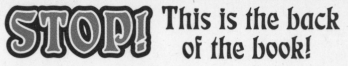

STOP! This is the back of the book!

This manga collection is translated into English, but arranged in right-to-left reading format to maintain the artwork's visual orientation as originally drawn and published in Japan. If you've never read comics this way before, take a look at the diagram below to give yourself an idea of how to go about it. Basically, you'll be starting in the upper right-hand corner, and will read each word balloon and panel moving right-to-left. It may take a little getting used to, but you should get the hang of it very quickly. Have fun! If this is the millionth manga you've read this way, never mind. ^_^

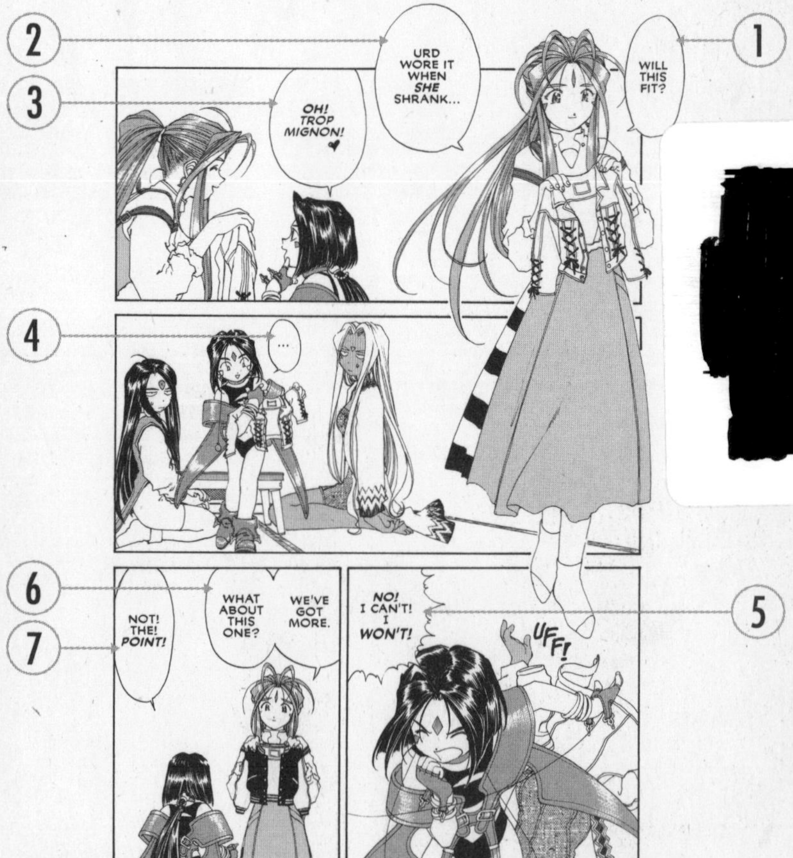
1
WILL THIS FIT?
2
URD WORE IT WHEN SHE SHRANK...
3
OH! TROP MIGNON!
4
...
5
NO! I CAN'T! I WON'T!
UFF!
6
WE'VE GOT MORE.
WHAT ABOUT THIS ONE?
7
NOT! THE! POINT!

[redacted]